Exploring Experience Design

Fusing business, tech and design to shape customer engagement

Ezra Schwartz

BIRMINGHAM - MUMBAI

Exploring Experience Design

First published: August 2017

Production reference: 1290817

Published by Packt Publishing Ltd.
Livery Place
35 Livery Street
Birmingham
B3 2PB, UK.

ISBN 978-1-78712-244-4
www.packtpub.com

Credits

Author
Ezra Schwartz

Reviewers
Oz Chen
Scott Faranello
Ran Liron

Commissioning Editor
Ashwin Nair

Acquisition Editor
Reshma Raman

Content Development Editor
Mohammed Yusuf Imaratwale

Technical Editor
Murtaza Tinwala

Copy Editors
Dhanya Baburaj
Safis Editing

Project Coordinator
Ritika Manoj

Proofreader
Safis Editing

Indexer
Mariammal Chettiyar

Graphics
Jason Monteiro

Production Coordinator
Shraddha Falebhai

About the Author

Ezra Schwartz is a multidisciplinary design leader with a holistic approach to experience strategy and design. He led projects in diverse settings, from Fortune 50 companies to start-ups in finance, healthcare, aviation, manufacturing, education, research, and other industries, and is the author of two books on prototyping.

Throughout his career, Ezra has been devising and refining qualitative and quantitative design methods, advancing rapid interactive prototyping techniques, streamlining iterative design guided by continuous user feedback, advocating for accessible design, and mentoring junior practitioners.

Ezra lives in Hyde Park, Chicago, where he draws serenity and often conceives design solutions while running along the shores of the magnificent Lake Michigan.

Acknowledgements

Many of my colleagues, family, and friends have contributed directly or indirectly to this book--I wish I could mention you all. I would like to extend my special thanks to Ruth and Doron Blatt, Mary Burton, Ritch Macefield, Marci Campbell, Dino Eliopulos, Julia and Eitan Gauchman, Hedva Golan, Jim Carleton, Caroline Harney, Christine and Scott Marriott, Ayelet and Alon Fishbach, Galila Spharim, and Yigal Bronner, for their support and encouragement over the years.

I would like to acknowledge the remarkable fellow practitioners who responded so generously to my request to share their personal journeys in Chapter 7, *The Design Team*-- Marlys Caceres, Eddie Chen, Dino Eliopulos, Jay Kaufmann, Ritch Macefield, Saikat Mandal, Christine Marriott, Ross Riechardt, Derik Schneider, Ginger Shepard, Courtney Skulley, Ken Stern, John Tinman, and Richard Tsai.

Kudos to my friends and colleagues at TandemSeven who provided numerous opportunities to engage in insightful conversations on various topics covered in the book and beyond.

To my wife Orit, who helped me shape many rough ideas, for her insights, expert contribution to Chapter 5, *Experience - Perception, Emotions, and Cognition* and thoughtful edits of the final draft.

I am grateful to Scott Faranello and Oz Chen who reviewed early drafts of this book; Ran Liron, for his detailed, honest, knowledgeable, thoughtful, and generous comments; and Marlys Caceres for her assistance with images.

Last but not least, I want to thank the people who are behind the scenes of this book--the editors and staff at Packt Publishing, and especially Reshma Raman, Mohammed Yusuf Imaratwale, Murtaza Tinwala, Ashwin Nair, and Narendrakumar Tripathi for their patience and continuous encouragement throughout this project.

About the Reviewers

Oz Chen is an experience designer who works with start-ups and companies with a mission to create a social impact. In 2013, he founded UXBEGINNER.COM (`http:/ / www.uxbeginner. com/`) to help students transition into the field of user experience design. When he's not designing for clients, publishing content, or mentoring designers, Oz loves to travel, practice Spanish, and attend life-changing festivals.

> *To my mom, my benevolent creator, thank you, with deep love.*

Scott Faranello is a usability expert with over 15 years of experience in product design, web production, product strategy, and quantitative measuring of user behavior. Having worked closely with a wide and diverse array of clients and teams over the years, he has focused on delivering valuable and predictable outcomes that satisfy both end users and business goals. Scott is the author of two books published by Packt: *Practical UX Design* and *Balsamiq Wireframes Quickstart Guide*. He currently resides in CT with his wife and two boys.

Ran Liron is a veteran UX leader, operating in Israel. He has more than 20 years of hands-on experience, balancing considerations of users' needs, technical limitations, and business objectives. Ran has planned and executed a wide variety of projects for all types of clients and markets, including large international corporations and start-ups, such as B2B and B2C, finance, cyber-security, government, military, e-commerce, IT, telecom, insurance, health, education, social networks, and advertising.
Ran is very passionate about evangelizing UX best practice and methodology, in organizations he had worked for, in the IT community, and as a mentor in Google's Launchpad for start-ups.

www.PacktPub.com

For support files and downloads related to your book, please visit www.PacktPub.com.

Did you know that Packt offers eBook versions of every book published, with PDF and ePub files available? You can upgrade to the eBook version at www.PacktPub.com and as a print book customer, you are entitled to a discount on the eBook copy. Get in touch with us at service@packtpub.com for more details.

At www.PacktPub.com, you can also read a collection of free technical articles, sign up for a range of free newsletters and receive exclusive discounts and offers on Packt books and eBooks.

https://www.packtpub.com/mapt

Get the most in-demand software skills with Mapt. Mapt gives you full access to all Packt books and video courses, as well as industry-leading tools to help you plan your personal development and advance your career.

Why subscribe?

- Fully searchable across every book published by Packt
- Copy and paste, print, and bookmark content
- On demand and accessible via a web browser

Customer Feedback

Thanks for purchasing this Packt book. At Packt, quality is at the heart of our editorial process. To help us improve, please leave us an honest review on this book's Amazon page at https://www.amazon.com/dp/1787122441.

If you'd like to join our team of regular reviewers, you can e-mail us at customerreviews@packtpub.com. We award our regular reviewers with free eBooks and videos in exchange for their valuable feedback. Help us be relentless in improving our products!

To my mother, Eda Schwartz, and to the memory of my father, Zeev, for their sacrifices and for exemplifying the power of determination and optimism

To my wife Orit for being my loving partner throughout our joint life-journey

To my sons Ben and Yoav for showing me how talent and creativity evolve

To Tsippi and Shlomo Bobbe for their love, support, and inspiration

Table of Contents

Preface

For as long as I can remember, I've been designing one thing or another. My earliest recollection is of a newspaper my friends and I put together during summer break before third grade. That publication lasted only for a couple of limited-edition issues; limited, because, in addition to writing articles about soccer, my job was to *design* the paper. This meant that I had to come up with a head mast, writing the few articles we put together neatly, tracing photos into a simple layout, and finally, manually copying each issue a few times. Altogether, this was a tedious, time-consuming effort, which took a while to compete, since we were lured into playing soccer outside. Yet, the joy of turning a blank sheet of paper into a meaningful *product*, which we distributed (handed out) to our beloved family members for money to buy an ice cream, planted the seeds that eventually blossomed to become my lifelong career in design.

Over the past three decades, I have made my living as a professional designer of a wide array of products. I designed physical objects, such as print publications, including magazines, books, advertisements, and posters; exhibition booths and gallery exhibits; time-based content, such as interactive learning materials and animated films; and eventually, moved to design user interfaces for desktop applications, websites, and apps.

Experienced designers arrive at their careers by a variety of paths. Some go to school to study one of the design disciplines, whereas others learn on the job by observation, trial, and error. Some designers plan and premap their career, whereas others more or less stumble upon it and are drawn by the interesting challenges and creative opportunities of design work. Experience design attracts practitioners from diverse educational and professional background, who are united not by a single skill set, but rather through their shared interest in multidisciplinary exploration, problem-solving, and creative team work.

The time spent on writing this book has often felt like building a sandcastle on the beach. I spent long pleasant moments pouring sand, shaping it, creating and fortifying the structure. All the while, I imagined that the castle and its formidable walls can withstand the approaching tide, but I accepted the inevitable--the entire construction would be gone in the morning. What's left is the anticipation and excitement of starting over, constructing a new castle--better than the preceding one. It is difficult to define experience design neatly and precisely. I have tried to construct a clearly organized and comprehensive description of what is experience design, the concepts underlying this field of practice, and the processes it typically utilizes. However, experience design is an evolving field, and the structure of its "castle" is in constant flux--definitions, practices, strategies, and tools are evolving continuously.

This book is my attempt to present what I see as the foundation of experience design, which, despite the inevitable waves of change, has an interesting history, a solid structure, and certainly an intriguing future.

I wrote this book for those who are curious about experience design and seek a general understanding of its evolving multifaceted nature. This is not exclusively a prescriptive set of answers. In fact, the central themes of this book are interesting questions, which are yet to be answered--how does an impersonal relationship between companies and market audiences turn into a very personal product experience? What is the role of design and designers in fusing intangible motivations, needs, and emotions of companies and people with concrete products, to form a strong, lasting emotional connection between an individual and a product or brand?

The discovery process undertaken in this book involves forming a historical perspective. I reviewed relevant milestones throughout human evolution, which are like the lights marking a runway for a safe landing on a dark night. The seeds of much of what is done today, while appearing to be taken right off the pages of a science fiction book, have been planted a long time ago. Other important topics include the stakeholders, processes, methods, and tools that are involved in the practical, day-to-day activity of product design.

Finally, this book is also about the notion that while constant change, uncertainty, and ambiguity can be unnerving, these aspects of experience design are countered by opportunities for open-mindedness, curiosity, and creativity.

Due to space limitation, I can list only a few of the works that inspired and shaped my thinking over the years here: Daniel Kahneman's "Thinking Fast and Slow", Richard Thaler's "Nudge", Atul Gawande's "The Checklist Manifesto", Don Norman's "Design of Everyday Things", Ross King's "Michelangelo and the Pope's Ceiling", Fredrick Brooks's "The Mythical Man-Month", Ken Albala's "Food: A Cultural Culinary History", Jacques Pepin's "The Apprentice", Anthony Gotlieb's "The Dream of Reason", Edward Humes "Door to Door", Nassim Taleb's "The Black Swan", Robert Cialdini "Influence", Stanley Milgram's "Obedience to Authority", Dan Ariely's "Predictably Irrational", Maryanne Wolf's "Proust and the Squid", Steven Levitt and Stephen Dunbar's "Freakonomics", Steven Pinker "The Language Instinct", James Gleick's "The Information", and Paul Walker's "The Feud that Sparked the Renaissance".

What this book covers

Chapter 1, *Experience Design - Overview*, introduces the reader to the emerging field of experience design (XD) and its evolution, by demonstrating the manifestations of XD in everyday life using contemporary and historical examples.

Chapter 2, *The Experience Design Process*, is a journey through the evolution of the product design process and the changing dynamics between its core entities--business, products, customers, technology, and design.

Chapter 3, *Business and Audience Context*, explores motivations, vision, and constraints that influence a product's experience strategy from a business perspective.

Chapter 4, *The User and Context of Use*, describes qualitative and quantitative research methods and modeling tools, such as personas and journey maps, that XD practitioners use to research the needs, desires, and expectations of their intended users.

Chapter 5, *Experience - Perception, Emotions, and Cognition*, is a panoramic, very high-level pan over key physiological and psychological building blocks of human experience, and also includes a discussion of how designers fuse sensory inputs with cognitive processes to build desired emotional experiences.

Chapter 6, *Experience Design Disciplines*, dives into the evolution of disciplines that specialize in designing surface, space, time, motion, and virtual product experience.

Chapter 7, *The Design Team*, covers the multidisciplinary nature of XD through an overview of professions and roles that originate in the various design domains. At the heart of the chapter, practitioners share their personal journeys through a career in design.

Chapter 8, *Delight and Engagement*, explores the characteristics of great experience, which amplify a product's desirability, engagement, conversion, retention, and reputation.

Chapter 9, *Tying It All Together - From Concept to Design*, is a sweep through concept development and the techniques that help designers communicate the design to stakeholders and validate their approach with target users.

Chapter 10, *Design Testing*, focuses on the important phase of testing to confirm that the experience meets the needs of the business and users.

Chapter 11, *The Design Continuum*, concludes the book with a focus on managing design, from an evolutionary refinement through governance to revolutionary overhauls that unseat traditions.

Who this book is for

This book does not assume any prerequisite training in or knowledge of design, business, or technology. I wrote this with the following audiences in mind:

- General readers who heard about experience design (XD) through the media and are interested to learn more about it
- High school students who are researching inspiring careers in technology and design
- Readers who wish to enter the field of XD, but want to understand which of the many possible specializations might best align with their interests, current skills, and training needs
- Organizations that want to build internal awareness among leadership and employees around core concepts of XD
- Non-designers who want to get a *big picture* of XD and collaborative design models that involve developers throughout the design process, not just at the end
- Anyone who wants to understand the differences between XD and UX, CX, IxD, IA, SD, VD, PD, and more importantly, their convergence in XD

Reader feedback

Feedback from our readers is always welcome. Let us know what you think about this book-what you liked or disliked. Reader feedback is important to us as it helps us develop titles that you will really get the most out of.

To send us general feedback, simply email `feedback@packtpub.com`, and mention the book's title in the subject of your message.

If there is a topic that you have expertise in and you are interested in either writing or contributing to a book, see our author guide at `www.packtpub.com/authors`.

Customer support

Thank you for purchasing this Packt book. We strive to do our best to ensure that you get the most from your purchase:

Downloading the color images of this book

We also provide you with a PDF file that has color images of the screenshots/diagrams used in this book. The color images will help you better understand the changes in the output. You can download this file from `https://www.packtpub.com/sites/default/files/downloads/ExploringExperienceDesign_ColorImages.pdf`.

Errata

Although we have taken every care to ensure the accuracy of our content, mistakes do happen. If you find a mistake in one of our books-maybe a mistake in the text or the code-- we would be grateful if you could report this to us. By doing so, you can save other readers from frustration and help us improve subsequent versions of this book. If you find any errata, please report them by visiting `http://www.packtpub.com/submit-errata`, selecting your book, clicking on the **Errata Submission Form** link, and entering the details of your errata. Once your errata are verified, your submission will be accepted and the errata will be uploaded to our website or added to any list of existing errata under the Errata section of that title.

To view the previously submitted errata, go to `https://www.packtpub.com/books/content/support` and enter the name of the book in the search field. The required information will appear under the **Errata** section.

Piracy

Piracy of copyrighted material on the Internet is an ongoing problem across all media. At Packt, we take the protection of our copyright and licenses very seriously. If you come across any illegal copies of our works in any form on the Internet, please provide us with the location address or website name immediately so that we can pursue a remedy.

Please contact us at `copyright@packtpub.com` with a link to the suspected pirated material.

We appreciate your help in protecting our authors and our ability to bring you valuable content.

Questions

If you have a problem with any aspect of this book, you can contact us at `questions@packtpub.com`, and we will do our best to address the problem.

1
Experience Design - Overview

"The only source of knowledge is experience."

- Albert Einstein

What is experience design, and why does it matter?

To find something about anything, many begin by Googling it, as over a trillion Google searches in 2016 alone suggest. The results for "experience design", for example, appear almost instantly, and a discreet grey line at the top of the results list indicates "about 1,270,000,000 results (1.03 seconds)". So many results, in so little time, with so little effort on my part--what an awesome user experience!

On second thought, spending just one minute to evaluate each result would take anyone interested in doing this over 200 years, working 24 hours a day. So, perhaps, so many results are useless and the experience is not that awesome?

On the first results page, the fifth listing is a link to Wikipedia, which many consider to be a trusted source of information. Google's algorithm not only finds an enormous set of results, it also ranks them, placing results it considers to be most relevant higher on the results list. This saves the user a lot of time. So, perhaps the experience is pretty good after all!

Except that occupying the most valuable real-estate on the page are the four results above Wikipedia. These are paid ads with links to commercial products. The highest bidders for the keywords that make up the search term win the top-most ranking. That's how Google makes money off the free search service it offers, and the user experience it provides prioritizes Google's needs above user needs. This situation is very different from the company's original approach.

In the late 1990s, Google, a small, new, and unknown company, entered the highly competitive internet-search market. Within a few short years, the company took over decisively as the global leader in search. In the process, Google eliminated or greatly diminished most of its rivals because its search experience was second to none. To find out how this happened, we need to step back in time.

It may be hard to believe today that back in the 1990s, search was generally the domain of experts such as reference librarians and professional researchers. It was nothing like the almost trivial activity performed by the general public worldwide billions of times each day. Back then, the search experience was technical and frustrating--one had to create a "query" by typing keywords into specialized search fields and use logic terms to expand or restrict the search. Even when done well, one often ended up with no results, or with the task of sifting through irrelevant results in search of a relevant one.

Internet search companies' approach to solving this experience problem was to reduce the need for user-run search altogether. Instead they offered curated links to popular categories, such as travel, sports, health, and many others. The assumption was that, since people were not used to search, clicking through ready-made links to useful search result pages would shield users from having to perform searches and provide instead an easy, satisfying browsing experience.

Consequently, home pages featured a plethora of links while obscuring the search field. Users often clicked through a sequence of links that ended in a dead-end. Links that worked well were usually limited to those curated by the search companies, but user-initiated searches were often a mixed bag of irrelevant results.

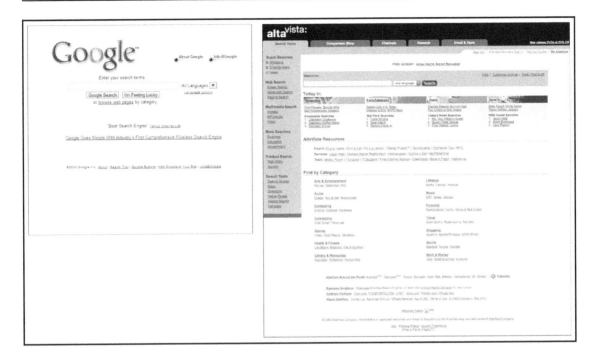

From the get-go, Google's search user experience offered a dramatic departure from prevailing conventions. Instead of a busy screen saturated with links, the user was presented with an almost empty, pristine white screen that featured a single search field and two buttons: **Google Search** and **I'm Feeling Lucky**.

User-initiated search was the only option Google offered. Moreover, astonished users quickly found out that typing in what they were looking for, immediately yielded relevant links on the first page of the results, often close to its top. Soon after, Google introduced features such as **Did you mean**, which resolved major search frustrations caused by misspellings of the search term, and "type ahead", which suggested possible search terms while the user typed in the search field.

Google revolutionized the search experience by placing the user in charge of search and demonstrating that search can be easy, fast, and productive. Fast forward to the present. The growing unease about how Google uses the personal information it collects from search activity has shifted the context of the search experience and created an opening for alternatives to Google. For example, DuckDuckGo, maker of a search engine of the same name, assures its users that it does not collect or share any personal information, does not store search history, and therefore has nothing to sell to advertisers that track users activity on the internet.

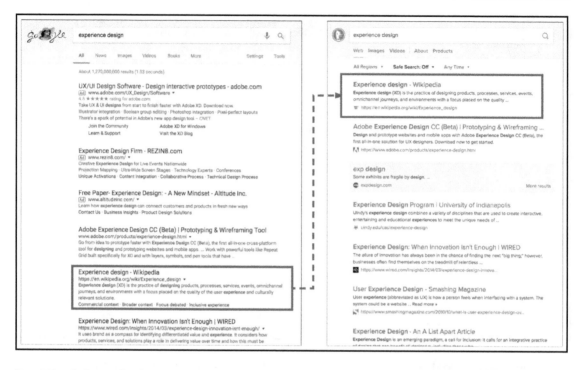

DuckDuckGo and other contemporary search engines have access to fewer resources than Google and lack its advantages in search technology. Yet, as previously suggested, millions of links to a search are useless. Ultimately, informed users assess a search engine's user experience by considering both the quality of its first results page and the extent of lost privacy.

As illustrated in preceding screenshot, searching `experience design` with DuckDuckGo places the link to Wikipedia at the top of the search results page. Isn't this experience better than Google's?

The brief journey through the maturation of internet search illustrates the evolution of product experience in the context of competition and the intersection of personal and commercial interests. The main thrust of this book, is the attempt to piece together the intricate puzzle of motivations and perspectives that shape product design, either physical or virtual. What makes this an exciting and perhaps futile effort, is the fact that the number and shape of the puzzle pieces constantly changes, and the number of possible images tor the assembled puzzle is infinite.

Nowadays, many people are getting increasingly cozy about holding a conversation with their devices-- talking to Siri, Alexa, Assistant, or Cortana. Such conversational interfaces represent an emerging experience that, until very recently, has been confined to the realm of science fiction. In fact, as more products are becoming "smart" thanks to embedded processors, artificial intelligence, and ubiquitous hi-speed network connectivity, the sun seems to be setting on the beige box and monitor known as a personal computer and the experiences that gave raise to existing technology giants such as Google.

This is a perfects segue to the Wikipedia entry for "Experience design". The Wikipedia page, as viewed in early August 2017, is curiously short. The definition is reproduced here verbatim:

> *Experience design (XD) is the practice of designing products, processes, services, events, omnichannel journeys, and environments with a focus placed on the quality of the user experience and culturally relevant solutions. An emerging discipline, experience design draws from many other disciplines including cognitive psychology and perceptual psychology, linguistics, cognitive science, architecture and environmental, haptics, hazard analysis, product design, theatre, information design, information architecture, ethnography, brand strategy, interaction design, service design, storytelling, heuristics, technical communication, and design thinking.*

> *- Wikipedia*

A few additional paragraphs discuss various aspects of experience design. Overall, though, this is what we learn about XD:

- A highly interdisciplinary, collaborative and iterative approach to product design
- What is being designed is defined very broadly, ranging from physical to digital, from material objects such as buildings and devices to non-material entities such as processes and journeys
- Understanding, predicting, anticipating, nudging, influencing and ultimately changing user behavior through engaging product experiences is what binds business, technology and design.

As of August 2017, the search for more specific and authoritative definitions of experience design has not yielded reliable results. There are scores of personal opinions, musings, and debates. Many of the results point to related terms, such as "user experience design". Perhaps this limited range of findings reflects the fact that currently, only a handful of academic settings offer programs in experience design. It is worth noting, though, that programs that teach the key components of XD exist under various other titles.

For example, the Illinois Institute of Design in Chicago (IIT) is a graduate design school.

One of its programs, a Masters of Design, lists the wide-ranging backgrounds of the 2015/16 student body on the program's overview page for 2017/18 prospectives:

- Architecture
- Business consulting
- Chemical engineering
- Communication design
- Computer science
- English literature
- Economics and finance
- Education
- Fine arts
- Humanities
- Industrial design
- Interaction design
- Marketing
- Mechanical engineering
- Non-for-profit management
- Philosophy

The page then lists a sample of the careers and professional directions pursued by program alumni:

- Brand strategist
- Planner/strategist
- Innovation methods
- Interaction design
- Product development
- Strategy and new business development
- User research
- Information architect
- Innovation strategist
- UX designer

Similar programs across the country and the world share comparable interdisciplinary characteristics. Of course, people enter the field of experience design in a wide variety of ways, and many deliberately skip formal academic training, preferring instead to gain hands-on experience in any of the diverse opportunities offered by this emerging domain.

A day in the life and experiences of M

Experience design is concerned with developing a holistic understanding of the relationships between person and product over time--meeting needs and exceeding expectations in ways which users perceive as valuable, effortless, and emotionally satisfying. Key to an emotionally satisfying user experience is the speed of need fulfillment--a product's ability to meet needs as soon as possible, or better yet--anticipate needs before they arise.

To illustrate the evolving nature of experience design and the role it plays in the life of individuals, this section presents a few highlights from a day in the life of *M*, told as a series of positive and negative experience touch-points with products and technologies. Some of these are probably familiar. Note how your experiences with these touch-points are similar to or different from *M*'s.

Similarities and variations in individuals' experience highlight an essential aspect of experience design--it transforms simple daily activities most would consider both trivial and intimately personal, into a shared social and commercial experience. When we engage with our smart products throughout our daily routines, our interactions and experiences generate a new type of industrial raw material: Data, lots of it. Our individual data is transmitted, and aggregated with data from millions of other users, to reveal common patterns and trends.

And so, the following examples focus on typical mundane activities we perform routinely, activities that feel almost automatic. But, are they really almost automatic? As you read about *M*'s experiences and compare them to yours, think about the subtle but powerful ways in which product experiences can effect behavioral and emotional change, what might explain this power, and what are its limitations.

The importance of usability

M wakes up at 6 am every morning and drinks a glass of filtered water from a refrigerator that was purchased less than a year ago. A prominent digital display on the freezer door informs *M* about the temperatures inside the refrigerator and freezer compartments, and the status of the replaceable air and water filters. These indicators turn from green to orange when it is time to order new filters, and to red when the filters need to be replaced. The refrigerator can order these filters automatically from Amazon, but *M* is not yet comfortable with having a kitchen appliance make purchasing decisions.

In fact, *M* is disappointed with the expensive refrigerator. The external water/ice dispenser was the key feature that led *M* to choose this particular model because *M* is concerned about of the quality of tap water in the residence, and all members of the household drink a lot of water throughout the day. In the refrigerator models that feature water dispensers, many are internal. The users have to keep the refrigerator door open while pouring water into a glass or water bottle. The model *M* selected was one of the few with an external dispenser, promising convenient and energy-saving access to filtered water.

As it turned out, filling water bottles from the refrigerator water dispenser is difficult and messy due to a design flaw. The plastic nozzle from which water is dispensed is hidden from sight, making it difficult to align the opening of the water bottle with the nozzle. The result is spilled water. Everyone in *M*'s family refills their bottles with water several times a day. Water spills, the kitchen floor gets messy, and someone has to mop a few times a day.

Design flaws in product features that are frequently used become amplified by repeated experience of the adverse consequences. *M*'s positive opinion about the refrigerator's brand, based on 15 years of satisfying use with the previous refrigerator owned by the family, has now turned less favorable. While the old model did not feature a fancy digital display, its water/ice dispenser worked flawlessly.

Less can be more

M boils water for coffee in a recently purchased electric kettle. Inexpensive and easy to use, *M*'s previous kettle was safe and easy to use. It had a single-purpose function, time-to-boil was fast, and the appliance automatically turned off once the water boiled, or when it was nearly empty. After several years of frequent daily use, the kettle malfunctioned.

Captivated by the latest generation of kettles, *M* had a hard time selecting a replacement among models with features such as precise temperature control, adjustable temperature control, multi-temperature control, keep-warm controls, and remote control via wireless smartphone app. Moreover, the prices of advanced kettles seemed reasonable given the added capabilities, and yet, they were twice or three times more expensive than the single feature kettle. *M* wondered whether the swell of technology features was an overkill for the task of boiling water.

M settled on a cordless model with pleasantly glowing blue buttons, keep-warm feature, and precise multi-temperature controls. The kettle's options included boiling the water or heating the water to lower temperatures recommended for white, green, or black tea. The appliance's price was triple that of a simple boil-the-water electric kettle.

Although *M* and family members frequently drink tea, they don't bother with the various tea-related temperature settings on the kettle. *M* is concerned about the energy wasted when the kettle is set to keep-warm and so this feature is also rarely used. However, the layout of the multi-temperature buttons is confusing and often M and other family members unintentional switch from boiling to a lower temperature setting. As a result, they end up with a luke-warm beverage and find this very annoying.

At home, *M* likes to drink instant coffee which, despite the popularity of home roasting, grinding, and brewing of coffee beans, accounts for half the sales of coffee worldwide. *M* prefers instant because:

1. It is easy and fast to prepare
2. No special equipment is needed
3. *M* has full control over how strong is his coffee
4. Each cup is fresh
5. *M* finds the warmth of the drink pleasurable
6. *M* happens to like the flavor and taste
7. *M* likes coffee, but is not fussy about it
8. *M* has been drinking instant coffee since youth and is emotionally and sentimentally attached to the beverage

This is M's list and it cannot explain why *M*'s good friend *A takes an opposite* approach to coffee. *A* roasts small batches of raw beans in an artisanal roaster, grinds a few beans for each cup in a high-end burr grinder for ultimate freshness, aroma, and flavor, and makes the coffee with a high-end Italian espresso machine. It may seem irrational to use this expensive and time consuming process for each cup of coffee. Compared to *M*'s, *A*'s coffee is:

1. Not easy to prepare
2. Requires special equipment
3. Time consuming

To understand the motivation behind *A's* coffee-making efforts, let's look back at *M*'s list of reasons for preferring his instant alternative. Asking *A's* opinion about items six through eight on *M*'s list would reveal that:

- *A* does not care for instant coffee
- *A* is very particular about coffee
- As a young person, *A* also drank instant coffee, but he never liked the taste and was happy to discover other coffee options.

A also greatly enjoys having full control over the coffee-making process and he enjoys experimenting and tweaking its various aspect. The end result is extremely satisfying to *A*, as are the complements received from family and friends. Seen from *A*'s perspective, expensive and effortful coffee making is completely rational.

Across town, *M*'s brother and sister-in-law just stick a cartridge of high-quality coffee into an espresso maker that they keep in their bedroom. Like *M*, they want to minimize the time and effort involved in the preparation of their morning cup and, like *A*, they appreciate excellent coffee and dislike instant.

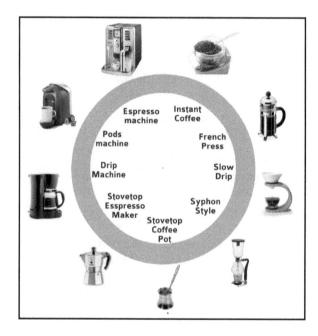

M's colleague, *G* prepares coffee using a simple aluminum stove-top espresso maker, a coffee making method favored in Italy. *G* uses roasted beans purchased from a local coffee house that takes pride in its freshly roasted, high quality, fair trade beans. It took a little time to figure out the stove-top coffee pot, but after that, *G*'s coffee making has been a fast and easy process.

We saw four different ways to make coffee. Each choice and process drives an industry geared toward offering consumers a product that responds to needs, desires and preferences more complex than the basic act of preparing and drinking coffee.

What we learn from this example is that:

- People are distributed across a wide spectrum of innate preferences and attitudes towards the experiences that satisfying their needs. Some examples are:
  - From artisanal, do-it-yourself users to those who prefer ready-made solutions
  - From casual users of a product, to power users
  - From a desire to tinker, tweak, and customize every aspect of a product to being complete oblivious to how it functions
  - From prioritizing price and value to prioritizing aesthetics and experience
  - From being influenced by fashion and social trends to strongly individualistic choices
- The importance of recognizing the motivations and preferences of individual users:
  - Members of *M's social circle* share many demographic traits, such as education, income level, the type of neighborhood where they live, and so on. Yet even with relatively homogeneous groups, paying attention to individual variations and unique characteristics, helps designers create product experiences that better meet users' needs and desires.

Task density

One morning, *M* noticed that coffee will probably run out by the end of the week. Within seconds, *M* switches from skimming an article in a newspaper app, to the Amazon app. *M* scans the coffee jar's bar-code, selects the matching product in the search results, and uses the **1-Click** purchase option to pay. A new package of coffee will be delivered the next day and *M* is back to the newspaper, waiting for the water in the kettle to boil.

M is not an impatient or impulsive person, and yet, when it comes to spontaneous purchases that occur at a point of need, *M* has a propensity for bypassing more rational and economical ways to purchase goods. These include options such as combining multiple items in a single order, price comparison, and exploration of new options--the type of actions that characterized *M*'s shopping behavior only a few years ago.

Grocery shopping, which for *M* used to be a time-consuming weekend activity that included preparing a shopping list and making trips to several stores, has now blended flawlessly into *M*'s daily bursts of atomic online purchases, often of a single item.

In fact, during the 10 minutes that pass between waking up and taking a sip from the first coffee of the day, *M* completes numerous tasks, some compound, other micro-tasks, some sequential and other simultaneous. Here's a partial list:

1. *M* is brushing teeth while scanning the news, Skype, and WhatsApp notifications that popped overnight on *M*'s smartphone's screen
2. *M* is filling the kettle with water, turning it on, and adding a teaspoon of instant coffee to a coffee cup, al the while scanning the list of unread email
3. While waiting for the water in the kettle to boil, *M* is deleting unwanted email, reading new email, ordering coffee online, responding to emails when a brief response appropriate, and scanning the breaking news section on a newspaper app
4. As soon as the kettle beeps, *M* is getting the milk out of the refrigerator, pouring boiling water into the cup and adding the milk. These activities are done using the left hand, because the right is holding the phone so that *M* can continue reading the news
5. While drinking this first cup of coffee, *M* is quickly checking the weather app, then switching back to the news and beginning to prepare a second cup of coffee
6. While all of this is happening, *M* is thinking about the day ahead -- meetings and deadlines at work, evening plans with the family, and the contents of the emails and news scanned earlier

Just reading the list is exhausting, and yet *M* makes no mental effort to perform so many simultaneous tasks in rapid succession.

Experience designers spend a lot of time understanding tasks in order to optimize, simplify, and if possible, eliminate extraneous aspects. Tasks can be prioritized by the frequency of their occurrence, how dependent they are on other tasks, whether they take precedence over other tasks, their complexity, and so on:

- Tasks that require multi-step processes and take longer to complete are divided into subtasks
- Bursts of independent tasks are squeezed into available slots between the subtasks of multi-step ones
- Many subtasks are more demanding then they appear to be. For example, pouring boiling water into a cup requires coordination and care to avoid bodily injury, and sorting through a list of work-related emails requires concentration and snap judgment.

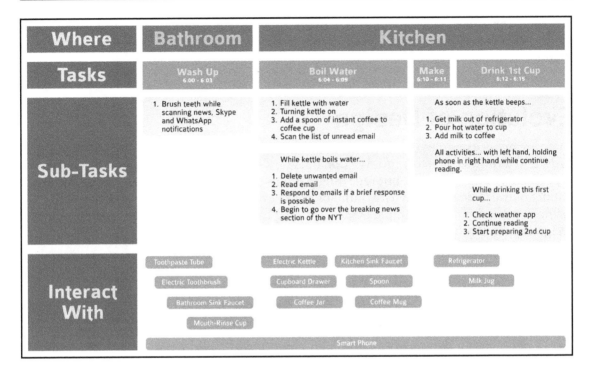

Another observation about the sequence of tasks *M* completes in the morning, is how unique it is to our times. *M*'s primary activity is preparing and drinking coffee--an experience that is centuries old. Interspersing morning coffee with a complex array of personal and work related tasks performed in quick succession--this reflects a behavioral change enabled by the fusion of technology and experience design.

The availability of all manner of content on demand - anytime, anywhere - is powerful. Our habits and behavioral patterns change as we fold into our lives the devices and activities that deliver this rich access at a relatively low cost. We adapt and learn to fill the gaps between life-sustaining activities with bursts of new activities.

And so, *M* can accomplish a lot while idling. Throughout the day *M* keeps checking news and other social network sites regularly. Various apps send notifications to *M*'s phone, which can be accessed from *M*'s laptop, phone, and iPad. *M* still subscribes to the home delivery of the Sunday edition of the New York Times. It used to be an anticipated weekend leisure activity, but the truth is that nowadays, *M* never finds the time to sit down and enjoy the paper. In fact, *M* begins to feel stressed from the intense and seemingly never-ending interaction with technology. Technology, which was supposed to save time and money, seems to be all consuming and, micro transaction by micro transaction, also expensive.

In recognition of user fatigue and mental overload, experience designers must develop and continually evolve engagement strategies that deal with task fragmentation and shorter attention spans.

Evolution of Design

There are many examples of animals that build amazingly intricate structures--honeybees, birds, and termites come to mind. We don not know whether the animals have an aesthetic appreciation of their designs, but repeating patterns suggest that they follow some internal instinct. We also do not know why humans create art or attempt to infuse products with aesthetic value, but there is ample evidence dating back to prehistoric times to suggest that design is an innate human trait.

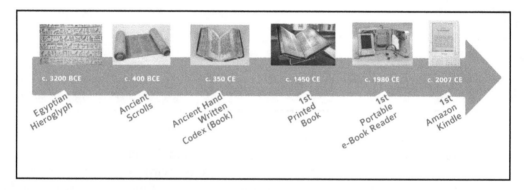

Archeological remains and historical documents capture an essential aspect of design patterns: They are the outcome of continuous cycles of refinement, evolution, decay, and revival. The diagram above illustrates the journey of the book from clay tablets used thousands of years ago by the ancient Egyptians to the Kindle, an electronic tablet that echoes the stone version. Of course, we now have even more ways to experience books, including audio books, books in Braille, and interactive digital books.

Despite the significant evolutionary and revolutionary changes in the book-reading experience, three fundamental dimensions have been preserved during thousands of years of change:

- **Sensory dimension:** The book experienced through the physical features that address the senses--format, size, material, weight, tactile quality, typography, and visual imagery. Audio books are experienced through the sound of the narration, and Braille books, by touch.
- **Temporal dimension:** The book experienced through the duration of engagement (reading, listening, looking at pictures) and the impact of the ongoing interaction with the book on cognitions, emotions, moods, and mental perceptions.
- **Content dimension:** The book experienced through the information it contains (fiction, non fiction, poetry, etc.)--understanding, contextualizing and responding to the content.

The three dimensions of experience are not limited to books. For any product, the intersection of the physical, temporal and content dimensions creates a unique experience signature that binds a particular person to a particular product. When a single product supports multiple experience signatures, the products is transformed from a mass-produced item into an object of personal significance. This does not happen to every person with every product, but experience designers strive to achieve this type of emotional attachment as frequently as possible.

Experience design seeks to transform mundane ingredients, such as business requirements, budgets, release schedules, and deadlines, into experiences that create an enduring emotional attachment to a product. To make this possible, the processes, methodologies, tools, and techniques of experience design draw from a wide variety of disciplines.

There are dozens of specialized design disciplines today. Each one has come into being in response to emerging needs. Some disciplines, like architecture and tool making, go back thousands of years, while others, like sound or game design, are very recent. The boundaries between these disciplines are not as clearly defined as their title suggest. Automotive design, for example, includes the design of both exterior and interior of the vehicle.

The interior include seats, which are furniture, and sophisticated dashboards, which are essentially computers.

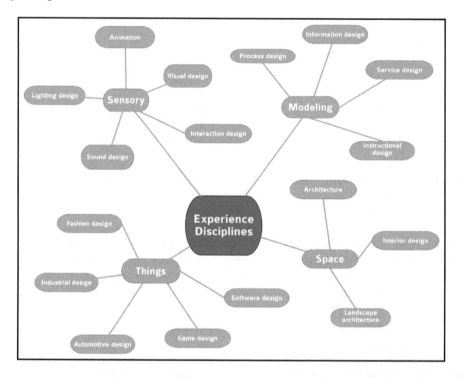

The division of various disciplines into sub-specialties reflected a need for subject-matter expertise and specialized design approaches to address design challenges and opportunities in highly specific situations. The automotive dashboard design is a good example. Experience design, on the other hand, emerged in response to the converging needs of multiple product categories. The fusion of physical, digital, mobile, and virtual experiences within a single product, requires close multi-disciplinary collaboration. Since many of the specialized design categories share similar approaches to design methods, it is possible to envision them folded into a single unified discipline of experience design. These changes in disciplinary boundaries reflect a number of fast moving trends in the global and social economy.

- **Computing**: Significant advances in computing performance at much reduced costs to companies and consumers; including hardware, software, data centers, and so on.
- **Manufacturing**: Advanced materials, miniaturization at the atomic level, 3D printing, and other innovations in manufacturing technology.

- **Global shift to mobile computing**: Aided by inexpensive smart devices, affordable hi-speed broadband and wireless networks, and high-precision global GPS coverage.
- **The logistics revolution**: The invention of the shipping container, fleets of mega container ships, and the complex operations that make it possible to scale manufacturing capacity to vendors all over the world, maintain low inventories with on-demand assembly, and move massive amounts of products around the world fast and reliably.
- **The democratizations of the means of production**: The creation and distribution of products and content is now within reach of individuals and companies regardless of size. Social networks and the emergence of a new type of user, who is activity engaged on a global level by creating and publishing content, from blogs to feature films.
- **The Internet of Things**: Billions of embedded chips in a wide verity of products and objects collect and transmit continuous streams of data. This data, aggregated and processed in real-time, reveals patterns that help develop insights about people and societies on scales never imagined before.
- **Artificial intelligence**: AI endows systems and devices with reliable cognitive capabilities, such as correct interpretation of human communication and decision-making, leading to new types of sensory experiences with sensory and conversational interfaces; complementing, and potentially phasing-out the need for manual input

These trends open up tremendous opportunities for individuals and companies, who can tap into the vast and relatively inexpensive design and development space, and dream up product experiences that respond to demand for engaging productivity, content, and entertainment. Experience design is no longer regarded as a non-essential "creative" sub-activity that is relegated to specialists.

Summary

Experience design means different things to different people, and a profusion of acronyms and passionate opinions regarding their exact scope and meaning further complicates things: CX, HCI, IA, IXA, PD, SD, UCD, UEA, UI, UX, UXA, VD and XD, to name a few. Additionally, changes in the industry are so rapid, that even during the year in which this book has been written, new experience trends have emerged, existing one solidified, and others faded out. Striving to capture an enduring snapshot of experience design, the following themes are revisited throughout the book:

- **Scope**: Experience design is not limited to websites, apps, or mobile devices. Rather, it is an attempt to consider the entire spectrum of manufactured experiences, from architecture to products and services.
- **Historical perspective**: "Innovation" seems to be applied indiscriminately and trivially these days. This diminishes the value of true achievements. We explore experience design as a point in a continuum going back thousands of years, providing context and linkage.
- **Diversity**: Many established disciplines originating in academia, business, design, and technology, contribute to what is still an evolving approach to the creation of product experience.
- **Art versus design**: Art for art's sake is beyond the scope of this book primarily because the underlying motivations, approaches, and techniques in art as such are usually different from those found in the experience design disciplines.
- **Privacy**: For the first time in history, intimate behavioral, physiological, and social details about hundreds of millions of individuals are captured continuously and in great detail by numerous corporations: what we eat, our sleep patterns, exercise routines and associated vitals, multitude of our personal preferences, who we talk to, what we say, and much more.
- **Inter-connected world**: Billions of devices that make up the "Internet of Things" are connected to the network, tracking vehicles, homes, devices, conditions on Earth and in pace, as well as individuals.
- **Data science**: Data is a raw natural resource. Processing it makes new services and products possible, such as analysis of past events and predictions of future trends. Insights from matching data patterns reveal potential affinity clusters, which connect individuals to other people, companies or organizations.
- **Artificial intelligence**: Great advances in artificial intelligence are impacting human decision support processes and infusing predictive guidance based on statistical probabilities derived from vast data collections.

- **Taking over**: Product designers use technology, data and design to drive the simplest, easiest interaction paths for users, reducing the need for learning and decision making. increasingly, humans are being replaced altogether by products that perform autonomously--from vacuum cleaners to cars and airplanes.

The recognition that experience design is an emerging discipline calls for embracing its fast evolving nature. While no one knows the full potential of XD domain, science fiction and dystopian visions provide a wide range of scenarios from hopeful to dire.

And yet every day, experience design work is being done. Multi-disciplinary teams are assembled, strategies are set, research conducted, requirements gathered, concepts developed and tested, and products released to market. While shaping our world and being shaped by it, time-tested methods and tools are being used, while new ones are introduced to meet changing needs. A journey through the experience design process is presented in the next chapter.

2

The Experience Design Process

"Do the difficult things while they are easy, and do the great things while they are small."

- Lao Tzu

This chapter addresses the following questions:

- What is the experience design process?
- How does experience design fit into the broader product development process?.

We tend to think of processes as linear entities, just like stories--with a beginning, an arc of action, and an end--in our case, a successful finished product. Indeed, from a bird's eye view, experience design fits this model well, neatly positioned as the middle phase of the overall product development process:

Define > Design > Build

There is practically an endless variety of products in the world--physical, digital, and hybrids. Zooming in on each phase of the overall development process reveals a spectrum of variation just as wide. The fact is that a single unifying approach to design process does not, and probably cannot, exist. Understanding how experience design processes fit into the flow of product design is like putting together an intricate puzzle—arranging an interplay of motivations, objectives, constraints, stakeholders, practitioners, users, methodologies, and tools--in and across phases.

There are, however, common approaches and methods that evolved over time, and have been continuously refined and reinvented by each generation of designers. Without this vitality, mass production would not be possible. Still, participants in the design process often feel as if they are the first ones to go through the journey. The reason for this is that in product design, doing everything right has never guaranteed product success, just as doing things wrong has not necessarily negated the possibility of big commercial success for a poorly designed product. Of course, this contradicts the basic premise according to which repeating a process formula should lead to consistent outcomes. The following key points should be kept in mind while exploring the evolution of design as a function of product development:

- Design processes have evolved over millennia, both instigating and in direct response to major social and technological changes, such as the agricultural, industrial, and information revolutions.
- Changes that took decades or even centuries to take effect can now occur in months and weeks. To keep up and, better yet, to thrive, product owners, designers, and developers are motivated to experiment and evolve their methods and processes.
- The faster the process, the more critical it is for all participants in the process to collaborate effectively. This drives the formation of multi-disciplinary teams and rapid iterative design processes, which are informed by continuous team communication and ongoing feedback from real users.

Although this chapter looks at physical products, many of the events and examples described here are equally relevant for experience design of software-driven tech products. Technological innovations have increased the significance of experience in the products they made possible in the past as well as recently, as is the case with the internet and smart mobile devices. As a consequence Design has emerged as a critical element that unifies the entire lifecycle of a product.

Processes and change

The design of products and experiences is closely connected to the processes underlying user-product interaction, which in turn are influenced by ongoing social and technological changes. In this section, we will explore the relationship between the evolution of products and changes to the nature of the user experience they engender.

The world transitioned rapidly from the industrial age to the information age. Today, many products and services are digital and data driven, as is the manufacturing of most physical products. Slow and linear human-controlled processes have been replaced by real-time, parallel, computer-controlled processes. Some of the trends that have emerged are as follows:

- Highly personalized products, which are tailored to the preferences of each individual customer and are manufactured on-demand by robots and 3D printers, are sun-setting mass-production of impersonal cookie-cutter products.
- From industrial machines to cars and home appliances, electro-mechanical products that operate as isolated islands are being phased out as the **Internet of Things (IoT)** ushers in an era of sensing products that are knowledgeable about the environment in which they operate, connected to the network, and actively exchange communications with other products and their owners.
- Profitability, which was tied directly to efficiencies gained through long-term planning, well-defined segmented roles, and sequenced processes, shifted toward flattened organizational hierarchies, multidisciplinary teams, and just-in-time planning and manufacturing.
- Slow and inefficient workflows that relied on heavy use of paper forms processed manually by a large clerical staff have been replaced or eliminated by web forms, which are processed by rules-driven business software. This trend has enabled organizations to streamline their processes and improve their client experience.

Another emerging trend is that experience design is becoming essential for the development and success of products because of new experience-centered demands. Technology products depend on design expertise to translate raw data and computing power into something more than slick, easy-to-use, hi-tech devices. The desire is for products with which you can have a relationship, products that are experienced as an extension of the self. Once an emotional tie is established between a user and a product, getting the user to switch to a competing product is very expensive. This is one of the reasons why some of the largest corporations in the world have realized that they must compete with start-ups that beat them in the experience game. Manufacturing giants, such as General Electric, 3M, Procter & Gamble, and Phillips are emulating software giants, such as Apple, Google, Microsoft, and others in standing up design-innovation centers where the focus is on bridging the gap between technology and people through experience design.

Product advantage has shifted from the practice of trying to win the longest features list in the market to projecting the capabilities of a product through a lens of a unified emotional experience. This last feat is what experience designers do, and consequently, designers are now usually integrated into the product's lifecycle right from its inception, much earlier than ever before.

A case in point is the consumer-grade dishwasher. In the early years of this century, reasonable expectations from a dishwasher included energy efficiency, reliability, durability, and, most importantly, that the dishes come out clean. Interaction design focused on the unit's operational controls and its shelving system—both areas where direct interaction between user and machine occurs. It was simple to use and utilitarian:

1. Load the machine with dirty dishes after rinsing them from any grime (even though this appears to contradict the premise of an automatic dishwasher).
2. Add the detergent.
3. Move a dial over to start or select the button that corresponds to the wash cycle you need.

At this point, the machine begins doing its job and the next interaction happens after the wash cycle is completed and it is time to unload the clean dishes. As long as the dishes came out sparkling clean, there is not much engagement between the dishwasher and its owner.

Figuring out how to operate the machine could be a frustrating experience without a manual--which buttons to push, or which program to choose? The source of perplexity has been oversimplification--manufacturers attempted to capture great many features in just a few buttons or dials, often using just icons to indicate options for cleaning cycles such as the following:

- Fully loaded or lightly loaded machine
- Length of a cleaning cycle
- Cycles that use hot or cold water
- Sanitation cycles
- Cycles that match the type of items loaded--pots or plates
- Cycles for heavy or lightly soiled dishes

These are great many options. They provide a competitive edge during the research and sales phase of the product. After all, it is only natural to desire the maximum features for the price. It is also pleasing to know that one's dishwashing machine can tackle any conceivable dishwashing situation one might face. Despite this, the tendency, in the end, is to use just one cycle option most of the time.

After the dishwasher has been installed in the kitchen, many users stick to the single operation they know or remember. It is too difficult to figure out based on the user interface additional and maybe better ways to use the dishwasher for cleaner dishes and greater energy savings. This leads to disappointment in the purchase--a negative experience-- especially because the more features the appliance offers, the more expensive it tends to be.

Most people do not want to spend time reading the user manual in order to get the most out of their product--they just want clean dishes.

In contrast to the dishwashers of the past, the goal of more recent products is to ensure that customers have a great experience throughout their relationship with the product and its brand. Appliance makers such as Bosch, GE, and Whirlpool offer *connected* and *smart* dishwashers that take full advantage of experience design.

The manual tasks of loading dirty dishes into the machine and unloading clean ones after the machine completes its task have not changed (even as we fully expect household robots to do these for us in the future). Yet the experience of using the dishwasher is much more pleasing because understanding and utilizing the machine's various features has become easy. In fact, there is no need to enter the kitchen to check on the progress of the dishwashing cycle. Instead, the machine communicates and engages the user through an attractive mobile app.

From a manufacturing and experience perspective, the benefits are considerable. If controlling the unit can be relegated to the app, it is possible to eliminate most of the controls that are currently placed on the actual dishwasher. These controls can be replaced with internal sensors that allow data transmission to and from the app and to the user.

With less physical controls there is also less concern about the corrosive effects of water, detergent, and heat. It is possible to increase the reliability of the product while also designing a slick-looking, easy to use product. Any operational confusion is resolved by the app.

The mobile app propels the experience of using a dishwasher from the completely unglamorous to the sphere of the trendy and stylish in modern hi-tech devices. The appliance app can look as stylish and sophisticated as any other app users have on their phone. Most importantly, the user is in full control and can maximize their personal satisfaction with their purchase decision because they can maximize the utility of the appliance via the app.

The example of the dishwasher demonstrates the decoupling trend that is transforming many industries and products. Physical button and dials are replaced by their digital equivalents in mobile apps and web-based applications, which offer better experience and engagement. However, to be successful in such transformations, business people, engineers, and designers must collaborate throughout the phase of product development.

Next, we will review in more detail the evolving role of design in the production process and the shift in the meaning and importance of user experience.

Evolving roles and processes

The period known as the Industrial Revolution spanned the 18th and 19th centuries and introduced mass manufacturing on scales never experienced before. Manufacturing was governed by a strict division of labor and a top-down hierarchy of social status and influence over how products and services are created. In comparison, out times, the information age, are marked by a trend toward an elimination of division of labor and hierarchies. What seems like a revolutionary change, however was an evolutionary process.

In the traditional manufacturing industries, the business and production sections of a company were associated each with a distinct and often disconnected cluster within the organization. This split is rooted in early manufacturing practices, and as we will see, it has been preserved in modern companies in the hi-tech and service sectors to this day. In many cases, the separation between the business and production sections was not only functional but also physical. It has been common to find offices of a company located in different building, cities and sometimes countries and continents from the production. This reasons for this physical separation were initially practical--factories had to be close to ports, railroads, and main transportation routes, whereas business people had to be close to banks, lawyers, and other business people who tended to concentrate in larger urban centers. Emerging zoning and environmental regulations further distanced the *business-end* from the *production-end* of a company.

The nature of production work itself further added to the split. The work environment, skills, and tools needed for running the business differed greatly from those used in factory work. These differences, captured by the white, ironed shirts of office workers, and the oiled-smudged blue overalls of the factory workers, became commonly used terms in which *white collar* and *blue collar* distinctions signify not only distinct job descriptions but also a clear socioeconomic division. When Steve Jobs and other highly influential executives began wearing jeans, t-shirts, or turtle necks to work and important company events, they signaled a symbolic shift away from the deeply rooted traditions of the industrial world and toward a flattening of hierarchies based on divisions of labor.

Mass production created a design paradox. On the one hand, mass production required a lot of design thinking. Raw materials had to be formed and tooled into parts that fit together with precision and withstand significant stresses. Just think about the design challenges posed by the immense steam locomotives, ocean liners, or today's heavy trucks. On the other hand, the design flexibility and focus on aesthetics that characterized hand-crafted products in previous centuries were severely restricted by the heavy use of industrial machinery, which dictated a *cookie-cutter* approach and had fewer design options.

Design tasks became highly dependent on a deep knowledge in material science, physics, and applied mathematics. The people who had education, training, and experience in these domains were not designers but engineers. Filling the need, engineers became responsible for the appearance and aesthetics of the final product, as well as the user experience it delivered.

Despite the common stereotype that presents engineers as lacking an appreciation for design, we are surrounded by fine examples of great designs created by engineers who did not have what today would be considered a formal design training. This makes sense because design, like engineering, is essentially an advanced form of problem solving, and many design problems require engineering solutions. How to keep production costs low and sticker prices competitive? How to fit a more powerful engine into the narrow space that was contained for the previous engine? How to land people on the moon and return them to earth safely in the smallest vehicle possible?

Yet, design and engineering were often in conflict because engineers and designers were considered to have very distinct objectives:

- The engineer is trained to focus on finding the best solutions for how something works—how to get the product to function as planned or better, within relevant business and technical constraints.
- The designer is trained to focus on the best solutions for how something looks and feels—how to get the user to satisfactorily gain the most out of the product's functionality, within relevant business and technical constraints.

The trend today is to narrow the gap between the fields. In the earlier history of product development, and especially when there were a lot more engineers influencing the design of products than there were designers, the usability needs of people took a secondary place to the product.

The shift in development focus toward the experiential needs of end users began with the emergence of modern advertising in the 1950s, but hugely successful, productive and efficient products were in existence long before.

Consider the consumer washing machine, another home appliance that shaped modern life. Prior to the invention of the washing machine in the late 1700s, the manual task of laundry mostly fell on women. It took about two more centuries before washing machines became an affordable household feature. Early models were perhaps simple, but they helped usher a shift toward new gender roles.

Household chores are hard and time-consuming. The washing machine, vacuum cleaner, and other appliances changed the lives of many women, whose time and energy were no longer consumed by hours of daily manual housekeeping labor. Social change is slow, and women continue to carry most domestic responsibilities in many families. Nonetheless, common household appliances have contributed to profound changes in the social norms regarding the roles of women in and outside the home.

As home appliance became more affordable and common household items, their novelty wore off. Competition among manufacturers has turned to a race over features—more cycle options, more timing options, more temperature option, and so on. As we saw, however, more features resulted in more complexity and more frustrated customers. Even everyday products that could be found in most households presented usability obstacles. Mastering the full operational scope of your washing machine, cooking range and dishwasher took effort and then, the knowledge did not transfer easily to operating the same type of appliance made by a different manufacturer. This was a poor state of usability and eventually, it led to a shift toward greater involvement of designers in the product development process.

Early models of design process

Design does not occur in a vacuum. It is a part of the product lifecycle continuum. The continuum is usually dominated on the one hand by business functions that initiate, finance and propel the product development forward, and on the other hand, by engineering functions that build the desired product. Design, for the most part, has been an insignificant player.

The high-level process models in the following diagram capture common configuration that reflect the sequencing of design in relation to business and engineering:

- The gaps that separate business, design, and manufacturing represent isolation and communication gaps between teams
- Shape sizes represent the relative organizational concentration of resources in terms of people and budgets dedicated to each phase
- The sequence of placement represents the order in which the perspectives of each entity are being considered

In these models, the business phase is always at the front, followed by engineering. The placement of design is variable as is the impact of the configuration on the overall process.

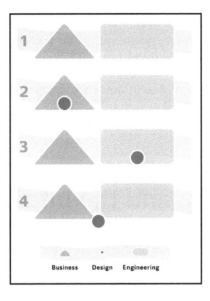

The process models are:

1. No design or end user input is involved in the process whatsoever--business stakeholders develop the requirements for the product, including the ones that impact design and usability. Requirements are handed down to engineers, and the end- result is a product that includes minimal consideration of important aspects of user experience, such as efficiency, productivity, or satisfaction.

2. Designers are affiliated with the business side of the product, typically with the product managers or the marketing group. Business stakeholders and designers have little or no contact with engineering while they develop the requirements for the product. These are handed down for execution with little consideration of technical implementation issues. Consequently, the engineering group must modify the design to accommodate budgetary or technical constraints at a point when consulting with designers is useless due to production deadlines.

3. Designers are affiliated with the engineering side of the product, and have limited access to the business group. Product requirements, often at high level and without any feedback from end users, are handed down to designers who are directed to prioritize technical constraints over usability and experience considerations.

4. Design is a small entity within the company, supporting business and engineering in the maintenance of existing products. The team must abide by inflexible workflows and can make only small, incremental improvements to the products assigned to it. As in the other models, teams work in silos, with each team focused only on its responsibilities. In such cases, the fragmentation can often lead to a complete neglect of the end product's user experience.

These four models are still common, but in many product and service categories, the trend is toward user experience as a primary competitive measure. Companies and organizations that employ these models recognize that they need to reorganize if they want their products to survive and thrive.

Design, process, and the internet

In 1989, a single invention set off a chain of events that transformed the world and consequently, lead to the recent prominence of user experience design within the product development process.

Tim Berners-Lee invented the **World Wide Web** (**WWW**) in 1989. The invention standardized how documents and other resources can be identified, searched, and accessed on the free internet. While it enabled people and organizations to connect with other people and organizations without limitations of place and time, it introduced technical limitations associated with the hardware and software that made access to the internet possible; it was all quite technical.

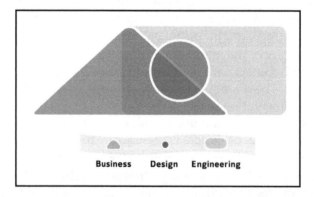

Initially, the internet was viewed as an entirely virtual space, distinguished from the physical "brick and mortar" world. The model in the preceding diagram illustrates a change in role of design, as companies and organizations moved into the digital domain and software development business.

Traditional "brick and mortar" entities, such as banks, insurance companies, retailers, organizations, and government agencies, found themselves owning, creating, and supporting complex software and hardware, which were necessary to extend their products and services over the internet. Initially, support for all things "computers" rested with IT departments, which previously handled office equipment. Software was often created internally, or purchased from vendors, but was not considered to be a critical part of a company's core mission or competency. It took several years for organizations to fully appreciate the magnitude of the shift in the importance of software and user experience and the opportunities they held. In the meantime, increased costs on customer support, and low customer satisfaction, became expensive evidence of the negative impact poor software interfaces has on the organization's bottom line, its reputation and its competitive edge.

Differences in professional culture, lingo, skill sets, tools, and compensation kept business and engineering isolated from each other. However, it turned out that designers can break the silos between the two groups. Increasingly, companies turned to professional designers to help with improvements to their desktop and web applications, as the latter became closely associated with a brand's public identity and financial success.

An emerging methodology, user-centered design, required greater collaboration between business and engineering teams, in order to sync up on end user needs and priorities. Design became the unifying thread that could lower cross-departmental barriers, as company focus shifted to the user experience. Still, it took years to change the view of design as it was necessary but insignificant over all, and this attitude was reflected in small budgets for design.

Software projects were treated as "one offs," and once the design was delivered to the development team, there was no need to keep the interface consultants around. Consequently, the permanent software developer staff was assigned with maintenance of the software. Developers added required features and functionalities wherever there was space on the screen, even if that screen bore no relationship to the function at hand.

Not familiar with the actual needs of end users and seeing the product's core value in an expanded functionality, developers produced many software packages that were bloated and, for the most part, unusable. The 80/20 rule, also known as the Parto Principle, became a popular description for software that had 80% of its users, and use only 20% of its functionalities.

The implications on the profitability of companies grew in significance:

- Software maintenance costs increased with the increase in features and complexity. Moreover, companies found it difficult to adjust the software quickly in response to market demands.

- Companies that purchased enterprise software to run critical functions, such as sales, accounting, inventory, or human-resources, often encountered software vendors who were reluctant to customize the software or were slow to update it, and found it difficult to migrate the data to a better vendor.
- The more complex and unintuitive the software, the higher its learning curve and the costlier its training. Instructor-led classroom training was common, but involved instructor fees and the expenses related to employee travel and missed days of work.
- User manuals were notoriously detailed, but only few people could figure them out. Those who did figured out the software, developed work-arounds, and undocumented ways to get it to do what they needed. Some organizations found themselves in the precarious situation where only a single person knew the ins and outs of a critical software, and the risk of losing that person threatened to disrupt the entire company.

Browsers, search, and design

Mosaic, a free web browser with a **graphical user interface (GUI)**, was first released in 1993 and quickly became the first web product to spread via word of mouth, a phenomena known today as a viral success--the panacea of every investor in technology start-ups.

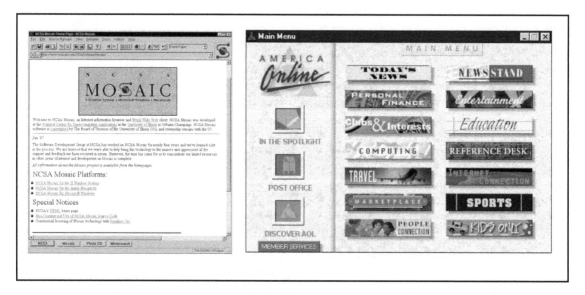

It was not Mosaic's graphical user interfaces, nor its ability to access the internet that made it so successful--successful precedents were already established:

- Apple, Microsoft, and IBM brought personal computers within the reach of the general population. When Mosaic was launched, the graphical user interface featuring windows, icons, and the ability to interact with software using a mouse had already been well established.
- America Online dominated the online services market, offering millions of people a graphical user interface, affordable monthly subscriptions, and the now legendary "You Got Mail" audio announcement, which at the time delighted users--after all, who does not like to get mail?

Rather, what made Mosaic so successful was the ease of use it introduced--the ability to browse the WWW freely, in a standardized and uniform way. AOL, CompuServe, and Prodigy were successful online services, which were also easy to use. However, they were also gated communities of sorts; Mosaic appealed to a growing audience who wanted independent access to the internet.

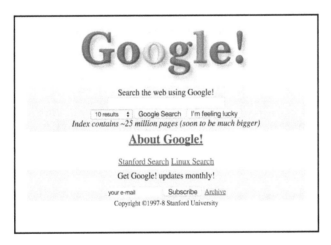

Google's search engine. Circa 1998

Another important development occurred in 1997, when Google introduced what at the time was a revolutionary user experience for search engines--a single search field, which had the most accurate search results ever experienced before.

"Accurate" is perhaps not the right word to describe Google's revolutionary search. Instead, it was the ease and speed with which the search returned the right result at the top or within the first page of the results list. A common experience with other search engines was often frustrating because of the following reasons:

- Users had to build a search query using the Boolean modifiers AND, OR, NOT (Flights AND Paris OR Rome), which many people found confusing
- The results often did not return what the user was looking for

That is why, prior to Google, performing internet searches has been a professional activity performed by librarians and research experts in specific domains, such as travel agents.

Sadly, these days the first page of Google's search results is almost exclusively filled by paid advertisements as opposed to "organic" results. This results in a poor user experience and offers a classic example of prioritizing profits over user needs.

With these and associated events, the floodgates of business opportunity burst wide open and it became apparent that the internet is the new frontier for individuals and business. The DOTCOM period between 1997 and 2001 that swept investors' imagination with the promise of fast and unimaginable riches was analogous to the US gold rush of the mid 1900s. While it turned out to be a bubble, which caused the industry a temporary setback when it burst, it was also a time of intense creativity that pushed forward the evolution of experience design.

Yet, throughout the first decade of this century, design was still considered an add-on rather than something that should be seamlessly integrated into the product development process.

From eye candy to user experience

The internet was created in the 1960s, and it spread gradually from government and academia, to commercial and personal use. Important milestones include the emergence of secure online payments via encrypted browsers, Amazon's shopping cart, advances in warehousing and shipping logistics involved in the fulfillment of online orders, media streaming, the emergence of social networks, and a transition from slow dial-up to fast high-speed connections, which radically improved the experience of being online. In developed countries, a reliable and persistent internet connection has tremendous importance. It is comparable to utilities and is needed almost like water and electricity. We will expand this point later.

Robust but relatively small, virtual communities formed in the 1980s through the early 1990s were propelled by the availability of personal computers and dialup connections to the network. The main form of interaction occurred on bulletin board forums offered by companies such as CompuServe and Prodigy. Many of the participants in these early virtual communities were hobbyists, who often built their own computers and had a high tolerance for the obscurities of going online.

The internet, which was treasured by many of its regular users as a noncommercial utopia, got quickly commercialized. The shift to a commercial internet placed a sudden and unexpected stress on the experience of millions of people:

- Secure and robust commerce demanded functionality that was not well supported by web browsers
- Monitors were expensive and small, with low resolution and limited colors
- Internet connections and computers were slow, especially in comparison to what we are used to today

Content creators attempted to limit the amount of information that could be displayed on the screen and minimize horizontal scrolling, since people were not used to it and it was considered a usability concern. The term "above the fold" was borrowed from the newsprint industry to signify important content that must be placed at the top part of the screen. Content had to be split into multiple pages to ensure faster loading and to avoid scrolling.

This approach backfired. It caused orientation and navigation problems, which in turn contributed to a fragmented and poor user experience:

- Navigating the websites of companies and organizations became a serious problem. Users bitterly complained about being unable to find the relevant information they need and getting lost in a maze of pages due to confusing navigation.
- Many paper-based forms, such as college or job applications, were ported unchanged to the Web, often resulting in a frustrating user experience:
    - Users lost time as well as the data they laboriously entered due to system time-outs, communication errors with the server, and other technical problems.
    - Data entry was tedious, confusing, and frustrating. For example, lack of instant field-level validation meant that a user could complete an entire form and, upon submission, receive an error message that the form cannot be processed due to input errors. In some cases, the error message did not identify the field/s that require corrections.

- For a while, browser manufacturers believed that dominating the web browser would lead to dominance over the internet. Browser wars ensued, resulting in the release of incompatible browsers by Microsoft (Internet Explorer), Apple (Safari), Google (Chrome), Netscape (Mosaic's successor), and Firefox (Netscape's successor). For a while, it became practically impossible to provide a consistent user experience for all users. Echoes of this problem still reverberate in modern browsers.

- Additionally, browsers made by a single vendor were not backward compatible. This meant that applications that worked in a certain version of a browser became useless on the next version. This was particularly true for Microsoft, which dominated the browser market for a few years. Microsoft IE 5, IE 5.5, and IE 6 were very different from each other and did not provide backward compatibility. We still see these issues today.

- Annoying advertisements polluted the user experience with unexpected and hard to remove popups, animations, and sound effects.

This list emerging issues in the early days of the commercial internet is just the tip of the usability iceberg that hit users. The situation posed serious challenges for companies and brought much frustration to their clients and customers.

As mentioned earlier, design was generally viewed as superficial beautification, or "eye candy", and not as a truly valuable investment in product quality. Budgets for user interface projects were small, schedules tight, and expectations unrealistic. Stakeholders had to be educated on the value and process of good user interfaces before they relented and approved design budgets.

A small group of people, who advocated for improving the usability of applications and websites, began to draw the attention of business and IT people. It took a couple of decades for the value proposition of design to sink in the corporate consciousness. Gradually, the recognition of design's importance propelled the business side, with marketing and sales often leading the charge to invest in user interface designers.

Needs to roles to processes

Software user interfaces were constrained by the limitations of hardware, operating systems, and programming languages. Advances in these areas, along with the continuous decrease in hardware and software prices, had a tremendous impact on how people interact with computers and software.

Until the mid 1970s or so, interaction with software and computers was the purview of programmers only in universities and government, or in corporate settings with access to room-size computers that were programmed using punch cards. This was a slow, tedious, and non interactive process, since the entire deck of cards containing the software had to be processed before the computer provided an output.

Just two decades later, personal computers were common in offices and households. These units mass produced, relatively inexpensive, and easy to place on a desk (hence the term desktop computer). Users interacted directly with the machine by looking at a screen and manipulating text and graphic objects using keyboard and mouse.

The popularization of computing placed the general population, of all age groups, in direct contact with products that were fundamentally biased toward programmers and professionals. With the advance of computer-based commerce and entertainment, hardware and software manufacturers faced increasing pressure to make computers easier to use.

A new profession slowly emerged in the 1970s. These professionals wanted to improve the experience of using computers. With the popularization of graphical user interfaces (GUIs) by Apple and Microsoft in the 1980s, the practice became known as User Interface (UI) Design. The term User Experience (UX) was coined by Don Norman in 1993. According to Don Norman:

> *I invented the term because I thought Human Interface and usability were too narrow: I wanted to cover all aspects of the person's experience with a system, including industrial design, graphics, the interface, the physical interaction, and the manual.*

The term became popular throughout the first decade of the 21st century. Eventually, both "interface" and "user" were dropped in favor of the generalized "**Experience Design (XD)**" to reflect a more holistic approach to the practice.

Design expertise branched into four domains, each of which serves both software and physical product design:

- **Experience research**: Specializes in activities that take place at the start of the project and focus on understanding the user and the context of use. Depending on the product, professionals study the physical, perceptual, cognitive, and emotional aspects of the experience for users. Research methods include various forms of qualitative and quantitative activities. Researches are engaged throughout the design process, performing contextual inquiries, usability studies, and post-launch tests with users. These topics are discussed in detail in later chapters.

- **Data design**: Specializes in information architecture, metadata, development of semantic aspects of data classification, and data visualization. Experts in this area also produce ontologies, taxonomies, and thesauri, which can impact, for example, the navigation structure in software.
- **Experience design**: Owns all aspects of the product's experience and forms the "glue" that binds all design activities, from engaging business stakeholders at the onset of a project, to defining the experience strategy, and closing collaboration with developers during production phase.
  Practitioners use a variety of methods, techniques, and tools to articulate and guide the design through iterations of high-level concepts, 2D and 3D models, sketches, wireframes, interactive prototyping, visual and interaction design, lighting, and material design.
- **Frontend development**: Specializes in programming the user interfaces based on experience requirements, while harnessing the best technologies available for the product.

Unified design process - experience is the product

Designers work with two types of products--completely new inventions and updates to existing products. Both can be catalysts for revolutionary changes in people's lives.

For example, Motorola produced the first handheld cellular phone in 1973. This invention changed the experience of voice and written communication for people worldwide. The first iPhone, a rethinking of the cellular phone, was introduced by Apple 34 years later, in 2007. The release of the iPhone marked another tectonic shift in the role of experience design in product and service development.

As described in Chapter 1, *Experience Design - Overview*, in the iPhone and the products that followed it, physical and digital experiences were fused into a powerful, beautiful, easy-to-use, multipurpose personal device that could handle work, personal life, and entertainment. This, of course, also meant a blurring of the boundaries that separated the personal and private from the public and work related domains.

Concurrently, advances in computing and manufacturing led to the Internet of Things (IoT). IoT is the idea that it is possible to collect and transmit data from and to any object, be it a car or an item of clothing, and make sense of this data using artificial intelligence.

These are early days, and many companies experiment with hyper-technologizing products and services in an attempt to improve experience. Some of these efforts may seem ridiculous today, but experimentation is the key to eventual advancement.

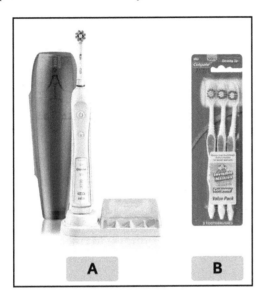

Take, for example, the "Oral-B Pro 5000 SmartSeries Dual Handle Power Rechargeable Electric Toothbrush with Bluetooth Connectivity Powered by Braun", (Yes, this is the product's actual name on the Oral-B website), shown in the screenshot above. In April 2017, its price on Amazon was $237.69. In May, the list price dropped to $159.99, with a promotional price of $97.92.

A set of three "Colgate Classic Clean Soft Bristle Toothbrush" (also shown in the preceding screenshot), can be purchased on Amazon for $6.80, or $2.30 per toothbrush. This simple product is 42 times cheaper than the Bluetooth product at sale price.

Each of the products offers a vastly different user experience. The bluetooth product benefits are as follows:

- Electric toothbrush with bluetooth communication between brush and smartphone provides real-time feedback on brushing habits, helping you achieve amazing results

- Floss action round brush head with micropulse bristles for a superior and interdental clean, which is not found in a regular manual toothbrush
- 3D cleaning action oscillates, rotates, and pulsates to break up plaque and remove more plaque along the gumline than a regular manual toothbrush
- Pressure sensor lights up the brush and the smartphone if you brush too hard
- Five modes--daily clean, gum care, sensitive, whitening, and deep clean

The manual toothbrush does not require charging, has no moving or electronic parts that can malfunction, requires very little space, convenient for travel, does not require an app, and keeps the daily routine of teeth-brushing simple and cheap.

However, does the expensive hi-tech product actually clean teeth better than the cheap manual product? Perhaps a clue to this question may be the fact that the **American Dental Association** (**ADA**) grants its seal of approval only to manual toothbrushes, and the manual toothbrush mentioned above is one of the approved products.

At the same time, it may be argued that the hi-tech brush provides considerable long term benefits because the device collects historical information about brushing frequency, use modes, and other habits. The collected data can help the user brush more efficiently and enjoy healthier teeth.

There is a growing number of devices that promise to track, collect, and analyze aspects of our daily functioning, mental states, and social interactions. This brings to mind a song by *The Police*, and it is becoming a reality:

"Every breath you take
Every move you make
Every bond you break
Every step you take

Every single day
Every word you say
Every game you play
Every night you stay

I'll be watching you"

Today, experience has become a major competitive edge and consequently also a strategic priority for organizations and companies. The implications for the role of design are illustrated in the following diagram:

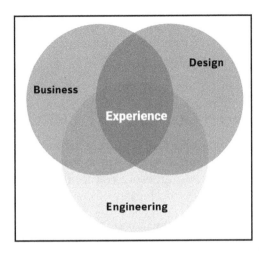

In this model, experience emerges as the fusion of business, engineering, and design. All major entities are synced throughout the product development lifecycle to ensure a lasting and unified outcome. The radical twist, however, is this:

Success of experience is measured throughout the life span of the user, not the product

For example, if you own an iPhone 6 or 7 and you like the experience this product provides, you are likely to purchase iPhone 8 when you are ready to replace your device. The iPhone is not unique-- many products and services build long-term loyalty that persists across multiple generations of product evolution. Such continuous relationship with a product and brand over a consumer's lifespan (or a phase of it) can be seen as an emotional bond created through consistently satisfying and quality experience.

The unified design process has two perspectives:

- A high-level product design perspective focuses on developing an overall experience strategy that would compel a target audience. Usually, the business side of the organization initiates these activities and engages experience strategists to envision a new or an updated product.

- A detailed product design perspective focuses on defining the product-specific experience qualities on the individual-user level. All design practitioners collaborating on the design share this perspective.

Unified experience design process model

A generalized model of a user-centered design process is illustrated in the following diagram. The design process in the model is product agnostic. It can be applied to physical or strictly digital products. The model suggests a continuous flow, which spans the life cycle of the product, from its inception to phase-out.

The product's user is at the center, positioned within the larger circle of the product's target audience. In `Chapter 3`, *Business and Audience Context,* we will zoom into these circles for a discussion about audience and user modeling.

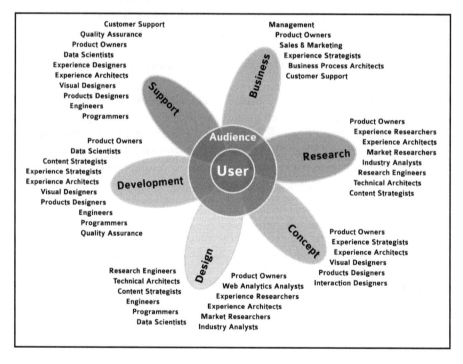

The general process flow of experience design

The product's user and audience stand at the core of the experience. Orbiting the core are six centers of design activity:

- Business
- Research
- Concept
- Design
- Build
- Post-launch

The centers are interconnected, and information flows freely in a meaningful way. This is not a top-down "waterfall" hierarchy. Each of these centers is a hub of multi-disciplinary activity that produces artifacts, and propels the process forward. Here are some of the disciplines that play an active role within each center:

- **Business**: Management, product owners, sales and marketing, experience strategists, business process architects, business analysts, and customer support
- **Research**: Product owners, experience researchers, experience architects, market researchers, industry analysts, research, engineers, technical architects, and content strategists
- **Concept**: Management, product owners, experience strategists, experience architects, visual designers, product designers, interaction designers, engineers, and technical architects
- **Design**: Product owners, content strategists, experience strategists, experience architects, visual designers, product designers, manufacturing, programmers, and data scientists
- **Build**: Product owners, content strategists, experience strategists, experience architects, visual designers, product designers, manufacturing, programmers, customer support, and data scientists
- **Post Launch**: Product owners, web analytics specialists, and experience designers

In various industries and companies, the grouping of the disciplines may vary somewhat, yet everywhere, the process requires active engagement and involvement of the entire organization, as well as a commitment to staying focused on the core--the user.

Key design activities that happen within each center are:

- **Business**:
  - The organization determines the vision and motivation for the project, identifies market needs and the competitive landscape, weighs the risks and opportunities, develops a roadmap, allocates budget and resources, and drafts a detailed project plan.
  - The organization considers the experience strategy for the product, and develops a prioritized list of high-level capabilities and business requirements.

- **Research**:
  - The organization conducts competitive market and technology research, assesses its own strengths and weaknesses, identifies ways to expand market share and extend its reach to a wider target audience; it conducts surveys and focus groups, if relevant.
  - Conducts qualitative and quantitative research activities, such as surveys and contextual inquiry sessions with individuals and small groups, in order to surface important needs, desires, expectations, barriers, and biases.
  - Reviews existing applications, documentation, and other materials to understand current state; models the user experience with personas and journey maps, and helps develop insights for future state.

- **Concept**:
  - Uses the artifacts produced by the business and research processes as inputs to visualize 2D or 3D explorations of the product and its underlying design architecture; some of the work begins earlier with content inventory, and strategy, information, and technical architecture.
  - Designers use various participatory methods, such as ideation workshops, to brainstorm the approach; visualization is developed iteratively, advancing from sketches and rough wireframes, to high-fidelity concept prototypes that can be validated by users.
  - User feedback and validation; continuously revising the work, based on feedback from actual users, ensuring that the approach meets needs and expectations.

- **Design**:
  - Uses all the work produced previously as inputs to concentrate on a detailed design for the various components that make up the product; documents the experience by creating specifications, pattern libraries, design guides, and interactive style guides. For physical devices, continued logistical planning for appropriate machinery, suppliers, distribution channels, and human, capital, and supporting resources.
  - Usability testing--ideally, several cycles of testing with real users; the feedback used to improve the design.

- **Build**:
  - Programming the front and back ends of the system, detailed documentation, and manufacturing.

- **Post launch**:
  - Track and analyze usage, run customer satisfaction surveys, conduct follow up sessions with customers, and fix defects and bugs.
  - Continue work on the product's next phases and releases, extend features and capabilities based on input from all of the above activities and ongoing feeds from the market.

Summary

New scientific knowledge leads to new technologies, commercial opportunities, and eventually to social changes and individual adaptation. Changes in the role of design were presented in this broad context. This chapter followed the trends that lifted design from a supporting role in a fragmented product development process to that of an equal partner in a process that is unified by design.

The trend toward multi-disciplinary design teams that collaborate throughout the entire product lifecycle, allows teams to partner around a unified process that is infused with multiple forms of feedback from users. However, the most radical change that occurred in this context, was the evolution of experience design processes, methodologies, and tools, which helped create a new emotional framework for the relationships between people and the smart products that know something about them.

Increasingly, experience design helps transform products from being mere artifacts to becoming extensions of their users. Designers help companies articulate desired emotional connections between customers and products that can be sustained and nurtured for a long time.

The next chapter is a journey through the first step in the design process--a deep-dive into the formation of experience strategy at the business level.

3

Business and Audience Context

"If your customer base is aging with you, then eventually you are going to become obsolete or irrelevant. You need to be constantly figuring out who are your new customers and what are you doing to stay forever young."

- Jeff Bezos

This chapter addresses the following questions:

- Why do organizations invest in experience design for their products and services?
- How do designers help organizations form an experience strategy?

First, let's consider an example of a successful product experience strategy. Back in 2006, before the iPhone launched the mobile revolution, chatter about an exciting and revolutionary camcorder swept news outlets, social media, and dinner conversations around the world. The product did not represent a breakthrough in advanced, multi-featured videography. On the contrary, the video camera, called **Flip**, was about the size of a deck of cards. It had a big red button to begin recording and a couple of other buttons that handled basic functions such as replay. Early models captured only low resolution video.

However, until 2011, when the company was sold and the product discontinued, Flip was the best-selling video camera on Amazon, accounting for nearly 13% of all camcorders sold.

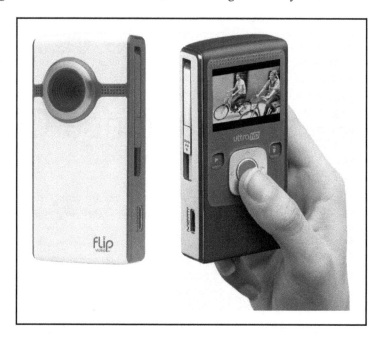

The success of the Flip success had everything to do with its experience strategy, which, in a nutshell, was *less is more*. The strategy focused on a single-feature, easy-to-use, anytime-anyplace-anyone approach, which availed the Flip to the broadest audience possible.

People have an instinctive desire to capture and preserve precious fleeting moments in their lives. They want to preserve, remember and share their memories.

Prior to the Flip, camcorders were fairly complicated to use, relatively expensive, and usually purchased by men. Typical camcorders recorded videos on tape cassettes. Manufacturers competed by packing the largest amount of features into the smallest footprint possible, but even the smallest camcorders were significantly heavier and bulkier than the Flip, which recorded video to a built-in memory chip.

The following list details the experience features, which differentiated the Flip and explain why it became a worldwide hit despite being technically inferior to most other camcorders in the market. As you read through this list, consider how each of these features could apply to a successful experience design strategy for any product:

- **Size and weight**: The Flip was small, sturdy, and light--a good ergonomic fit for single-handed use in most hands, and it could be easily placed in one's pocket, ready for immediate use in all circumstances.
  In comparison, even the smallest camcorders were not very practical to carry around, nor did they conveniently support single-hand recording. They were bulkier, heavier, and required a carrying case because they were fragile. Their most frustrating limitation, however, was the lost opportunities to capture unexpected meaningful moments--either these moments had passed before the device was removed from the case and turned on, or people left the camcorder in their car, hotel room, or home.

- **Ease of use**: The Flip's narrow case and few buttons ensured simple and easy operation for children, adults and the elderly.
  Typical camcorders attempted to bring features of expensive professional-grade camcorders to the general consumer market. Consequently, they were much more complicated than the Flip, with multiple modes, settings, options, and buttons. Since most users of these camcorders were not professional videographers, the complexity of these devices frustrated them. While fiddling with various buttons and multi-layered menu options, they ended up missing the precious moments they wanted to videotape.

- **Power**: The device used ubiquitous 2 AA batteries. This is an important advantage for travel around the world and in remote areas. Typical camcorders used a proprietary battery pack, which required frequent charging. With no access to electric power to charge a drained camcorder battery, more frustration ensued as the device was rendered useless after a few of hours of use during travel or outdoor activities. This problem is familiar to any smartphone owner today.

- **Durability**: The Flip had a built-in flash memory, which enabled the storage of 1 to 2 hours of video, and its zoom feature was digital, not optical. Consequently, the device was energy efficient and durable because there were no moving parts. Additionally, there was no need to spend more money on tapes. A typical camcorder was compatible with a specific tape cassette size. This made research and purchase decisions confusing for many consumers. The cassette and zoom mechanisms required many moving parts, which drained the battery faster, and made camcorders delicate and prone to damage. Also, of course, there was a need for continuous purchase of new blank tapes.

- **Post recording ease of use**: The Flip had a built-in folding USB connector, which made it extremely easy to transfer video clips to a computer for further editing and sharing on any popular video editing software.

  Typical camcorders required proprietary cables--which were easy to misplace or lose, and occasionally, proprietary software to transfer the movies from tape to computer. Getting the computer to identify the camera was prone to failure and confusion, and when successful, the transfer time was equal to the length of the tape. For example, an hour long tape required one hour to transfer. Occasionally, the process failed due to a software glitch or other technical problems. Consequently, people often never got around to transfer their movies; the tapes were left to gather dust, and the memories were never viewed or shared.

- **Design**: The Flip was available in several colors, including blue, orange, pink, silver, white, and black. These were playful little boxes with rounded corners--a shape that was both practical and pleasing to adults and children alike. The device's distinctive design made it stand out in store displays and online. Traditional camcorders were offered in black or sliver, with very little visual differentiation between brands and models, and the assortment of buttons and input and output ports made them appear more complicated.

- **Cost**: The Flip was inexpensive, which made it an affordable personal purchase and an ideal gift. It was sold online and in drugstores, such as CVS, and other popular venues. It was not a complex purchase--there was no need for tedious technical feature comparisons or visits to an electronics store.

  Tape camcorders were often significantly more expensive, and sold primarily in stores that carry electronics or online. Figuring out which model to purchase was complex due to many brand and model choices.

As is obvious from the list, the Flip's success, as the success of any product, can be attributed to many practical features such as its ease of use, size, simplicity, durability, and cost. However, for customers and users, a product has to addresses both practical and emotional needs. In the case of the Flip, these were capturing moments to preserve as memories and share with others. Good product experience leads to good emotional experience, which in turn leads to a positive emotional bond between a user and the product. This company making the product benefits in the short and long terms.

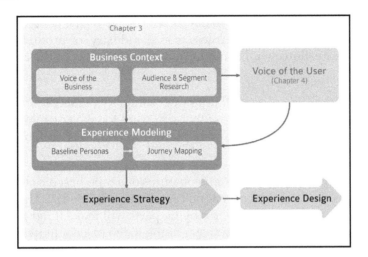

Before designers determine which emotional aspects should guide the experience strategy of a product, they focus on putting together an intricate puzzle. To assemble the puzzle designers conduct a series of discovery and research activities, which are presented in this chapter and in `Chapter 4`, *The User and Context-of-Use.*

The objectives of discovery and research activities are:

- Understand the company-business context
- Understand the product-audience context
- Understand the customer-user context

After the analysis and synthesis of the data is complete, designers move on to working with the product's stakeholders to determine the appropriate experience strategy for the product and its intended users, and for meeting the company's vision and objectives (see the preceding diagram).

Defining the business context

Companies strive to be as profitable as possible. Simply put, profits are any funds left after the company paid off all its obligations. Profits compensate employees and shareholders, attract new investors, and fuel investments in new products, which, if successful, would generate more profits, and so the cycle repeats. Without profits, companies shut down.

The question, "How will our product(s) make us profitable?" is the generic survival challenge shared by all companies, regardless of size, industry, or product. The business context of each company, however, is unique, and so is its impact of the product experience strategy.

Suppose that you are the CEO of a small unknown company, which is similar to Pure Digital, the maker of the Flip, and suppose that you want to take advantage of cheap memory cards to create a tapeless camcorder. Here are a couple of options for a product approach:

- Create a camcorder that has all the features of a tape-based camcorder, including similar look and feel, except that no cassette-tape is needed. The product would have a competitive edge--fewer moving parts will make it lighter, cheaper, and more durable. Additionally, transfer of the video to a computer is significantly simplified. However, the product would have to compete with the established giants in the camcorder market, such as Sony, Panasonic, or Canon. If your product begins to show signs of success, these other companies will release products similar to yours, well before your company changes to recoup its initial investments.
- Create a product that is a complete departure from typical products. Your product will address all the frustrations people have with current products, and provide a compelling, easy to alternative. If it is successful, its distinctive look and feel would be associated with your brand. By the time the competition release their own products, your product would dominate the market for this segment.

Which option will you choose? Both have their risks and opportunities. If the second option is the right one for your context, note how much it depends on a successful experience design. Thanks to the experience design of the Flip line of products, Pure Digital was able to popularize and dominate the *pocket camcorders* market and win over many customers from the tape camcorder market.

Another question all companies face is--"What's next?". The question may emerge in various situations, such as changes in company leadership, opportunities to implement new technologies, new ways to implement the existing technologies, decreased sales of current product(s), customer dissatisfaction with existing products, and many others.

Sometimes, a company and its products are very successful, yet its leadership fees that it is urgent to invest profits in the development of the next generation of product(s). Often, however, funds and resources for future products are limited: Short and long term priorities must be aligned:

- **Pressures to increase spending**: Investing in the future requires spending in the present. Long-term vision requires companies to make significant investments in product research and development, with no guarantee the future profits due to an increased competitive edge or larger market share, will materialize.
- **Pressures to reduce spending**: Investing in the future reduces the funds necessary to compete in the present. Immediate budgetary constraints and competitive pressures require companies to focus on maintaining or improving market position and quarterly results: Continued investment in the current product line is critical.

How well future and present priorities are aligned, is a measure of multiple factors. Some would argue that the most important factor is a mutual trust between employees and management. Trust is established with transparency, good communication, fairness in compensation and treatment, and a belief in a shared vision for the present and the future.

Mutual trust plays a critical role in flattening the hierarchical structures inherent to companies. The success of good experience design strategy depends on internal company dynamics of trust.

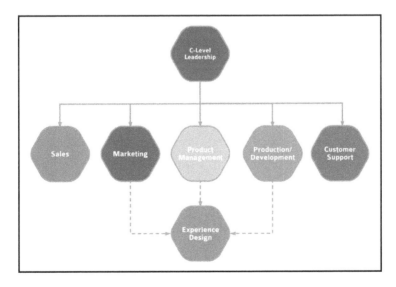

The preceding diagram, of a top-down structure reflects a couple of common characteristics that influence trust:

- The larger the company, the more layers separate senior decision-makers from the product. Some executives may not be familiar with critical issues with the product or may disagree on priorities, an intervention which sometimes leads to internal fragmentation.
- There is an unavoidable compartmentalization and specialization, as each group members within the company must focus on their responsibilities for a specific aspect of the organization. Regardless of the company's size, division of roles and responsibilities is often the culprit of dispute over issues of turf, product vision and priorities.

As discussed in Chapter 2, Experience Design, as a functional unit, is often hierarchically nested under another unit, such as marketing, product management, or engineering. In highly compartmentalized organizations, trust is sometimes an issue, and designers, who depend on the cooperation and agreement of all stakeholders, have a hard time aligning competing visions for the product.

In such scenarios, in is not uncommon for an exciting vision for a product experience strategy to get defused of fizzle out all together, due to imbalance caused by political in-fighting, over-dominance of one department or stakeholder which leads to lack of motivation and input from other stakeholders.

The following diagram shows the flatting effect that a culture of mutual trust has on successful design. Experience strategists, with a mandate from leadership, can reach out to each of the groups within a company, synthesize the various inputs, identify internal gaps in vision and priority, and help all stakeholders embrace a unified vision going forward. Such unified vision is often referred to as the **voice of the business**.

Over the past couple of decades, a growing number of organizations recognized the value of integrated design by forming in-house experience design departments and led by a senior designer who report directly to the CEO. Celebrated examples in the automotive tech and manufacturing industries include BMW, Apple, and Herman-Miller. The results of an integrated design are expressed in the quality of their products, improved sales performance, and increased customer satisfaction.

Although the trend points toward fully integrated design capabilities, there are still many organizations--that for various reasons, such as size, budget, or lack of skilled resources-- prefer to partner with design consultants which help them guide their product experience strategy. Design consultants can be effective when given autonomy and active support from leadership.

Business needs - research activities

Experience strategists conduct a number of research activities during the first phase of their experience design project. The purpose of the research is two-fold:

- It helps designers understand the company's vision and objectives for the product; that is, understand what is at stake. Based on this context, they work with stakeholders to align product objectives, obstacles, and success criteria for the project.
- Once an organizational alignment is achieved, research insights can help develop a product experience strategy that is aligned with agreed upon company objectives.

Research activities include:

- Stakeholder and subject-matter expert (SME) interviews
- Documents review
- Competitive research
- Expert product reviews

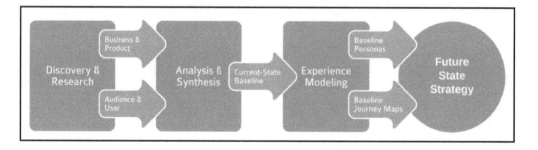

Stakeholder and subject-matter expert interviews

Stakeholders are typically senior managers and executives who have a direct responsibility for, or influence on the product. Stakeholders include product managers, who manage the planning and day-to-day activities associated with their product, and have a direct decision-making authority over its development. In strategic projects, it is not uncommon for the executive leadership from the chief-executive down, to be among the stakeholders.

The purpose of stakeholder interviews is to gather and understand the perspectives of individual stakeholders, and align the perspectives of all stakeholders around a unified vision regarding the scope, purpose, outcomes, opportunities, and obstacles involved in undertaking a new product development project. Gaps among stakeholders on fundamental project objectives and priorities will lead to serious trouble down the road. It is best to surface such deviations as early as possible, and help stakeholders reach a productive alignment.

The purpose of **subject-matter experts (SMEs)** interviews is to balance the strategic high-level thinking provided by stakeholders, with detailed insights from experienced employees, who are recognized for their deep domain expertise. Sales, customer service, and technical support employees have a wealth of operational knowledge of products and customers, which makes them invaluable when analyzing current processes and challenges.

Prior to the interviews, the experience strategist prepares an interview guide. The purpose of the guide is to ensure that:

- All stakeholders respond to the same questions
- All research topics are covered if interviews are conducted by different interviewers
- Interviews make the best use of stakeholders' valuable time

Some of the questions in the guide are general and directed at all participants, others are more specific and focus on the stakeholders' specific areas of responsibility. Similar guides are developed for SME interviews.

In-person interviews are the best, because they take place at the onset of the project and provide a good opportunity to build rapport and trust between designer and interviewee.

After a formal introduction regarding the purpose of the interview, and general questions regarding the person's role and professional experience, the person is asked for their personal assessment and opinions on various topics. Here is a sample of different topics:

- Objectives and obstacles
- Prioritized goals for the project
- What does success look like?
- What kind of obstacles the project is facing, and suggestions to overcome them
- Competition
    - Who are your top competitors?
    - Strength and weaknesses relative to the competition

- Product features and functionality
    - Which features are missing?
    - Differentiating features
    - Features to avoid

The interviews are designed to last no more than an hour and are documented with notes and audio recordings, if possible. The answers are compiled and analyzed in a report which points out consensus areas, gaps in vision and priorities, and other risks. The report is one of the inputs that feeds into the development of an overall product experience strategy.

Product expert reviews

Product expert reviews, sometimes referred to as heuristic evaluations, are professional assessments of a current product, which are performed by design experts for the purpose of identifying usability and user experience issues.

The thinking behind the expert review technique is very practical. Experience designers have the expertise to assess the experience quality of a product in a systematic way, using a set of accepted heuristics.

A heuristic is a rule of thumb for assessing products. For example, the 'error prevention' heuristic deals with how well the evaluated product prevents the user from making errors.

The word "heuristic" often raises questions, and the method has been criticized for its inherent weaknesses due to:

- Subjectivity of the evaluator
- Evaluator's lack of domain expertice relevant to the evaluated product
- Cultural and demographic background of the evaluator

These weaknesses increase the probability that an expert evaluation would reflect the biases and preferences of the evaluator and result in different conclusions from different evaluators.

Still, expert evaluations, especially if conducted by two evaluators, are an effective tool for experience practitioners who need a fast and cost-effective assessment of a product, particularly digital interfaces.

Jacob Nielsen developed the method in the early 1990s. Although there are other sets of heuristics, Nielsen's are probably the most well known and commonly used. His initial set of heuristics was first published in his book, *Usability Engineering*. It is presented here verbatim, since there is no need for modification:

- **Visibility of system status**: The system should always keep users informed about what is going on, through appropriate feedback within reasonable time.
- **Match between system and the real world**: The system should speak the user's language, with words, phrases, and concepts familiar to the user, rather than system-oriented terms. Follow real-world conventions, making information appear in a natural and logical order.
- **User control and freedom**: Users often choose system functions by mistake and will need a clearly marked "emergency exit" to leave the unwanted state without having to go through an extended dialogue. Support undo and redo.
- **Consistency and standards**: Users should not have to wonder whether different words, situations, or actions mean the same thing. Follow platform conventions.
- **Error prevention**: Even better than good error messages is a careful design which prevents a problem from occurring in the first place. Either eliminate error-prone conditions or check for them and present users with a confirmation option before they commit to the action.
- **Recognition rather than recall**: Minimize the user's memory load by making objects, actions, and options visible. The user should not have to remember information from one part of the dialogue to another. Instructions for use of the system should be visible or easily retrievable whenever appropriate.
- **Flexibility and efficiency of use**: Accelerators--unseen by the novice user--may often speed up the interaction for the expert user such that the system can cater to both inexperienced and experienced users. Allow users to tailor frequent actions.
- **Aesthetic and minimalist design**: Dialogues should not contain information which is irrelevant or rarely needed. Every extra unit of information in a dialogue competes with the relevant units of information and diminishes their relative visibility.
- **Help users recognize, diagnose, and recover from errors**: Error messages should be expressed in plain language (no codes), precisely indicate the problem, and constructively suggest a solution.
- **Help and documentation**: Even though it is better if the system can be used without documentation, it may be necessary to provide help and documentation. Any such information should be easy to search, focused on the user's task, list concrete steps to be carried out, and not be too large.

Competitive research and analysis

Companies operate in a competitive marketplace, and therefore, having a deep understanding of the competition is critical to a company's success and survival. Here are few of the questions that competitive research helps address:

- How does a product or service compare to the competition?
- What are the strength and weaknesses of competing offerings?
- What alternatives and choices does the target audience have?

Experience strategists use several methods to collect and analyze competitive information. From interviews with stakeholder and SMEs, they know who the direct competition is. In some product categories, such as automobiles and consumer products, companies can reverse-engineer competitive products and try to match or surpass their capabilities. Additionally, designers can develop extensive experience analysis of such competitive products, because access to and experience with the product is possible.

In some hi-tech products capabilities may be cocooned within proprietary software or secret production processes. In these cases, designers can glean the capabilities from an indirect evidence of use.

These days, the internet is a main source of competitive information - from direct access to a product online, to help manuals, user guides, bulletin boards, reviews, and analysis in trade publications. Occasionally, unauthorized photos or documents are leaked to the public domain, and they provide clues, sometimes real and sometimes bogus, about a secret upcoming product. Social media too is an important source of competitive data in the form of customer reviews on Yelp, Amazon, or Facebook. With the wealth of such information it is easier to focus the thinking of a differentiating and superior product experience.

For example, Uber, the car hailing service, generated public controversy which led to dissatisfied riders and drivers who were unhappy with its policies, including - until recently - its resistance to allowing riders tip their drivers: By design, a tipping function was not available in the app - the primary transaction method between rider, company, and driver.

Research indicates, however, that tipping for service is a common social norm, and that most people tip because it makes them feel better. Not being able to tip places riders in an uncomfortable social setting and stirred negative emotions against Uber. The evidence of dissatisfaction could be easily collected from numerous web sources and interviews with riders and drivers.

For Uber competitors such as Lyft and Curb making tipping an integrated part of their apps provided an immediate competitive edge that improves the experience of both riders, who have an option to reward the driver for their good service, and drivers, who benefit from an increased income. This, and additional improvements over the inferior Uber experience, become a part of an overall experience strategy focused on improving the likelihood that riders and drivers will dump Uber in their favor.

Defining the product - audience context

A number of models attempt to map out the relationship among companies, their products, and their target audience. In 1991, *Geoffrey Moore* suggested one influential model in his book, *Crossing the Chasm*.

This model helps company and product leadership think about the target audience for their upcoming product by segmenting people according to their attitudes toward a new technology - an important consideration, since technology plays a major role in many products.

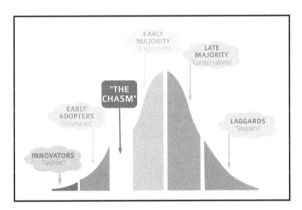

The preceding bell-curve diagram depicts the technology-adoption life cycle of a product. The center portion of the curve represents the largest number of potential customers, and their numbers decrease as the curve slopes down left and right. The curve is divided into five portions, each representing one of the following clusters of people:

- **Innovators**: On the far left of the curve are people who are not afraid of taking risks with products that at the 'bleeding edge', featuring new and sometimes untested technologies. The products may be so new that they are classified as Alpha or Beta releases, terms that refer to early versions of products still undergoing considerable development changes.

Innovators often also create new technologies themselves, and generally understand what they are getting themselves into with such products. "Techies", as the model refers to people in this segment, represent a small portion of the overall target audience.

- **Early adopters**: To the right of the innovators is a larger segment of people who love technology, have an interest in being early trend-setters, or enjoy the exclusivity and prestige that is associated with owning products. Back in the 1990's, for example, products in the category included large-screen plasma televisions and hybrid cars - items are are common place today, or in the case of plasma TV, have been nearly pushed out of the existence due to LCD displays. Early versions, however, tend to be expensive because they are produced in smaller quantities at higher costs per unit, and their distribution is limited. *Visionaries*, as the model refers to people in this segment, are influencers, since their product choices tend to be followed.

- **Early majority and late majority**: Occupying the center of the curve are two groups that represent the largest portion of total audience for the product-- people who are likely to purchase once it's value has been proven by the previous segments.

  As the buzz around the product reverberates through word-fo-mouth and social network, its position as a desirable status symbol firms up, as does its value and cost preposition. It gains critical mass as the early majority of customers, the 'pragmatists', buy it in droves. The curve peeks, and as time passes, the product matures, evolves and becomes a 'safe bet' which appeals to the second big wave of customers - the 'conservatives', as the late majority is referred to in the model. The curve continues to slope down: as the product becomes more popular, it becomes less exclusive and eventually early adopters move on to the new-new thing, and the cycle begins for a new product.

- **Laggards**: The segment on the far right of the curve represents people who are diametrically opposite to the innovators and early adopters segments. They are generally suspicious of new technology and refuse to consider it unless they must. Instead, they stick with the products they own until they can no longer be repaired or replaced by a similar product. Often, the source of their resistance to change is not related to financial means and ability to afford the new technology, but because they see no value in doing so. They are *skeptics*, as the model refers to the group, whose size in the model equals the combined two segments on the far left of the curve.

A major unknown question for a company often centers around the adoption rate of its new product--will it be liked by early adopters, and if so, how long will the transition to the early majority segment take? The transition gap between the segments is the chasm that must be crossed for the product to become a commercial success. If the transition does not happen, or it is too slow, the product and possibly the company might fail.

Over the past three decades companies tried various approaches to gaining success in an attempt to capitalize on the market's appetite for the latest technological trends. In recent years, however, this appetite has flattened out as customers became more interested in ease of use. Experience design has emerged as a significant contributor to helping companies bridge the adoption gap.

Companies are pressured to deliver new versions of their product every year or two, because their revenue is realized by selling more items each year. Customers, however, reach a point of saturation, satisfied with the version of the product they already have, they don't feel that a few new features justify the effort and cost of replacement.

Think about going to the best restaurant in the world. You are served the best food you have ever tasted. It is an "eat as much as you can" buffet, and you eat until you can no longer put anything in your mouth. Once you are full, any additional food, regardless of how fantastically great it is, will not be enjoyable. In fact, overeating will hurt your overall dining experience.

When loyal early adopters and early majority customers reach a saturation point and are disinterested in upgrading their existing product, they are probably ready for a new, different, and refreshing alternative. Increasingly, new options are not similar products with more features. Instead, they make an existing product experience obsolete.

For example, the experience of using software products inevitably involved purchase and update steps, which had a couple of major drawback for customers and software maker:

- When a new version of the software was released, the customer had to pay for an upgrade, and sometimes, pay the full cost of the new version if their old version no longer qualified for a discount.
- Installation of software was often complicated by lost licenses, hardware incompatibilities, and other technical glitches. Software updates involved reinstallation, which was too complicated for many users, and even when web-based automatic updates became common, many customers did not keep up with the latest patches and updates.
- The customer had to pay the full price of the software even when they needed it only for a single or infrequent use.

Cloud-based **software-as-a-service** (**SaaS**) has emerged as a solution that eliminated those three issues. In 2005, the start-up, Upstartle (later acquired by Google), created a browser-based word processor called Writely, which has since been renamed **Google Docs**.

Google Docs was one of the pioneering products to compete with a powerful market leader (Microsoft Word, in this case) and essentially changed the entire way most software are experienced today. It has eliminated the cost of software--it was free, no installation was involved, because it was hosted on the cloud and accessed through most web browsers, which also meant that new features and updates appeared immediately upon release.

Within a decade, Microsoft had to switch its entire Office suite to the cloud, as the old model of software ownership faded away. The trend towards a subscription-based model has expanded from software to the products, as companies are experimenting with applying the model to physical products, such as cars and large appliances. The customer gains all the benefits associated with owning the item, at a fraction of a cost, while the company gets to extend the number of subscribers and offer a scaling model of features. Such a model provides a basic set of features and capabilities as a low introductory price, often for free.

The low cost translates to low risk for the customer who is trying out the product, and everyone wins: The most basic access is often offered for free, while more expensive subscription tiers provide more features and functionalities focused on meeting the needs of professionals, teams and enterprises, as illustrated the following screenshot of LucidChart.com, a could-based charting software:

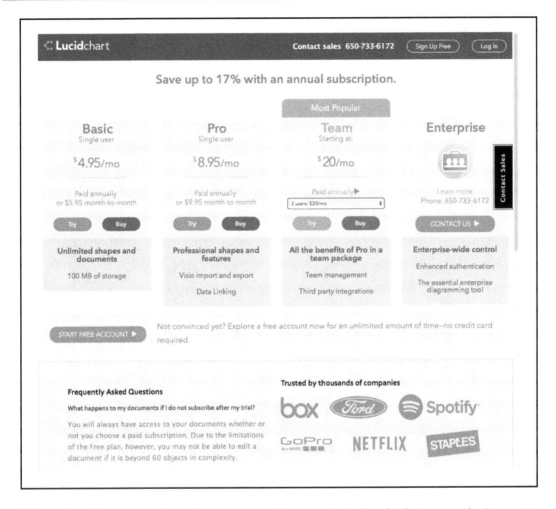

Additionally, this approach addresses a core design principle which stresses the importance of reducing the overload and complexity of the experience.

Features versus experience

Another influential model has contributed to the emergence of experience design as a leading strategy for product success. A core element of the 'Treacy Value Proposition Framework', which was created by Michael Treacy and Fred Wiersema, is an idea of *customer intimacy*: Essentially building a life-long relationship with customers by developing a deep understanding of a specific audience segment's needs. Customer engagement and brand loyalty are outcomes of product experiences that reflect this understanding.

Another way to think about the approach to product design, is to consider features vs. experiences using a car as a product example, as illustrated in the models below:

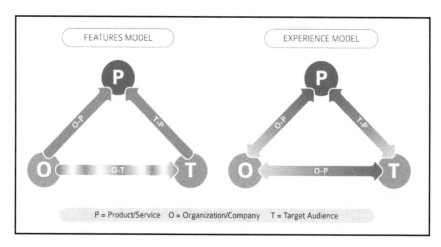

- The path **T-P** illustrates the relationship between a target audience and the product. In the features model, the target audience evaluates the supply of all available cars and chooses the car that most fits its needs. For example, people who needed a reliable car for tough winters seem to prefer cars by Subaru, which has a standard four-wheel drive; families with young children seem to prefer the space, convenience, and utility of Honda Odyssey minivans; and so on.
- The path **O-P** connects the company to the product. In the features model, the company evaluates the supply of all available cars and identifies the various audience segments according to their choice of products by their features. In the case of cars, features include four-wheel drive, or a minivan. The company competes with others on providing cars that have more or better features that will attract their target audience.

- The path **O-T** connects the company and its target audience. In the features model, the link is weak: The company can easily gauge its competition and decide which popular features to imitate and improve upon. Audience research and expensive R&D efforts could be minimized because that effort has already been taken by the competition.

However, a weak link between the company and its audience only works when technical features are involved: If the competition releases a device with a 6" screen, the company can release a 'better' product with an 8" screen at an equal or lower price, and so on. But as the focus shifts to product experience, offering a larger, more powerful yet cheaper hardware does not cut it any more. To understand how to improve upon competing experiences, the company must invest in building a direct strong link to its customers. The right triangle in the diagram above illustrates an emerging experience approach in which all the connectors--**TP**, **OP**, and **OT** are bi-directional, as constant communications flow between the company and its users through data-driven products. With that data, the company can gain exclusive insights into use patterns, preferences and needs, and continue improving its products with the confidences of measurement and feedback.

Feedback from users flows directly back into the product in the form of data usage analytics, and to the company, through social networks. Companies often have up-to-the-moment data that identifies changes in patterns of use. This intimacy level of knowledge at the user level makes possible on-the-fly adjustments to the user-experience in order to reverse or strengthen various patterns of use and improve the person's satisfaction.

In the complex market reality we live in, most companies struggle to find an approach that endures, due to constant change. Fresh approaches are required as a response to new trends, or due to the desire to set them. While more companies engage in developing a unified experience approach for their products, the notion that the product IS the experience is still novel in many boardrooms. Traditionally, marketing builds product demand, and the 'front-end' of the experience in the form of emotional anticipation. Customer service deals with the tail-end of the experience by addressing issues customers have with the product post purchase. Not much has been invested in the *middle* pat--the actual experience of using the product.

Next, we will move on to an exploration of research and modeling activities that are focused on understanding the needs and expectations of product users. This phase of the project is informed by and builds upon the outputs from the *voice of the business* phase. Its focus is to find and express the voice of the user to the project team.

Audience Research

Potential investors want to know who might purchase the product, why, at what price, and how many potential customers are out there. Experience strategists set out the research similar questions to understand the audience context. This information leads to an understanding of the individual people who might purchase the product, and eventually to the development of a product experience strategy.

The following diagram maps out an audience funnel that connects a company and its product to the individual consumer. The term "funnel" is in reference to the narrowing of the total market for the product down to specific audience segments.

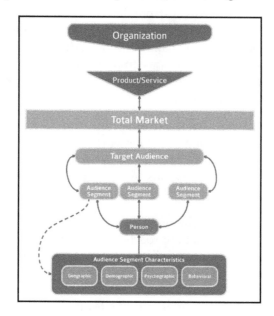

The total market for a company's product is the largest possible cluster of people who may share common interests or needs, which are addressed by the product, or will be addressed by a new product the company plans to offer in the future. Total markets can appear to be deliciously large. For example, the audience for a product such as the Flip camcorder is potentially everyone in the world who wants to make videos. That's a lot of people and a lot of camcorders to manufacture and distribute in the hope that all will be sold.

When taking a closer look at the total market, it actually begins to shrink significantly: Not everyone in the world who wants to make video can afford to purchase the device, or care enough to actually purchase the device. There are professionals and hobbyists for whom the product's video quality is unacceptable, others may already have a camcorder, or plan to purchase a tape camcorder, and so on.

The remainder of the total market is the product's target audience, people who are attracted to the product due to the combination of its experience design, simplicity, and low cost-- those who are frustrated with the complexity of the camcorder they own, others who will purchase it in addition to their camcorder, those who planned to purchase a new camcorder and like the simplicity of the product, those who will purchase the product as a gift, and so on.

Historically, the notion of targeting audiences and audience segments has gradually evolved from the advent of the industrial revolution in the mid-eighteenth century. Mass manufacturing coincided with many other emerging trends. Steam locomotives and steam freight ships made it possible to move large quantities of goods from factories to urban centers and large quantities of fresh produce from the countryside to cities, quickly and inexpensively. Proliferation of jobs in factories and services led to a raise in the disposable income for many workers in industrial countries.

For the first time in human civilization, it became possible for millions of people to spend money on products that are not essential for survival.

Fast-forward to our times, marked by a global economy, network-connected high-tech products, advanced logistics, product miniaturization, and huge markets for companies. Facebook, a social network company, has over a billion and a half users. According to http://www.internetlivestats.com/, Google executes over 1.2 trillion search queries annually, and Microsoft claims that more than 1.2 trillion users around the world use its Office product, in 107 languages.

However, reach of this magnitude is not limited to digital products and services. Many manufactures of physical products, such as Ford, Walmart, and McDonalds, established global production and distribution centers, which enable them to reach hundreds of millions of people. The latest trends in manufacturing, such as 3D printing, open up such opportunities to small companies to compete on a global scale, because printing products locally significantly cuts the cost and complexity of manufacturing and distribution.

The total potential market for many companies operating today is a large portion of the world's entire population. It is remarkable that only a century ago, just a handful of companies could imagine such an outlook, and a century before that, such an outlook was inconceivable. Coupled with the broadening of reach, is the transformation from mass production, limited product variety, and minimal personalization - to fully personalized production on demand. The trend is toward each individual customer ordering their unique version of the product.

Naturally, the larger the markets and audiences, the more robust the competition. This benefits individual users because with competition comes a wider choice of product options and price-points. Companies that are able to deliver a user experience that builds a strong emotional connection between users and their product stand a chance to dominate their market.

For example, like previous Apple products, its first generation of iMac computers was revolutionary in targeting a slice of the overall market for personal computers at the time. iMacs helped Apple greatly expand its share of that market, blending its B2B and B2C audiences--individuals, families, and users at corporations and educational institutions worldwide were mesmerized by a personal computer that was drastically different from anything else offered by its competitors.

Compared to computers that were packaged in uninspiring beige boxes, the iMac offered a set of competing experiences:

- It was shaped as an egg shell, whereas PCs of that era were shaped as rectangles.
- It came in five translucent colors, which made it possible to see its inside. Considering that computers are very visible in the home and in the office, the unique shape and choice of colors, coupled with the ability to see the computer's inner parts, made the iMac a delightful piece of home furniture to look at. Keep in mind that at the time, beige boxes wholly dominated the personal computing market.

- It delivered on the promise of true plug-and-play: get the product out of the box, connect keyboard and mouse, connect modem cord to the phone jack, plug to electricity, and start using your new computer!
  For Apple customers familiar with Macintosh computers, this and other iMac experiences further strengthened their emotional attachment to the company and its products. For new Apple customers, the elegant unboxing experience provided a powerful first impression even before turning the computer on.
- The "i" in the iMac's name further connected the emotional and intimate aspect of the person-machine relationship.

Audience segments and their characteristics

An audience segment is a subset of a product's target audience - a collection of individuals with shared characteristics along four dimensions:

- Geographic
- Demographic
- Psychographic
- Behavioral

We began this chapter with the Flip, a successful camcorder that coexisted with the iPhone and competing smartphones during the later part of this century's first decade. While it was selling well when it was discontinued at the start of this decade, the product's eventual decline could be predicted by the rise of smartphones: Many experience features that made the Flip a success, were matched or surpassed by camcorders built into smartphones, and as these became ubiquitous, the single-purpose Flip would have become redundant and irrelevant.

In the coming example we will look at how another small and simple camcorder was able to capture a segment of the camcorder audience DESPITE the availability of good camcorders in smartphone.

GoPro is a company that makes wearable video cameras, which are popular in the outdoors and sports community. While the Flip made it easy to take videos using a single hand, GoPro cameras are mounted, and thus enabled a user to shoot videos without using their hands at all.

With the camcorder attached to helmets, headbands, and other gear, parachutists, divers, climbers, cyclists, runners, auto racers, and others can record high-quality video of their activity from their point of view or other unusual vantage points--an option that was unattainable before without specialized professional gear.

The product enables its owners to document and share the beauty and excitement of their remote, and sometimes dangerous outdoor adventures with family and friends, on the web, and on social networks - a unique and compelling feature. Coupled with the reliability of the product under a wide range of extreme conditions, it helps build an emotional connection between the person using the camcorder and the product, a bond which can be difficult for a competing product to break.

What would a hypothetical segmentation of GoPro's audience look like?

- **Geographic**: Because the product can be used everywhere, its audience is not restricted to a specific geographical area. To narrow the field, it is logical to focus on mountains (climbing, ski, snowboarding, or hiking) and beaches (sailing, kayaking, fishing, surfing, or diving).
- **Demographic**: There is no particular restriction on age, gender, education level, marital status, occupation, or religion. To narrow the field, it is logical to focus on segments such as extreme sportsmen, men and female, and between the ages of 18-40.

- **Psychographic**: Active life style is a characteristic that helps narrow the audience for GoPro products. Although other video recorders, including those on every smartphone, satisfy the needs of most people, they are not a good fit for certain outdoor activities and extreme sports. Another characteristic is shared values, and for people who value independence, the ability to self-record and share a great footage is essential.
- **Behavioral**: To expand beyond the active outdoors segment, the need to capture precious moments and preserve important memories makes GoPro cameras perfect for documenting special occasions, such as birthday parties, vacations, or weddings in a special and engaging way.

The GoPro example demonstrate how a small company with a product in an over-saturated market such as camcorders, can be successful by focusing on a product experience strategy that caters to untapped needs of customers in special segments, such as active life, extreme sports, and outdoors adventure. The product's audience can be expanded to other segments, such as documenting special occasions, on the strength of its reputation with its core audience segments.

Audience needs - research activities

Most successful companies know their product's target audience and it segmentation. However, rapid technological advancements, sweeping changes in customers' attitudes and expectations, and the rise in the importance of product experience leave many companies scrambling to understand how the changing landscape of customers' preferences impacts their new or redesigned products.

Since it is the role of marketing departments to identify and engage product audiences, they are constantly researching their markets. This research helps shape the brand's identity and mission statement, develop advertising campaigns, deal with competition, guide the direction of products, and identify new market opportunities. Marketing research supports experience research and is crucial in shaping the product's experience strategy, which explains why marketing departments typically champion investments in experience design.

Occasionally, an organization might discount the need for early research, claiming to have a good understanding of its audience. This may be true in some cases, but generally, forgoing research is a risk. Fast rate of technological change makes it difficult for business stakeholders busy running their organization, to sense changes in sentiment toward their offerings, or identify the emergence of a serious competitor outside of the known field of existing competitions.

Experience strategists focus audience research activities on collecting quantitative and qualitative data on people's needs from a product and their experience expectations. The methods used include online surveys and visioning workshops. The latter promises to be more effective for experience research than traditional focus groups, because designers get to actively engage users in imagining the future of a product in a workshop.

Online surveys

You have most likely participated in a marketing survey. Perhaps, you were asked to provide feedback on your satisfaction with a recent hotel stay, a service you used, a product you purchased, and so on. You were asked questions that had you convert your experience into numbers--questions, such as on a scale of 1 to 7, with 1 being terrible, and 7 being great, please rate the cleanliness of the room you stayed at or the attitude of the service representative or the sound quality on your new headset.

Companies such as Survey Monkey, Typeform, Survey Gizmo, and others, helped popularize the survey method. Improved survey authoring, publishing, collection, and analysis tools, combined with free or otherwise affordable subscription options, greatly reduced the need for professional researchers. Experience designers were early to identify the possibilities and incorporate surveys into the design process.

Of course, the direct consequence of surveys being so popular has resulted with us all being constantly bombarded with them. Survey "fatigue", leading people to ignore participation in surveys, has had some impact on overall response rates, but in general, if the request relates to a product or service people care about, they are more likely to respond.

With surveys, designers can form a measurable understanding of people's needs, attitudes, expectations, and concerns. They use the results to map out *the gaps* between the current version of a product and the expectations of the product's target audience. Understanding the gaps helps develop a holistic experience product strategy. Additional surveys during the user research and concepting phases focus on specific product features.

Survey examples

Here are a few examples of experience attributes that audience research can effectively explore in the context of an e-commerce website or app. Each attribute in the example is tied to a sample question in the scale of 1 to 10, with 1 being the most negative response, 10 is the most positive. Note that in practice, designers and researchers use a variety of scales, such as *Agree/Disagree, Low/Medium/High, Like/Dislike/Neutral, Totally Disagree/Disagree/Somewhat Disagree/Neutral/Somewhat Agree/Agree/Totally Agree*, and so on.

- **Attribute**: Sense of security
    - **Question**: How does the site make you feel about the security of your personal information, including credit card details?
    (Scale of 1 to 10. 1 = Extremely concerned, 10= I fully trust the site)
    - **Explanation**: When the current site lacks the latest security features such as a two-factor authentication, the customer may interpret the experience as an evidence of lack of competency on the company's side and abandon the transaction. The opposite is true if the experience aligns with the user's expectations for security.

- **Attribute**: Overall look and feel
    - **Question**: Thinking about your experience on the site, what is your overall impression of the company?
    (Scale of 1 to 10. 1 = Underwhelmed, 10=Highly Impressed)
    - **Explanation**: Polished and well-executed experience is evidence of a technology-savvy company, a proof of the product's value and quality. Experiences that trend to the opposite project negatively on the company's image.

- **Attribute**: Experience consistency
    - **Question**: Thinking about your experience on the site, what is your overall impression of the company?
    (Scale of 1 to 10. 1 = Underwhelmed, 10=Highly Impressed)
    - **Explanation**: When a site or app are patched together to incorporate old and new sections, the user might be confused by inconsistent navigation, layouts and content placement. Consistency helps the user orient quickly, and makes the site easy to use. On mobile devices, inconsistent experience often means that some pages are not responsive, while other pages are. The first situation may generate negative impressions of the company and its products, while the second leads to positive feelings.

- **Attribute**: Clarity of content
  - **Question**: Do you agree with the statement "Finding the model I needed was easy"?
    (Scale of 1 to 10. 1 = Strongly Disagree, 10=Strongly Agree)
  - **Explanation**: When content on the site is well organized, well written, and is available in context, it increases the user's feeling of comfort, and helps in making purchase decisions with confidence, adding to their trust in the company and product. This is especially important for companies with multiple types of products, which require comparison in order to find the best fit. The opposite leads to user hesitation, frustration, and abandonment of the site.

- **Attribute**: Mobile experience
  - **Question**: Do you agree with the statement "Using the site on my phone is easy"?
    (Scale of 1 to 10. 1 = Strongly Disagree, 10=Strongly Agree)
  - **Explanation**: Increasingly, commerce is conducted and content is accessed primarily online. Websites and apps that are hard to navigate, have incompatible or confusing content, are slow and unattractive - will reflect negatively on the company and its product(s), reducing the company's ability to generate revenue through its online channels.

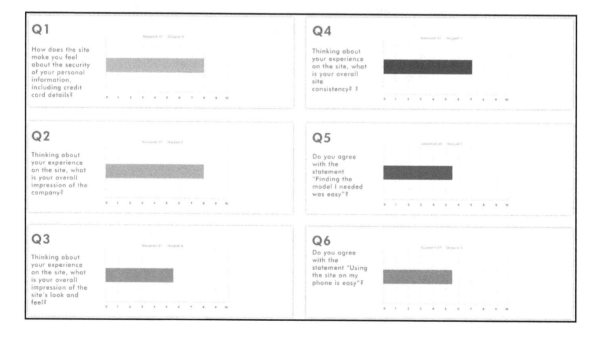

For this example, let's suppose that the survey results show the following:

- 20% of all survey respondents felt that the site is not secure; there were no 10s or 9s responses at all
- Of all survey respondents, 45% felt underwhelmed by their overall experience on the site; only 20% of users rated 9s and 10s
- Of all survey respondents, 52% felt underwhelmed by the company, due to significant inconsistencies in their experience; only 5% of users rated 9s and 10s
- Of all survey respondents, 60% didn't find the product they needed on the site easy; only 8% of users rated 9s and 10s
- Of all survey respondents, 70% didn't feel that the mobile experience was easy; there were no 10s or 9s responses at all

- These are pretty awful but not unusual results. Surveys often confirm what the company leaders already know, and support the case for a redesign effort. Typically, however, few companies let their important online assets reach this point. In fact, many invest in continuous and frequent refreshes and updates, in order to maintain their competitive edge.

Summary

All the activities described so far were meant to enable designers to fuse business and audience perspectives, and emerge with a product strategy that is focused on user experience as a means to achieving product success.

Getting to this point can take between a few weeks and a few months, depending on multiple factors, such as the complexity of the product, the number and types of research activities, size of the design team, and so on.

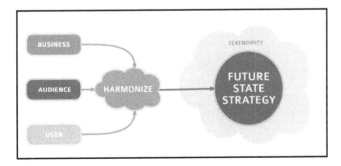

Research establishes a starting point for the design, a baseline understanding of the product's audience and audience segments. For existing products, it is an assessment of the gaps between the product's promise, the expectations it builds, and the customer's assessments of has been delivered. The wider that gap, the higher the risk of weakening a hold, or losing market share.

The next chapter takes on the topic of a user-centered discovery and research activities-- activities that complement and expend the contextual foundation designers must establish in order to form an experience product strategy.

4

The User and Context of Use

"All generalizations are false, including this one."

-Mark Twain

The primary questions this addresses are:

- What are the methods and tools that experience designers use to learn about the user they are designing for?
- What kind of user and use information is relevant to the experience design process?
- How can the specific needs of an individual user be generalized to the product design, yet reflect the diverse needs of many other individual users?

We will be shifting from research activities focused on the product's maker, audience, and segmentation that we explored in the preceding chapter, to research activities focused on the product's individual user--from understanding what the company hopes and expects to get out of its investments in design, to understanding the experience, features, and capabilities that will engage the user with the product and provide the most value.

Thinking about user needs and desires

Products and services existed for centuries, but user research is relatively new. In the past, the needs of most people were limited to the bare essentials. Most needs were supplied locally, and exposure to nonlocal goods has been limited to sporadic visits of traveling salesmen and their small inventory. The wealthy were exposed to exotic materials, spices, and foods, which were imported in small quantities from other lands.

Over the past three centuries, the advent of industrialization, mixed with improved economic conditions and increased prosperity of large populations in developed countries, led to exponential growth in manufacturing capabilities, consumer demand for nonessential products, and companies that make and sell them. With the increase in the number of companies came competition, which requires companies to differentiate themselves and their products from similar offerings.

A common form of differentiation used to focus on beating competing products over technology with new features and a dazzling list of functionalities, often, at a lower price. However, over the past few decades, both the consumer and commercial market have reached feature saturation. Additional technological improvements no longer entice consumers to replace what they have.

For example, when television sets became popular in the 1950s, few companies produced them. Demand increased despite the fact that early models were expensive, screens were small, and the image was in black and white. With an increase in demand came an increase in the number of competing manufacturers--screens got larger, image quality improved, and prices went down.

When color television sets were introduced, consumers rushed to purchase them despite the fact that their black and white sets were still fully functional, and color models were expensive. Shortly after, even more manufacturers were competing in that space, by offering larger screens and better image and sound quality--at lower prices. A similar cycle happened with digital, flat-screen, and high-definition television sets. Over time, the trend has leveled: Consumers were reluctant to adopt 3D and Ultra HD sets, for example. The reason is that the viewing experience has not been compelling enough to motivate consumers to replace their relatively new sets whose image quality is excellent.

The strategy for gaining a competitive edge is shifting toward forging a life-long relationship and brand loyalty with the individual user. The thinking is that a company and product that create such an emotional connection will have an edge over competitors, as long as it can maintain and exceed the customer's expectations.

Understanding the user needs and expectations is becoming a primary focus for companies, and a key driver for experience design projects.

Robots and Pencils, a company that specializes in creating mobile apps, describes a few surprising research findings related to people's response to conversational user interfaces. In such interfaces, the user engages with a **bot**--an artificial intelligence agent that helps the user perform a task.

It turns out that people don't necessarily want the bot they interact with to appear human. So, while the technology makes it possible to create an experience in which a conversational interface could simulate a human, having access to user research helps companies to avoid creating experiences that are the opposite of what people actually want.

The following figure outlines personal needs on the spectrum of the user's financial means, from **poor** to **affluent**:

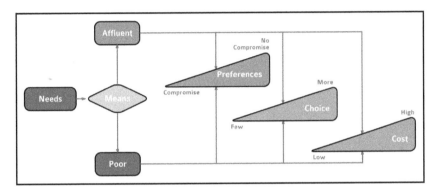

Needs can be prioritized from bare necessities to discretionary luxury goods. How much money one has, impacts one's ability to have not only what one needs, but also what one desires. With more money, there are a lot more choices to pick from. **Choice** is good, but, as research into happiness and satisfaction shows, having too many choices can be confusing, eventually leading to a sense of regret that the choice made was not the best.

- The poorer the buyer, the cost of the product is the first and primary filter used to narrow down the list of possible options. Personal preferences are the least relevant because choices are often limited, and people have to compromise. As the saying goes "If you ask about the price (of a luxury good), it means you cannot afford it."
- The more affluent the buyer, the less the need to compromise one's personal preferences. Personal preferences are the primary influence on the narrowing-down of possible choices, while the product's cost becomes least important.

Although it is true that many cheap products are inferior in quality to more expensive ones, scientific and technological advancements in materials and manufacturing has led to a wide availability of low-cost but high-quality products.

The following figure models the tension between needs and desires:

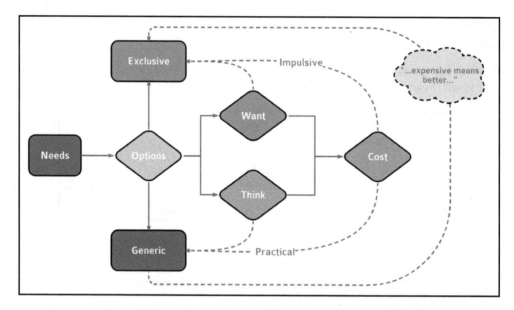

The image above illustrates the tension between needs and desire, in which expensive items are affordable to far fewer people, making them exclusive and alluring despite the fact that far cheaper substitutes address the same needs. For example, people tend to assume that expensive wines are better than cheaper wines, and therefore, will spend more than they would normally do, when purchasing wine as a gift. That, despite the fact that blind testing experiments have proved time and again that cheaper wines and expensive wines score similarly.

From an experience design perspective, making a product reflect exclusivity is often an important consideration. The choice of materials, quality of craftsmanship, choice of typography, and even colors can all add up to the appearance of true exclusivity. Attempting to imitate luxury and exclusivity risks making the product appear fake and cheap--"a wannabe"--which can turn off potential buyers.

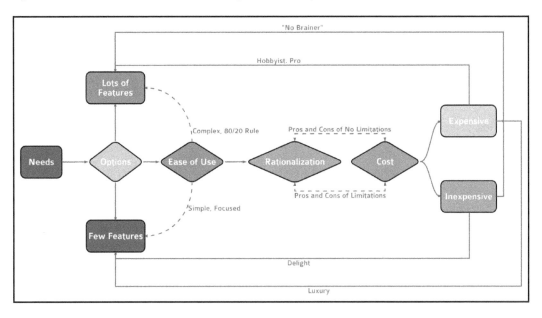

The preceding figure illustrates a dimension of experience, which focuses on simplification: User needs can be placed on a spectrum that ranges from a product that supports few features to one that supports many features. Consumers often think that the more features a product supports, the better it is--even if the user will not be using the majority of the features. The fact that the features are there creates an impression of value. This conflicting choices for many is made easy if the cost of the simple option is low--unless the simple option is also expensive, which then shifts it to a luxury category.

User research

Most companies conduct market research on an ongoing basis. The research helps identify, connect, and expand target audiences by guiding the development, evolution and change of a brand identity. While many of the methods used by marketers and experience designers are similar, their research objectives are complementary and not redundant. A close collaboration between the disciplines benefits both the organizations as well as the final product design.

One difference between marketing and experience research has to do with the number of participants in the research. The number of participants is known as the **sample size**. There are statistical methods to determine the sample size for a given research activity, which is important in scientific, social, and some commercial research/

Sites like Checkmarket.com, for example, provide calculators that help determine how many survey invites should be sent out, such that the number of those who actually respond, is representative of the entire target audience.

For example, if the target audience is 1 million, the sample size is 2,400. However, a lot more invites should be sent out, because few people respond. In this example, the estimate is that 12,000 invites will be needed to get to the sample size.

Very few experience design projects use quantitative research methods that require statistically significant samples. That's because:

- Tight budgets, schedules, and resources make it difficult to incorporate large-scale research activities in the development process.
- Often, in-depth conversations with a small number of participants is sufficient to surface clear and detailed use-patterns of needs and preferences.
- Quantitative user research methods, such as contextual inquiry, are not automated and require the direct involvement of the designer in the research activity. Obviously, this presents a scaling limitation.

Many of the products and services created today are data driven and have the capability to constantly collect massive amounts of use data. This is quantitative data, and it provides strong attitudinal and behavioral patterns of the entire user base. However, availability of such data is not an excuse to forego user engagement through direct research.

In Chapter 3, *Business Context and Experience Strategy*, we explored a number of research activities that focus on defining business objectives and product audiences, as initial steps to defining the best product experience. In the user research phase, the focus is on understanding the individual user and the context of use--why, when, and how a person will use the product or service.

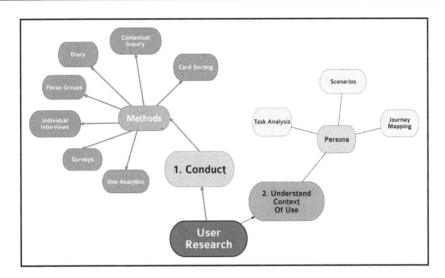

The preceding figure illustrates the cluster of user research activities that could be performed early in the design process. Research results help the entire team plan the project and develop concepts. Defining research objectives is the overarching theme that governs which of the methods to use, how to design the activities, and how they might be applied to the design.

Experience design research is critically important, but is considered a practice-based type of research, which means that it yields meaningful results without having to adhere to the rigors of scientific inquiry.

In the relatively short history of experience design, it has not been practical for most companies to conduct massive research efforts, and in some cases - any type of research. One of the major challenges that still confronts experience practitioners remains the need to convince their clients to include the time and expense associated with sufficient research activities in the product development timeline.

The following diagram shows common steps required throughout the entire research effort, which spans planning the research, conducting it, and analysis of results.

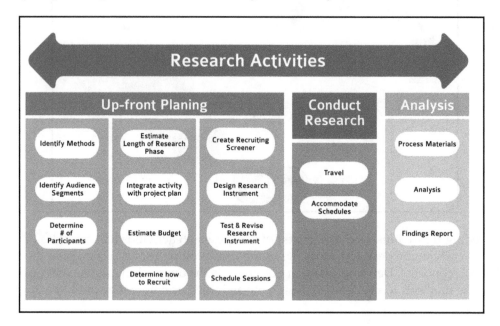

User research takes time, a major concern to the schedule of any fast pace design project. It can also be expensive if travel is required. For many organizations, this is a show stopper. Any research activity requires consideration of the following :

Upfront planning--research design:

- Identify the appropriate research method for the project
- Identify which audience segments should be researched and where participants can be found
- Decide how many participants will provide a sufficient coverage

Upfront planning--logistics:

- Determine how many days or weeks each research activity will take
- Sequence research activities in the overall project plan
- Estimate research budgets
- Decide how to recruit participants, and determine the need to use a recruiting firm

Upfront research design:

- Create a recruiting screener
- Design research instruments
- Test research instruments
- Schedule sessions and travel

Conduct research:

- Travel time
- Accommodate the participant's schedule

Post-research activity:

- Process research materials, such as transcribing a recordings tag, and taking notes
- Analyze research materials
- Create a report on research findings

Incredibly, all research methods mentioned so far are fairly simple, and do not require specialized tools. Professional tools and services are, of course, available, but fundamentally, the barriers for conducting user research are minimal, and that's fantastic.

Card sorting

At the time of writing this, *Spotify*--the music subscription service, lists about 1,500 genres and subgenres of music. The site `everynoise.com` offers an entertaining experience for exploring Spotify's genres using an algorithmic visualization. The site `musicmap.info` provides a beautifully engaging and insightful presentation of the history of hundreds of popular music genres from the 1870s to the present. The site `musicgenreslist.com`, which claims to have "The most definitive music genre list on the web", has a more traditional display of genres organized in hierarchical clusters.

The problem is that in music, as with fashion, technology, food, and nearly all areas of content, it is getting very difficult to be *definitive* when it comes to classifying, grouping and organizing new information. Wikipedia lists over 80 shoe styles, New Balance lists nearly 70 shoe categories, and Samsung offers nearly 70 TV models differentiated by technology, series, and size.

Key aspects of a great experience design involve fast discovery and easy navigation, which is challenging with so many content category options. Figuring out how to create navigation and organize content for discoverability, is part of Information Architecture, a topic is described in more detail in `Chapters 6`, *Design Disciplines*. Card sorting is a technique that helps designers figure out content organization questions.

Why use it in experience design?

Card sorting is an optional research activity, which works well for projects that involve presenting and navigating vast amount of structured data, such as in retail, manufacturing, construction, and other domains that involve finding items in large catalogs.

This method can help resolve very specific research questions for which the design team does not have a definitive answer due to ambiguity, conflicting approaches, or lack of sufficient knowledge. Examples for such questions are as follows:

- What should be the order of menu items of an application?
- Which terminology do users expect or prefer, especially in navigation elements and on call for action buttons--for example, Log In, Login, or Sign In?
- Of a list of features a product could support, which are the most important?

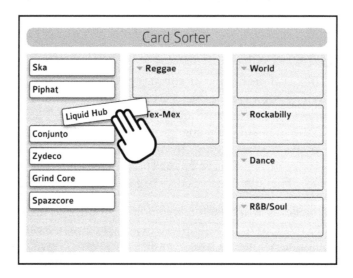

How to use it in experience design

When the design team understands that it is facing a problem that is suitable for the card sorting method, it needs to move quickly--the issues often impact the global structure of the product or the organization of key data elements and features. This dependency can delay concept development.

Typical planning steps for the formulation of research objectives for the card sorting method include:

1. State the design problem.
2. Determine who will participate in the research--internal stakeholders or potential users.
3. Determine whether the research should be facilitated by a person or automated; plan the logistics accordingly.
4. Based on decisions made using the preceding steps, create the cards--physical or using software.
5. Run the activity.
6. Analyze and present results, and come to an agreement on approach.

Pros

The pros of using card sorting are:

- The research problem may not be evident during the early phases of planning the project. Its low cost, speed of deployment, and flexibility make it a perfect tool for use at the time of need.
- It provides fast results and is relatively easy to analyze. Difficulties with analysis might indicate a disconnect between the designer's understanding of the product's and the user's need.
- Ability to use as a facilitated or non-facilitated exercise:
  - The facilitated approach works well as an activity moderated by designers during visioning workshops with stakeholders or users, and in focus groups.
  - The non-facilitated method has the potential to provide feedback from a large number of respondents.

Cons

When planned and conducted with precision, this method - cheap, easy and fast, has no cons.

Contextual inquiries (CI)

Simply put, **contextual inquiry** (**CI**) is a scripted interview with an individual user, typically coupled with an observation of how that individual performs tasks that the new design might address.

The idea behind CI is rooted in anthropological and sociological studies in which the subjects of research are observed in their natural habitat. To experience designers, this type of direct contact with users is invaluable. After spending long hours for months thinking about the product, it is easy for members of the product team to develop a myopic mindset in which the product is also the most important thing in the user's life. Contextual inquiry provides an opportunity to restore perspective, without losing the significance of the product in its context of use:

- A wide perspective that contextualizes the use of the product within a broader aspects of the user's personal or work life. For example, developers of lesson planning software for teachers get to understand how the use of the software fits into a teacher's busy schedule, which is consumed by hours of classroom time, meetings, curriculum development, and other professional activities. Within this broad context, the busy teacher who can access the tool only during short bursts of free time, needs the software to be as efficient, easy to use, fast and productive as possible.
- A deep perspective that provides a comprehensive understanding of how the product might be used for the purpose it is intended for--in the case of the software for teachers, the order in which teachers approach various tasks associated with lesson planning, such as resource gathering, homework assignment, test writing, and student assessment.

Why use it in experience design?

The closer experience designers are to their audience, the more successful their design will be. Contextual inquiry provides one of the best opportunities for designers to spend quality time with actual users and build an emotional connection that will be reflected in the design. The methodology provides a realistic picture of how the user currently interacts with a product or service, as opposed to opining on the use of a hypothetical product.

Although there is a practical limit to the number of people that can be interviewed, and that number is often in the low tens for many projects, the volume and value of detailed, nuanced data that gets collected is significant.

How to use it in experience design?

While the inclusion of contextual inquiry can be anticipated during the creation of the project plan, only basic assumptions, such as the number of interviews that will be conducted, can be made for the purposes of scheduling and budgeting. High-level scheduling should account for time needed to prepare for the sessions, for conducting the session, and for analyzing the data.

Typical planning steps for contextual inquiries include:

1. Formulating research goals:
   - The sequencing of processes and actions that define the user's motivation when using the product.
   - Detailed understanding of the processes that drive the user's interactions with the product, including inputs and outputs, dependency on other products, or sources of information.
   - How well is the product suiting the user's need?
   - Are there opportunities to improve processes by simplification or elimination?
   - Are there barriers for introducing change?
2. Determining which segments of the target audience are most capable of providing the relevant answers to the research, and should be tapped to participate. Also, determine the proportion of user types. This determination is often influenced by practical considerations--stakeholders typically have a good idea of who can be reached.
3. Determining the logistical challenges and a closer estimate of time and budget needs, based on the geographical location.
4. Determining who will do the recruiting--internal resources, or a third-party company who is specialized in recruiting.

5. Developing a screener based on the profile of segments of the target audience; a screener is a short questioner that helps recruiters find participants who match the required research needs.

6. Developing the CI facilitator guide. Contextual inquiry begins with a tight script that is intended to ensure:
   - Consistency across all interviews, regardless of the interviewee
   - That all topics that make up the research are covered

7. Preparing for the sessions:
   - Dry runs help iron out the flow of the session and the sequencing of questions.
   - Test recording equipment--in addition to taking notes, the sessions are typically recorded using an audio recorder, and sometimes, if possible and relevant, a video recorder. When the topic is software, screen-sharing and recording applications are used as well.

8. Conducting the activity:
   - It is essential to make the participant feel at ease, and express appreciation for the time they spend on this activity.
   - It is important to stress to the user when the CI is scheduled, and at the beginning of the session, that this is not a test of the user, but rather--a test of sorts for the product. This is very important because many participants may feel a need that their job or privacy are threatened.
   - It is also vital to ask the users to verbalize their thoughts as much as possible, and share with the researcher their motivation and thinking before, during, and after performing a task.
   - It is crucial to ask participants to be as honest as possible--for various reasons, participants may feel that it is rude or inappropriate, or risky to share their true feelings, and try to please the designer by glossing over the negative feedback.
   - A contextual inquiry, while structured, provides the designer with many opportunities to switch from asking pre-defined to asking context-specific questions that emerge during the conversation. These often lead to uncovering unexpected information which can be a turning point in thinking about the design.

9. Analyzing and presenting results, and coming to an agreement on the approach.

Pros

The following are pros of using contextual inquiries:

- It is very effective in helping designers develop a good understanding of a user's full spectrum of needs, pain-points, and desires regarding the actual use of the product. Participants are asked to provide an honest assessment of the product and the brand, their thoughts on competitive products and so on.
- It is very effective in detecting nuances and inconsistencies in patterns of use. The participant can demonstrate how the circumstances of a specific task might change how the user might prefer to perform it. Products that reflect such nuances provide a better experience and communicate to prospective users that the company cares about their specific needs.
- It is very effective in helping designers understand the flow of use, and what is important and less important to the user.
- Even participants who are critical about the product or the company, appreciate the fact that they are being asked to participate in an effort to improve the situation, and that they get to voice their opinion.
- CIs provide a unique opportunity to identify factors that might have a considerable impact on the design. These factor include the following:
  - **Exceptions and variability**: The more variable the interaction, the more difficult it may be to improve the experience through design alone, and business process changes might be needed.
  - **Workarounds**: Often, there is a gap between how participants describe the task they want to perform, and how they plan to perform it--to the way the task is manifested in the product. As a result, users tend to come up with their workarounds to close the gaps. Such workarounds are often valuable because point to a missing feature or capability which can be addressed in the new design.

Cons

This list appears to be significantly longer than that of the pros, but in practice, most of the logistical and cost issues can be resolved, and tremendous value is added:

- Face-to-face sessions are most effective, compared to remote sessions conducted over the phone or web sessions. Remote sessions are impossible with products that involve mobile users, such as farmers, various delivery and repair staff, health-care providers, and others. However, and that's a major concern, face-to-face sessions can be expensive since they requires the designer to travel to the participant's location. Further limits on conducting international research are due to cost and other complications associated with international travel.
- Documenting the sessions can be expensive and time-consuming. Although it is a best practice to include a dedicated note taker, it is not always possible. Moreover, note-taking is a skill that the designated note-taker might lack. Finally, even good notes will inevitably miss nuggets of really important information or context. Consequently, it is best to budget for professional transcription of the recordings, but the costs can quickly run up.
- The sessions require participants to give up an hour or two of their work or personal time. This poses a limitation on the availability of participants who might be too busy during certain times of the day or week, to take such a long break from their duties. Additionally, rescheduling and cancelations extend the original length of the time allocated to the research and/or reduce the number of final participants.
- This must be facilitated by a designer, which poses practical limitations on the number of sessions that can be conducted, and suspends all other design activities.
- An analysis of the research is time-consuming; for example, transcription of recordings, organizing notes, and reconciling the data from multiple interviews, can take up days and weeks, depending on the number of interviews.

- Dependency on the experience of the designer, their ability to guide the conversation so that the uncovered insights can be gleaned.
- Dependency on the cooperation and knowledge of the participant.
- A few outliers in a small sample of participants may yield an unbalanced understanding of priorities and needs.

The diary or log method

You may have kept a diary when you were a kid, and perhaps you maintain a journal now. The concept is simple--each day one records key events of the day. When used in research, participants are asked to log various research details, at specific intervals, as dictated by the needs of the research. This type of research is called longitudinal research. The method can be implemented with very basic means--as simple as a paper diary in which participants write the requested information at a given interval. A more practical approach is to have the participants use a cloud-based survey system, or a mobile app.

The method can be used:

- Before the product is designed. Given the time pressure on many projects, and the time investment associated with the diary method, its use is limited.
- After the product is designed, either in beta or finished form. It is now common that products automatically log all interactions. However, what is not captured is the user's feelings and emotions regarding the experience at each use.

Why use it in experience design?

The longitudinal nature of the method provides insights into the quality and consistency of experience over time. Each reporting point can be measured in relation to other reporting points along the entire period.

It is possible to quickly identify which tasks and actions the performed by the participant worked well, which did not and what was the overall experience each day, as illustrated in the following figure:

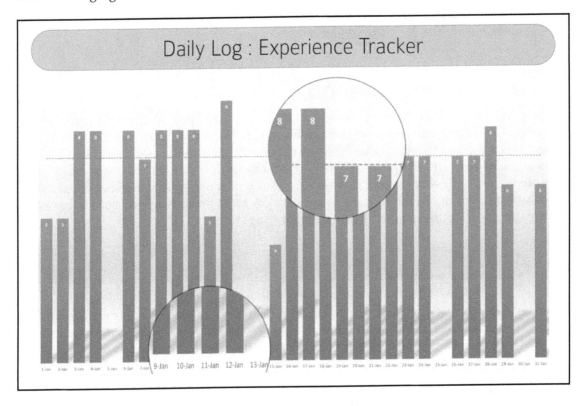

How to use it in experience design?

Typical planning steps for launching the method include:

1. Formulation of research objectives for the diary activity.
2. Determining who will participate in the research. The target audience should be capable of providing the relevant answers to the research; otherwise, they are not likely to provide meaningful information even if they do log regularly.
3. Based on the project's overall timeline, setting the duration of the activity--weeks or months.

4. Determining the frequency of inputs, and the maximum amount of time each participant should expect to dedicate to the effort. The shorter the time, the easier it is to get people to participate. For example, having to log activities three times a day, each day, over a period of a month, might be quite demanding. However, for some applications, it is exactly this type of detailed feedback which makes the diary method valuable.

5. Deciding on the appropriate compensation for participants. It should be proportional to the expected level of involvement and consistency of input. There is, however, a fine line between making the activity a fee for service, and a reward for participating in the research. The first might lead some participants to think about the effort as a job, or feel obliged to provide only positive feedback.

6. The more structured diary inputs are, the faster and easier it is to fill-out, aggregate and analyze.

7. Determination of the diary collection instrument, such as an online survey tool, ca special app, a physical paper diary, and so on. For example, for a company that develops specialized equipment for use in remote harsh conditions, electronic forms of data capture may not be possible.

8. Analysis and presentation of the results, including the identification of shared patterns across diaries.

Pros

The following are the pros of using the method:

- It provides a detailed breakdown of experience quality over time, which covers a range of product interactions, their frequency, sequence, duration, difficulty, positive and negative user reactions.
- It provides a good way to map out in detail sequence of events that lead to interaction pain-points and their proximity to specific tasks and processes.

Cons

The following are the cons of using the diary or log method:

- It requires sufficient lead time in the project to launch and conduct a significant longitudinal log.
- Logging information on a regular basis requires discipline and commitment, which is difficult to demand from most participants. It might be difficult to find enough participants.

- Special incentives are often required to keep people motivated. Ongoing monitoring to make sure that participants are logging regularly is also required.

Focus groups and visioning workshops

The method originated during the World War II, when it was used to check the effectiveness of propaganda films. Hollywood movie studios continue to screen movies to focus groups during production of a film, and use the feedback to modify characters, plot lines, and movie endings.

The use of the method has expanded to marketing and politics, and in the 1990s has become popular with technology companies who wanted to get early feedback on their existing or upcoming software or hardware products.

The visioning workshop is an exploratory research method that is more unique to experience development, in that designers and others who are involved in the product development process, join a group of potential users, and together they work through a series of exercises meant to yield the most desirable features the product should have.

Why use it in experience design?

Both focus groups and exploratory workshops can be helpful very early in the design process of an entirely new product or service, or when the team is conflicted about competing conceptual approaches. The sessions provide a structured setting where multiple opinions can be expressed, and the facilitator can guide a discussion that explores the attitudes of participants toward features and capabilities of a product or service.

How to use it in experience design?

Typical planning steps for defining research objectives for a focus group activity are:

1. Determine who will participate in the research. The target audience should be capable of providing the relevant answers to the research; otherwise, they are not likely to provide a meaningful feedback.
2. Based on the project's overall timeline, determine when is the best time to schedule the focus group activity, and how many sessions might be needed.

3. Consider possible venues to hold the session. In marketing and other types of settings, it is also common to use a research facility that is equipped with an observation room that enables designers and stakeholders to watch the sessions through a two-way mirror. In any case, the session needs to be held in a location that is easily accessible to participants, often in downtown areas.

4. Determine the compensation for participants. Because this method is quite popular, many potential participants know that a monetary reward is typical. Depending on the audience, the reward might be relatively high, because participants might be too busy to attend, and a small reward might not be worth their time.

5. Based on the decisions made in the preceding steps, design the diary. The more structured inputs are, the faster and easier it is to fill, and more importantly, make it easy to aggregate all responses.

6. Based on all the preceding points, determine the best way to use the diary--use an online survey tool, create a special app, distribute a physical paper diary, and so on. For example, for a company that develops specialized equipment for use in remote harsh conditions, electronic forms of data capture may not be possible.

7. Analyze and present the results, and come to an agreement on the approach.

Pros

The advantages of a focus group or visioning activity:

- It can be effective when presenting the group with something very specific to respond to, such as a working proof of concept
- It can be effective when asking the group to respond to alternative design approaches
- In some cases, putting a focus group together can be relatively easy, such as in university campuses, and when using coworkers as a sounding board

Cons

The following are the cons of using focus group or visioning activity:

- It is logistically complex to organize--the need to gather participants who share common attributes that match the needs of the research.
- It requires sufficient lead time in the project to plan the event, find an appropriate venue, and recruit participants.

- Geographical and space limitations pose a restriction on the number of total sessions that can be conducted and their location, and as a result, limits the overall pool of participants to those who are in close proximity.
- It often requires the services of a recruiting firm.
- It requires significant investment of time to create activities that will enable participants to provide feedback both as a group and an individual.
- It requires an experienced facilitator who can guide the discussions in an engaging way, and also control participants and ensure an equal voice to as many viewpoints.
- Focus groups are notorious for being easily impacted by group dynamics:
    - They are diverted to a specific direction by vocal and opinionated participants, and there is no contribution from shy participants
    - *Group Think*, where individuals in the group are adopting the majority view and are not voicing their own opinion
- Monetary incentives are often required to recruit participants. As with any research activity that is not voluntary, there is a risk that a participant's contribution is seen as a means to getting paid, as opposed to making a product better.
- Documenting the session is challenging--it is difficult to take notes when multiple discussions or activities are taking place, difficult to get a good video or audio recording in a room full of participants, and expensive - often impossible, to transcribe the recordings.

Many UX practitioners find the focus group's cons--which are listed here--to be so overwhelming that they reject this method altogether as a valid UX research method. Still, there are circumstances for which the benefits might justify this activity.

Surveys

It is highly probable that you will be asked to participate in one survey or another numerous times. Most likely you rejected many of the offers, even those that promised some reward for your time, and sometimes, you might feel compelled to respond.

For example, after a recent hotel stay, the hotel chain sent a follow-up e-mail with an invitation to provide your feedback on various aspects of your stay, from making the reservation, to checking in, attentiveness of staff, appearance of the hotel, the room you stayed in, and so on. Perhaps you were dissatisfied with the gym, and the survey provides you with an opportunity to comment on that.

The hotel chain, after analyzing the aggregated results from participants like yourself, can identify areas that require attention, and if a large percent of participants scored their gym experience as low, the chain might consider investing in necessary upgrades to their facility.

Why use it in experience design?

The survey method provides experience designers with a relatively easy way to collect feedback that is relevant to the design process, from a large number of individuals who are part of the product's target audience. Surveys make it easy to measure, with a high level of confidence, past experiences with a product, especially if the interaction is still fresh in the participant's memory.

For example, it is common to ask a website visitor to respond to a quick survey about their experience before they leave the site or to follow up a user after purchasing or using a product or a service, and ask about their experience, as shown in the following image:

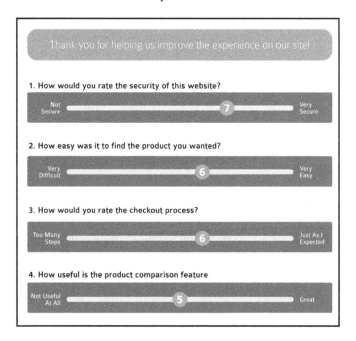

How to use it in experience design?

Typical planning steps include the following:

1. Formulate research objectives for the survey activity.
   - Determine the target audience that is most capable of providing the relevant answers to the research.
   - Determine how to reach that target audience:
     - For electronic surveys, e-mail addresses are needed. Some organizations tap into their relationship management systems for that type of information, others might be restricted from doing that due to regulatory constraints, and others might not have any lists yet, and need to work with a recruiting company.
     - Similarly, for paper surveys that are mailed to participants, mailing addresses are needed. Mail surveys are not very common in experience design because of the time it takes to collect responses. However, they might be needed to reach a population that does not have access to computers or mobile devices.
     - If the survey is conducted in person, the reach will be significantly reduced, but a sufficient number of responses can be collected by asking people to fill out electronic or paper forms at various public gathering spaces, such as cafeterias, airports, and university campuses.

2. Based on the project's overall timeline and type of delivery, determine when to launch the survey, and how long to keep it open for responses.
3. Determine the compensation for participants, if any, depending on the expected length of time needed to fill out the survey.
4. Based on the preceding decisions, design the survey. The more the structured inputs are, the faster and easier it is to fill, and more importantly, make it easier to aggregate all responses.

5. Test the survey and tweak the flow of questions, and how well the responses, when aggregated, meet the desired research objective.
6. Execute the survey as planned.
7. Analyze and present the results.

Pros

The following are the pros of having surveys :

-   A quick way to get feedback about past experiences, or thoughts regarding potential concepts
-   Can be designed to provide sample-appropriate quantitative data
-   Easy to put together and analyze response data
-   Relatively inexpensive

Cons

The cons of using surveys here are as follows:

-   Surveys often don't provide a good understanding of *why* responses are negative or positive. Often, a survey question might be phrased--"Rate your experience with our product on a scale of 1 to 10". The average of all responses might be 7, which might be interpreted as bad news--it may suggest that the experience is inconsistent because there are people who rate their experience at 7 or less, and people who rate their experience much higher.
-   Clearly, something about the experience causes the inconsistency in responses. Some survey tools allow survey designers to introduce a follow-up question to appear, especially if the rating is low, asking for more details. Unfortunately, people don't tend to provide much additional details to explain their rating, and often, if they do, their feedback may be obscure or incomplete.

Web analytics and customer support logs

Most companies have a customer support department which is dedicated to addressing issues customers have with the product. Issues and resolutions are logged, and over time, a historical record is created. This is a valuable knowledge base, which allows support representatives to quickly find appropriate solutions for customers who seek help using chat or phone.

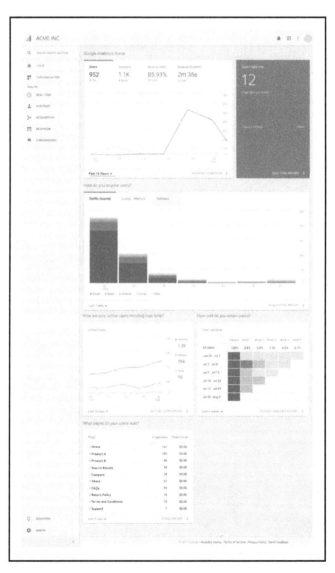

Web sites and application can gather a detailed log of each user session. The preceding image shows a typical screen of **Google Analytics**--a popular tool.

Web analytics is a dedicated specialization that helps stakeholders develop meaningful insights from the data. These insights correspond to key measures that businesses use to track the progress of their business, from the number of visitors to a website, the average time visitors spend on various pages, sections that are more popular than others, and much more.

For example, During the release phase of a new product, a company can track the effectiveness of marketing campaigns by following the increase of traffic to relevant destinations on its website. The number of visitors to such pages is then compared with the actual number of people who purchased the product. A big gap between visitors and purchasers might indicate a problem.

Why use it in experience design?

Early in the design process, designers focus on understanding the individual user. Customer service logs and web analytics data are often readily available, whereas other research requires planning, execution, and analysis. This is true for most design projects, with the exception of new companies or brand-new products, where a previous history is not available.

Service logs are records of individual instances that expose interaction issues. Aggregation of these records provides a high level understanding of how many issues are associated with a particular feature or task. Similarly, web logs reveal hotspots of interaction difficulty. Designers figure out ways to reduce the issues by eliminating the problem that caused it by tweaking the design.

Pros

The following are the pros of using web analytics and customer support logs:

- They are readily available, often easy to get, typically require relatively little time to review, and are free
- Often, they are summarized and organized by the department that, optimally, is staffed with knowledgeable domain experts; if not, this item is a candidate for the cons bucket
- The records are forensic evidence of actual interactions, issues, and resolutions
- The records are quantitative, reflecting trends and patterns of use, that often are relevant to the new design

Cons

The following are the cons of using web analytics and customer support logs:

- Large and complex circumstances require domain expertise to correctly set the software and manage it. As was mentioned in the preceding section, lack of knowledge can be a problem.
- Hasty response to the data might be premature, ineffective, or wrong, because underlying patterns or trends take longer to emerge. It is like focusing on symptoms of an illness, while the actual illness, which requires a completely different treatment, is left untreated.

Establishing the context of use

The following section explores methods and activities designers use in the process of forming a strategy and approach for the new design.

People interact with products and services to fulfill specific needs. The nature of that interaction is called **context of use**, and it is defined by three variables:

- The user
- The user's preferences toward fulfilling a need
- The product used to fulfill that need

Solving such a three-variable equation that involves people is like solving an extremely intricate puzzle, and although at first glance the challenge appears impossibly difficult, the work is being done every day. In this section, we will explore the foundation of approaching the solution.

Information about these variables and how they are interrelated is collected during research. After synthesis, research findings help designers think about the appropriate experience, and communicate their vision to stakeholders. The result provides both the approach to the appropriate experience and a system of managing the experience over time.

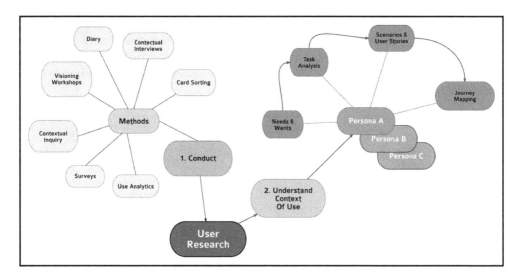

The preceding figure shows the flow of research inputs into models that capture the user experience, in context. Personas and journey maps provide the foundation for creating, communicating, testing, and evolving the product experience.

Personas

We are unique individuals, but typically not so special as consumers. We easily fall into all kinds of classifications, which we share with many other people. Ask yourself the following questions:

- Are you risk-averse, or a risk taker?
- Do you like to try new things, or prefer to stick with what you know?
- How sensitive are you to the cost of products?
- Are you a sports fan?
- Do you prefer coffee shops to bars?
- Which ice cream do you prefer, vanilla or chocolate?
- Would you rather tour a foreign country on your own, or join a guided tour?

It is highly likely that you will not have any problem answering these binary questions, but you should not worry about your individuality. It is common to group people by common traits, attributes, and interests, and when it comes to commerce, companies want to understand which groups are most likely to purchase their product, and why.

The persona methodology is credited to Alan Cooper, who wrote about it in his 1998 book, *The Inmates are Running the Asylum*. Back then, it was difficult to explain why interface design matters to business and engineering executives. Overtime, personas were found to be effective in helping executives make the connection between investing in better user experience and increased profits.

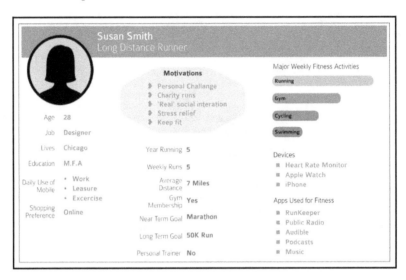

Audience research activities, combined with the information that designers collected up to this point in the project, guide the creation of personas. A single persona typically maps to a specific audience segment. Depending on the product, designers create a few personas, and the entire collection serves as a representation for the product's audience.

Personas reduce the anonymity of a faceless statistically-compiled market audience, and help establish a mindset focused on real people. A product strategy that is shaped by personas leads to produce design objectives that prioritize simplification and intuitive use.

A persona is not a person, but a generalization of an entire audience segment. It is a design artifact, which is used by designers to capture research-based qualitative and quantitative forms, the emotions, goals, motivations, and habits of a hypothetical user of the product. It is a tool that helps explain to everyone involved in a product design project why a particular design approach is appropriate to the types of clients represented by the persona.

As an analytical model, a persona is a tool that helps designers aggregate common behavioral traits and product-use patterns associated with major audience segments. Personas contribute to the overall design process in several ways, and at the start of a project, they help focus experience strategy on users' needs and desires.

Occasionally, those who are deeply involved in product planning and development become absorbed in adding features and capabilities to their product as a means of improving its competitive position in the market. Consequently, they lose sight of customers who will be using the end result. This is obvious in products that are complicated and difficult to use. Digital wrist watches of the type that predates the smart watches are a good case in point.

The following example features an experience common to digital watches, which is why I made some tweaks to the product and brand names. For the most part, the watches construction quality is decent, they are relatively inexpensive, and they pack an impressive amount of features.

The *Explorer VI* has five buttons--two on the left and three on the right. The watch is infused with features, including an altimeter, chronograph, countdown timer, date, lap timer, thermometer, alarm, and a glow light to view all if there is darkness.

The product's operating manual has 46 pages. The following figure shows one of these pages--a seven-step instruction on how to calibrate the altimeter. It is difficult to imagine anyone performing this task without closely following the manual, and it is unlikely they will consult the manual on one of the watch's numerous functions, while diving or climbing a mountain. In short, the target audience segment for this product--people who are engaged in intensive outdoor activities--will have a difficult time getting the product offers.

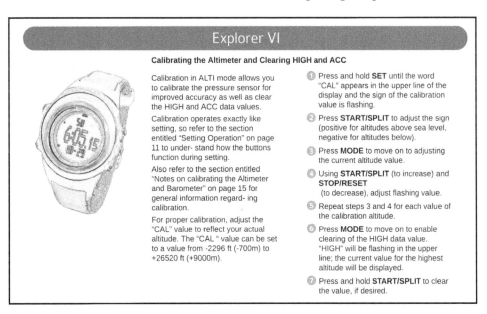

However, what if the team that designs products such as the *Explorer VI* had a design tool that helps keep the product's user front and center throughout the design process?

Persona development workshops

Workshops that focus on mapping out the experience prove to be significantly more helpful in forming an experience strategy that company leadership agrees with and fully supports than elaborate PowerPoint presentations, or long finding reports that no one reads.

The example that follows are meant to illustrate the value of persona workshops, and how their outcomes serve the design process. The example is by no means definitive, as there are many variations to nearly all the design activities.

Designers have several objectives from a persona workshop. First, they want to actively engage company leadership and relevant stakeholders. The workshops provide an opportunity to connect business and audience research activities outlined in `Chapter 3`, *Business and Audience Context*, with the user research process. Personas model audience segments whose attendees are very familiar with, but thinking about their customers from an experience-focused perspective is often new to them.

Next, designers might want to compare how company leaderships self-evaluates experience aspects of its product, to actual customer feedback collected through surveys, focus groups, and contextual inquiry sessions. This is how designers can assess and communicate expectation gaps that might exist between the current version of the product, and what customers expect.

As an example for one of the workshop's activities, the facilitator might ask participants to rate on a scale of 1 to 10 how well, in their opinion, the current version of their web-based product is performing against a set of experience themes such as the following:

- **Security and trust**: Does the product support the latest security features such as a two-factor authentication for personal identity verification? Can users provide alternative means of payment instead of their credit card information, such as PayPal or Apple Pay?
- **Overall look and feel**: Does the product look contemporary and professional across all its screens and across all devices?
- **Availability and clarity of content**: Does the product provide guidance and content that can help users perform various tasks, and is that content easy to understand, or heavy with terminology and jargon?
- **Mobile experience**: Is the product performing well, and does it look good on mobile devices?

Designers can then ask participants to rate on the same scale, what, in their opinion a customer's expectations are for the product, across the same experience themes. Often, the two sets of ratings--a self-evaluation of the product's current-state, and what customers expect, reveal a gap in the quality of experience, which the new design needs to bridge.

The team can then look at survey results, and compare self-assessment ratings, against actual customer ratings that were collected in the survey. At the end of such workshops, the personas contain qualitative and quantitative product experience information, which has been developed and confirmed with active involvement and participation of company and product leadership. Such direct involvement often leads to securing appropriate commitment, priorities, and budgets to the design project.

If there is one convincing way to advocate for investing in experience design, it is to show business leaders numerical evidence that represent aspects of the experience, such as customer attitudes, needs, pain-points, and goals.

The trend with persona documents is toward creating artifacts that can be updated and used continuously and iteratively throughout the products life cycle, from experience strategy, to post-release improvements.

Task Analysis

How do you brush your teeth? Before you articulate your response verbally, you "see" the task in your mind. You can clearly reconstruct the steps you take in your mind and provide a step-by-step flow without having to perform the task. Your explanation might be similar to how the American Dental Association breaks this down:

1. Place your toothbrush at a 45 degree angle to the gums.
2. Gently move the brush back and forth in short (tooth-wide) strokes.
3. Brush your teeth:
    - The outer surfaces
    - The inner surfaces
    - The chewing surfaces of the teeth
4. To clean the inside surfaces of the front teeth, tilt the brush vertically and make several up-and-down strokes.

5. Do this for 2 minutes, twice a day.

The task involves five steps and three substeps, not counting the step of putting the toothpaste on the brush before starting. Reading it makes the process very complicated:

- How to measure 45 degrees?
- How many seconds should be allocated to each substep in step 3?
- How many seconds should be allocated to step 4?

Our ability to contain in our minds numerous sets of actions related to daily activities, or work-related tasks, is helped by a cognitive ability called *mental models*. Once we are comfortable with a task, be it driving or creating pivot tables in Excel, we can easily access its mental model and be extremely fast and efficient in performing it.

That is why, the smaller the gap between the user's mental model for a task, and the task experience in the product, the more intuitive the product feels, and with it, our satisfaction with the experience increases. Consequently, experience designers spend a considerable amount of time understanding how user's use mental models regarding tasks. Task analysis is the methodology that documents mental models and aligns them with how the product experience will reflect them.

Task flow diagrams are used for task analysis. The flow diagram is a model, an abstraction of the ping-pong exchange that makes up a user-system interaction. These diagrams also play an important role in validating the sequence and logic of each task with business and technical stakeholders, and they are used to develop an agreement on which flows and parts of the flows should be prototyped.

The diagrams should be shaped by explicit context--given a particular user, the options afforded to the user by the system, and a particular user action, the system should respond in a particular way. While there are no set standards for UX flow diagrams, keep in mind that clarity, precision, and organization will help you during joint sessions with stakeholders.

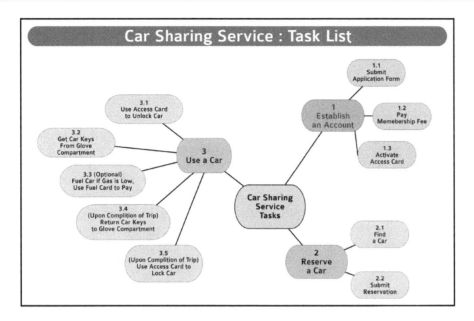

The preceding figure is an example of primary tasks associated with using a car sharing service. Such sharing services offer great benefits to their members and to the environment. For a low annual membership and reasonable hourly rates, local residents can use a car when and where they need one without the hassle and cost of ownership.

The list of tasks in the example is broken into three sequential primary tasks, and each has associated subtasks:

1. Establish an account (using the car sharing website):
   - Submit an application form
   - Pay the membership fee
   - Activate the access card once your membership is approved, and the card arrives in the mail

2. Reserve a car (using the car sharing website):
   - Find a car that is available on the day and time needed
   - Create and submit a reservation

3. Use a car (physical interaction with the car):
   - Use the access card to unlock the car
   - Get a car key from the glove compartment
   - Optional--fuel the car if gas is low using a fuel card, which is in the glove compartment

- At the end of the trip, place the car key back in the glove compartment
- Use the access card to lock the car

Experience designers evaluate each of the tasks to determine the best experience. In the preceding sequence, some of the tasks that are facilitated by the website are straightforward. For example, submitting an application involves filling out a form with the necessary details. Similarly, finding a car and making a reservation should be an easy and engaging interaction, but most users are familiar with the concept of making a reservation.

The challenging aspects of the experience is educating the driver about tasks that should be performed when accessing the car physically. This experience is different from the one most car owners are familiar with, and is different from the experience at a typical rental agency. The driver needs to remember to have their access card in order to open the car and then to find the keys, and if needed, the fueling card, and at the end of the trip, lock the car with the access card.

By listing in detail each task and analyzing its risks and opportunities, designers work with business stakeholders and developers to figure out how best to use the online experience to prepare the driver to do the tasks that will be needed to be done with the car itself.

Scenarios and user stories

User stories are brief statements that describe a functionality of the product, in the form of a single task, from the user's point of view. Typically, each story opens with the words "The user should be able to..."--for example, "The user should be able to access their inbox from any screen on the application."

The stories do not, and should not, attempt to suggest or define *how* to achieve the function, the user experience, or the technical approach. Their main purpose is to provide a complete inventory of a user-facing functionality, which can be prioritized and aligned with relevant project needs, such as their complexity and cost to develop, their importance from a business perspective, and their importance to the user.

While some tasks can be designed to be performed quickly and smoothly, there are many tasks that are more complex, due to exceptions or conditional logic based on the type of user or context of interaction. That is why, for each task, the optimal smooth flow, often referred to as the *Happy Path* or *Primary Path*, is considered the primary story. Then, for most happy paths, the designers should document alternate paths, which are variations caused due to various exceptions.

The product design must be able to handle these variations smoothly, and a great user experience is a result of anticipating many such alternate paths, and resorting disruptions in the flow toward a smooth conclusion.

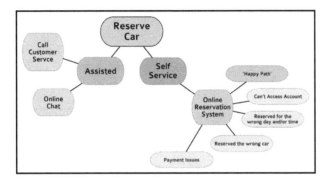

The preceding figure shows some of the variations possible for the "Reserve a Car" task. The primary flow, or happy path, is the one in which the user interacts with the online reservation system, and is able to complete a reservation satisfactorily. However, the reservation task is initially divided into *self-service* and *assisted* categories, and each of these has a number of versions for user stories or scenarios.

Journey mapping

Journey maps are used to chart the user experience with a product or service from start to end. Just as with geographical maps, journey maps can model discrete phases of interaction in great detail, or an entire end-to-end journey, with fewer details:

- Life-long engagement journeys are like small-scale maps, of say, a remote galaxy. The journey reflects the changing needs and priorities of customers as they mature, have families, and retire. Such maps are important to many organizations, from automotive, hospitality, construction, health care, banking, insurance, and more, because they model loyalty and attachment of the customer to the brand.

  From an experience perspective, it is important to acknowledge the changing needs in a design that are consistent across the entire spectrum. For example, younger adults may prefer the experience of small, sporty, and inexpensive cars. When they have a family, they may prefer the convenience and safety of an SUV, a crossover, or a minivan. When much older, they might want a totally different type of car.

- End-to-end engagement journeys are like large-scale maps of, say, a large urban center walking tour guide. The journey captures engagement phases from awareness through to purchase, use, and repurchase.

The map in the following figure is an example of a large-scale map inspired by the visualization of subway systems, to illustrate the navigational complexity of a government health-care website. For websites and apps, such maps that don't provide much additional details are very effective. The site's experience is evident from the layout of the map and the various routes, and their stations correspond to navigation menus and pages.

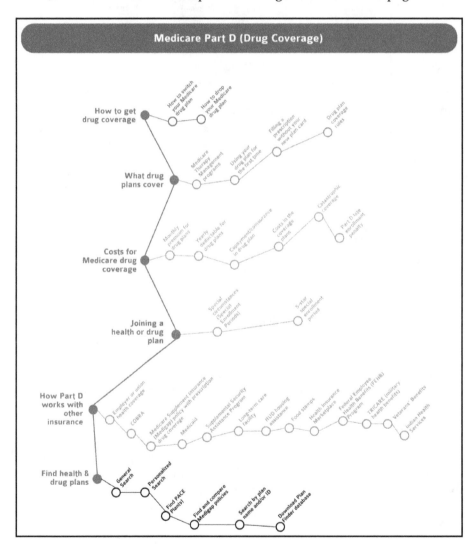

Journey maps are composed of three primary elements:

- **Persona**: Takes the journey.
- **Journey phase**: Often, it means the sequential steps the persona goes through along the journey. The phases correspond to business milestones, such as a purchase, and sometimes also to a life event in a persona's life, such as marriage, birth of a child, and so on.
- **Touchpoints** : This is a point where the persona and product meet. This is the most critical element of the map. A touchpoint may involve a direct interaction with the product, or a secondary experience, such as a reference on social networks, in an article, or during a conversation.

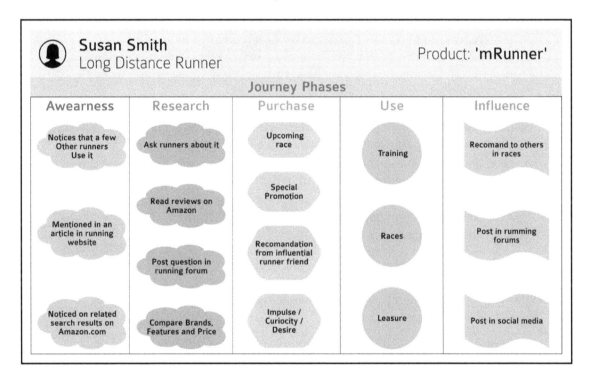

The preceding figure is an example of journey map that illustrates five key phases common in commerce and service products:

1. **Awareness**: In this initial phase, the person is passive. The potential customer may not know about the product, sometimes even the entire product category. The person may have little interest in the product, but through interactions with various sources of information, such as social interactions and informational resources, the person becomes aware of the product, and, sometimes, of direct or indirect competitors. Depending on the product or service, the length of this phase may be measured in years.
2. **Research**: The person becomes active as a result of a need for the product. The need may be urgent or further in the future, but the prospective customer begins to take an active role in identifying the right product that best fits their need, preferences, and budget. The depth of research varies depending on the product and the context in which it will be used. Also, the time between conducting the research and acting on it to purchase varies greatly based on the person's circumstances.
3. **Purchase**: The trigger for purchase might be attributed to many factors--the purchase timing may be planned, the need for the product becomes suddenly urgent, a special offer made the purchase a good deal, and so on.
4. **Use**: Once the prospect becomes an actual user, there are various settings in which the product experience is put to the test.
5. **Influence**: The satisfied customer who finds the product useful and the experience good, and becomes a champion of the product, actively recommends it on their social networks and commerce sites.

Not all the phases apply, and sometimes, the lines between the activities are blurry. Still, it helps to have a model that captures the information in a compact and easy-to-understand way. When used as a central repository for managing the use experience, journey mapping provides several benefits:

*   **Planning**: Journey maps help designers and stakeholders to look at the experience from different perspectives and prioritize on the area that needs to be focused on first. It is easier to be aware of and maintain consistency across similar touchpoints.
*   **Collaboration**: Maps are visual and typically self-explanatory. Since design is an ongoing, iterative process, personas and journey maps evolve with the design, and reflect the most current data regarding the experience. The continuity creates an important resource--an organizational experience memory that leadership and stakeholders can easily understand and use as a strategic tool to guide decisions around priorities.

- **Experience unification**: Journey maps help a designer leader focus on constant monitoring, assessment, and improvement of the experience.
- **Risk management**: Maps make it easy to identify the source of known and, sometimes, hidden problem areas in the experience and address specific touchpoints. The problem may be related to experience inconsistencies across multiple, similar user scenarios, and solutions may require design or business process simplification efforts.
- **Precision**: Journey maps provide a method to model with precision, the growth, sustainability, and strength of relationships with users over time.

Journey mapping workshops

A design strategy workshop is an activity that places designers, relevant decision-makers, and subject-matter experts, in a room where the walls are covered with long scrolls of paper. For a period of a few hours, everyone works collaboratively, using post-it notes and other simple aids, to map out the journey of customers from the time they become aware of the product, through their purchase experience, and throughout key usage points.

Participants use research data and their own experience to identify strength and weakness points along the journey. Journey maps are extremely efficient in concentrating large amounts of qualitative and quantitative information in a compact visual form which is easy to digest quickly. Journey maps are especially effective to visualize a high-level flow.

The primary goal of such workshops is to facilitate the creation of shared understanding among all stakeholders of the challenges and opportunities of moving towards a new experience strategy. The concentration of all pain-points in a single visual document makes a journey map a unique tool for thinking holistically through issues of experience continuity, re-sequencing of process, and prioritization of efforts. Think of the workshops as a decision support tool that addresses a couple of important issues:

- Leadership has to make hard, sometimes critical decisions around priorities, budgets, and resources. Ironically, the nature of such decisions place a distance between the needs of experience and the cold realities of practical management. It is easy to forget the end user when you look at an Excel spreadsheet.
- It is also best to reach an organizational alignment around the approach. However, because each group involved in the project has its own agenda, such an alignment can be difficult to attain, and relevant gaps around the experience are not likely to surface without an appropriate facilitation.

Summary

This chapter provided an overview of various user research methodologies, artifacts, and activities that experience designers regularly use in order to figure out the user whom they design for, the contexts the user engages with the product, and some of the experience attributes the product should support in order to make the user feel unique, despite the product being a mass produced.

This chapter along with--Chapter 2, *The Experience Design Process - An Overview* and Chapter 3, *Business and Audience Context*, provided a high-level overview of experience design processes, and methods. Design is never detached from the realities of business, yet, at the same time, it energizes and motivates organizations to reinvent themselves and their products. Design is a solution for moving forward that benefits everyone.

At this point, you should have a better understanding of the many considerations that get experience design going, and how the needs of an organization are aligned with those of your users through the design of a product.

We are experiential beings capable of consuming enormous amounts of sensory inputs from our changing environment and translating it into a meaningful understanding of our surroundings, other people, and ourselves. The upcoming chapter bridges the "why" and the "how" of experience design. It is an exploration of the nature of human experience through a review of perception, emotions, and cognition.

The next chapter will move toward a deeper understanding of the nature of experience, Chapter 6, *Experience Design Disciplines*--will take us through the disciplines that evolved to address diverse aspects of experience and Chapter 7, *The Design Team*, will explore those disciplines, and the various professionals and specialists who participate in the creation of the actual design.

5

Experience - Perception, Emotions, and Cognition

"The experiencing self, lives its life continuously. It has moments of experience, one after the other."

- Daniel Kahneman

This chapter addresses the question: Experience. What is it?

In a book dedicated to experience design, it is only logical to allocate a chapter to the nature of experience. The challenge was how to cover a topic that is like the ocean--enormously wide, deep and rich with mysteries. Despite thinking that spans thousands of years, fields such as neuro science, cognitive, social and organizational psychology, behavioral economics or artificial intelligence did not exist a century ago. Even the academic study of emotions is just a few decades old.

I am a practicing experience strategist, architect, and designer. Although the word "experience" is part of my title, much of what I learned about the physiology, psychology, and philosophy of experience, is self-taught, because my formal education focused primarily on screenwriting, filmmaking and animation. When I started to design software user interfaces in the early 1990's, the discipline was only emerging, the words "experience" and "design" have not yet been joined to describe it, nor could you get a degree in the field.

In 2001, the **Americans with Disabilities Act** (**ADA**) became law in the United States. At the time I was in charge of user interface design for a software company, and I had to start thinking about making our software accessible for people with impaired vision and other disabilities. As I was teaching myself about vision, it dawned on me that I know little of how any user--with or without disabilities, experiences interaction with software interfaces.

There are numerous good sources, both online and in print, to learn about any aspect of experience imaginable. This chapter could not even begin to address all of them. As a designer, however, I chose to present an informal journey along the pathways of experience, and the roles that these pathways perform when incorporated into commercial applications of experience design.

The senses

Perhaps the most confusing thing about our senses is that the data they transmit to our brain is being interpreted in contrasting and often conflicting ways, simultaneously objective and subjective, literal and metaphorical, real and imaginary.

For example, when I see the television set in a hotel room, I know it is a *real* object even if I interact with the device via a remote, and never touch it. Still, relying only on my eyes, I have full confidence that it is as real as the couch I'm sitting on, and that if I took the few steps separating the couch from the television, I will be able to touch it with my hands. I can even predict the smoothness of its surfaces, and the sensation of the heat it emits.

I also know that Superman and the rest of the characters in the movie I watch on the television, are not real, but that the actors portraying those characters are real. Little children, on the other hand, are convinced, until a certain age, that their beloved characters are real and that they live inside the television.

In their 1969 song *See Me, Feel Me,* the *The Who* beautifully captured the interplay between physically sensing something, and the mental perception of these experiences:

See Me
Feel Me
Touch Me
Heal Me
Listening to you, I get the music
Gazing at you, I get the heat
Following you, I climb the mountain
I get excitement at your feet
Right behind you, I see the millions
On you, I see the glory
From you, I get opinion
From you, I get the story

Songwriter: Pete Townshend

Primary senses include touch, vision, hearing, taste, and smell. They feed our brain with raw data. Specialized parts in the brain identify, interpret and contextualize this sensory information into perceptions, which form the foundation of how we understand the physical world we are part of, and our internal mental world, which is us.

Product experience is the result of purposeful design, and is meant to generate predictable, consistent, and repeatable behaviors and emotions with an individual user -- and reproduce those reliably, with all users of the product. For this to happen, a profoundly complex set of physical and mental processes is set into rapid motion, instantly fusing personal, social, and cultural preferences and biases. And yet, this remarkable occurrence repeats itself numerous times each second, all over the world.

Understanding the role that each of the senses plays in creating rich perceptual responses, is essential to designing good experiences. Until recently, most interactions with products relied heavily on the visual and auditory systems. Technological innovations increasingly draw the other senses into the arena of experience design:

- Speech recognition interfaces such as Siri and Alexa combine visual and auditory elements in new ways
- Touch screens ushered an era of tactile input and haptic feedback to the electronic products market
- We are well on our way towards sophisticated systems that incorporate fragrance and flavor with touch

In the following sections we discuss how the various sensory systems affect experience in both commercially-designed and natural settings. The objective is to present interesting examples that provide insights into the inner workings of human experience that are relevant to product design.

Vision and visual perception

When my son was quite young, we frequently visited the nature museum. The large exhibit of animals in their wild settings (preserved through taxidermy), both fascinated and terrified him. To his inexperienced mind, the visual information was confusing and consequently scary. While he could identify many of the animals he saw, how they related to each other and to him was less clear. These were not the animals he'd seen on the pages of his books. They looked like real things because, like him, they had volume and their furs or feathers were evidently material, like his skin and clothes.

In a certain sense, the animals were indeed real for me too, but I knew the limitations of their "realness", whereas my son had no such idea. No matter how hard I tried to convince him that the *real* animals are not alive, what he saw led him to believe that he was in danger. For his young mind, unable at that time to clearly differentiate the alive, from the merely looking alive--this experience was terrifying. There should have been a sign--*This exhibition will provide a pleasant and educational Experience only if you can understand that stationary animals behind glass no longer can jump on you.*

The visual system is in most cases, our primary information gathering tool. We collect a lot of information just by looking at things. When we look at a product, we try to infer its purpose and use. But vision alone has its limitations.

Take size, for example--the iPhone 6 Plus was Apple's response to growing customer demand and mounting competitive pressure to produce a phone with a larger screen. Streaming video and web browsing--the primary uses of smartphones--are better on a larger screen. But when the iPhone 6 Plus was released, some of potential customers who rushed to the stores to get it, they found that it was difficult to use with a single hand, if your hand happens to be small. Even a full-size photo of the device in an advertisement could not provide the actual experience of holding the device and using it.

Apple and other smartphone makers actually anticipated the problem, and developed a special one-handed solution (**A**). For those who still find the device too large, smaller models of course are an option, and for those who want the larger phones despite single-hand use difficulties, whimsical gadgets such as the "Thumb Extender" (**B**), come to the rescue.

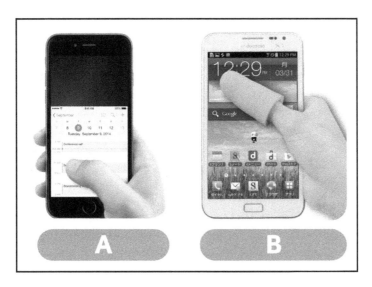

Vision mediates several perceptual and cognitive processes:

1. We assess the physical properties of products, and make snap judgements (often provisional) about their quality. If the product case is made of what appears to be plastic, we might decide that the entire product is of low quality, because we feel that aluminium is far superior--Which is why many products use plastic that looks like stainless-steel or aluminum.

2. We immediately run scenarios in our head about how we would use a product under various conditions. For example, editing a movie on a 17" laptop will be nice, but will I be able to use it in the tight space when flying coach? Will it fit into my backpack or will I have to purchase a new backpack as well?

3. We assign meaning to what we see. However, these ideas may be often wrong. Notably, most people firmly believed until just about three centuries ago, that Earth is at the center of the universe, since it appears that all stellar objects--Sun included--orbit it.

4. Vision streams data to our brain continuously (think about the difference between watching a movie, and looking at a slide show). Our mind adjusts to minor changes, and only a noticeable change will spring us into action--the gas gauge in my car's dashboard is slowly inching closer to the **empty state**, but I keep on driving. Only when a warning light goes orange, am I convinced that it is time to refuel or I'll get stuck without gas. Prompts, gauges, alerts, and status indicators are routinely used to focus our attention to a product we are using.

Product design is influenced by the power of first impressions formed by sight, because first impressions--within one to three seconds in some cases--generate assessment, trigger biases, value judgments, and expectations regarding the product's quality and experience of use. The smaller the gap between expectations and actual experience, the more effective the design.

The way we process visual information has a tremendous impact on experience, designed or not. Knowing what this processing entails can help design the experiences we desire and avoid undesirable experiential snafus.

We live in a physical three-dimensional world, and understanding it involves a continuous process of capturing, processing, analyzing, classifying, and organizing sensory data. Visual perception includes determining relative relationships among things and between things and ourselves. Relative classifications include:

- **Size**: Large and small
- **Height**: Tall, short, deep, narrow, or shallow
- **Position**: In, on, under, next to, between, behind, or in front of
- **Orientation**: To the left of, to the right of, above, or below
- **Distance**: Far or close

Most of the time, we depend on our visual perception of these relationships to provide accurate information. We automatically rely on this information as we form the thoughts and emotions that define our experience of what we see.

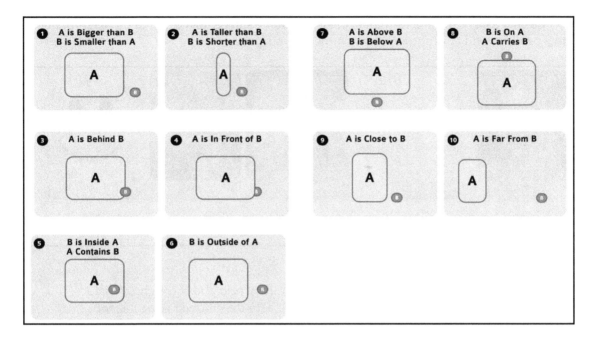

The illustration above demonstrates the instantaneous nature of visual perception in interpreting the relationship between two objects. You will probably identify the relative positions of block A to block B in each of the illustrations, well before you read the statement that accompanies it. Visual processing of spatial relationship is faster than reading.

We are used to the experience of immediately understanding what we see. Consequently, a product that keeps us guessing too many seconds about its use, will trigger in us feelings of concern and reservation.

Expressions

According to the *Harvey Ball World Smile Organization*:

> *The Smiley Face was created in America and has been part of American culture since its inception. Americans can be proud of the fact that the Smiley Face has since become the international symbol of good will and good cheer.*

It is odd that a basic form of human expression can be subject to a claim of ownership, made into a product, and appropriated for commercial purposes.

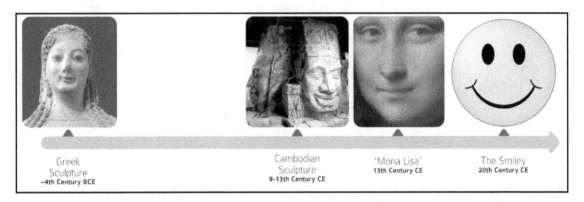

Representations of the smile can be found all over the world and throughout history, connecting Greek sculpture from the 4th century BCE to the emoticons we use for communication on social networks.

A smiling face is a universal bi-directional, social-communication device. Language independent, it is a compact, non-verbal, lightning-fast message that evokes feelings of friendliness, trust, and confirmation--even if the smiling face is a visual depiction, and not a live person--which explains why it is used so broadly in product advertising, design, and user interfaces. Here are some features of the smile:

- The smile can be intentional or automatic--infants smile instinctively, but as we get older, we learn to smile on-demand even if we don't feel like smiling. Combine the smile with a toy to *guarantee* a baby's happy smile:

- The smile does not necessarily reflect the smiler's mood. A tickling touch, a sound, or sight can trigger a smile that does not fit with our feeling in the moment. However, the act of smiling in itself can affect our mood, changing it for the better.

The smiley face demonstrates how designers use the rich cultural and psychological content of this image to create a variety of experiences, which can be based on a very simple visual stimulus.

We do not have to see a picture of a real person smiling, to perceive the meaning of the visual representation of a smile. This is true for other facial expressions as well. Two dots above a line on any surface or shape-depending on the curve of the line-express happiness, sadness, and other nuanced emotions.

You can think about this some more by reading the following interesting characteristics of smiles and smiling-how would you incorporate these characteristics to strengthen the design of an intended experience?

- When we see a person smile, we tend to assume something about their state of mind.
- We sometimes smile when others do, as a calculated response to a social situation.
- We sometimes smile inappropriately--we understand this, but can't help ourselves.
- Many different things make us smile, and some more than others. For example, little furry things.
- We smile in response to a memory, the present moment, or a thought about the future.

The first Apple Macintosh greeted its owner with a smile. The historical context is important, because in the early 1980's the personal computer product category was new. Computers were still viewed as office equipment rather than a personal productivity, entertainment, and communication hubs that they later became.

Apple's interface designers understood, instinctively, perhaps, that if the first thing one sees when the computer is turned on is a smile, it will instantly communicate the promise of a user-friendly, joyful, and heart-warming experience. This promise has been one of the Mac's principal differentiating features, in the competition with IBM and Microsoft on the hearts and wallets of consumers.

Gestures

Next to the smiley face icon, the visual representation of the *thumbs up* gesture may be the most widely used visual symbol, thanks to Facebook's *like* function. This non-verbal universal gesture is used as a status indicator that expresses one's positive or negative emotional response to something. The human ability to encode such social connotation in a physical gesture, and then abstract it in a graphic symbol, makes possible their use as icons in user interfaces.

From seeing to making meaning

What complicates the design of visual information is that responses to visual cues, while built into the visual-processing function of our brain, do not always produce the same reaction in all viewers.

The image of a white dove on a balcony banister, is an image with sufficient cultural content to elicit some anticipated responses related to a sense of beauty, nature, peace, freedom, and the like. Yet in addition to such generalized responses, the viewer's individual context can trigger completely different sets of associations, thoughts, and feelings.

For one viewer, the dove a reminder of a romantic vacation by the blue sea, while for another, an opportunity to contemplate a biblical story; and even with that, the focus can be religious and moralistic, or a secular appreciation of a delightful illustration created in the 1470s for the Nuremburg Bible.

While visual stimuli triggers thoughts and emotions that inspire creative new ideas, our mind sometimes imposes preset meaning to visual information we see--even if the objects depicted are completely abstract, and do not encapsulate the type of symbolic social context found in the smile or thumbs-up icons.

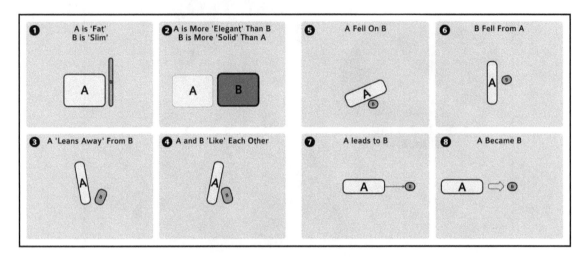

In the image above is a set of illustrations featuring blocks **A** and **B**. Read the captions that accompany each illustration and you will find that you can easily relate to their interpretation.

In addition to comparative assessments of objects **A** and **B** for their size, relative location, and so on, this illustration demonstrates our tendency to assign meaning. Even though the rectangles in the illustrations are inanimate and abstract, we tend to see a narrative: A story that includes emotional significance or even moral judgement:

- In illustration **3**, shape **A** is tilted to the left, away from shape **B**. Does **A** dislike **B**?
- In illustration **4**, **A** and **B** lean towards each other-these two might have made-up and are *friends*.

And so on. The stories of the relationship between **A** and **B** continue in the eye of the beholder. The viewer's role is active-they not only perceive the image, they reinvent and change it.

This characteristic of our visual perception is, of course, of crucial importance for the process of experience design. Anthropomorphism or personification are the terms used for our automatic tendency to assign human traits to inanimate objects and animals. This feature of the human mind explains why we can form lasting relationships with abstract ideas and products--from imaginary characters such as Mickey Mouse or Superman, to our phones, cars, favorite brands of household items, and so on. The image below, of a music school in Huainan, China, is a variation of a design approach called Skeuomorphism, in which some property of the original object - in this case, musical instruments, are preserved in the new one. In this case, it is an associative relationship that makes the obvious connections between the visual representation of the buildings, and their purpose.

The story that forms in the mind of the consumer ultimately guides the experience of the product. This story often originates with the sensory information sent to the brain when we see the product.

It should not surprise us then, that at some early point in our development as a species, we began using communication that relies on the visual sense. In painting and later in writing, people developed two dimensional representations of their three-dimensional world. Creating visual communication opened new possibilities since visual information can reach audiences without its creator being present. Visual information can be copied and spread. The experience it generates can exist simultaneously in many locations around the world, although it might be localized and adapted, gaining in the process added layers of cultural meaning.

Hearing and sound

We are immersed in noise, and sorting out meaningful signals from ambiance is an amazing capability of our brain. Although we do not have the advanced sonic capabilities of bats, owls, wax moths, elephants, dolphins, and other animals, human hearing is quite sensitive. How we process and interpret what we hear plays a central role in shaping our interpretation and experience of our surroundings. From helping us recognize danger, to assisting in relaxation--sounds trigger physiological and psychological responses that affect our behavior and interactions with the world around us.

Automatic defensive response is a central feature of all sensory systems. With vision, understanding that what one sees is dangerous, is learned from painful personal experience or preventive social guidance: Until we are thought that tigers can devour us, we have no reason to be afraid of the beautiful, furry animal.

The particular characteristic of a sound, such as volume, pitch, and tone, produce automatic physiological responses that reinforce or contradict the experience intended by those producing the sound. If you have ever sat through a wind-instruments concert performed by second-graders, you understand how auditory processing can work against the creator's intentions. On the other hand, if you ever jumped out of your chair to run downstairs in response to an ear-piercing fire alarm, the qualities of that sound have facilitated the intention of its designer very well.

Many products have an auditory component. The design of user experience for such products requires consideration of the physiological, emotional, and behavioral responses elicited by various characteristics of sound. Some examples are straightforward:

- Sudden sounds trigger an instant pause in whatever a person is doing. The sound maybe loud and high pitched like in an alarm system, or presented in short beeping bursts like when the car alerts the sleepy driver that it's drifting out of its lane.
- Continuous soft sounds of slightly lower pitch, such as ocean waves, are used in sleep-aid noise machines for their known calming effect.

The physiological responses to auditory stimuli are almost universal, and experience designers can usually count on eliciting reactions like the ones described previously because they trigger autonomic nervous system responses.

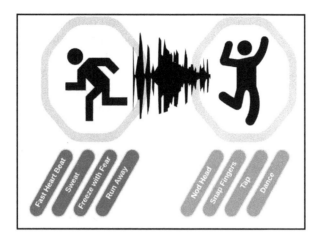

The image above illustrates two categories of sound qualities:

- Sounds that alert the body to danger (whether real or imagined). The physiological stress that follows might include sweating, pounding heart, freezing in place, or a desire to escape. We can put sudden loud bangs, explosions, screams, and sometimes an eerie quiet in this category.
- Sounds with qualities of rhythm, tempo, harmony, and melody that elicit pleasant and grounding response, and cause the body to relax and move in calming rhythmical ways.

But there are also significant individual differences in response to sounds. An individual's response to sound is affected by thresholds, habituation, and the personal-emotional and cultural context within which the auditory processing occurs.

While imagery is passive--we have to focus our attention on an object--sound waves spread in the air, and hit the eardrums of anyone within reach. Thresholds differ among individuals. For some, loud music is fun, while for others it is torturous. But loud sounds can be dangerous, and cause irreversible permanent hearing loss, which is why the design of volume-controls often includes a visual representation of the loud to quiet range, and portable music players in smartphones and other devices include an option to limit the volume level of headphones.

Kindergarten teachers need high thresholds for noise; otherwise they could not function in a classroom full of loud five-year olds. And if that teacher feels that sometimes even their high thresholds does not offer sufficient protection in the classroom, they can use products like the *Deluxe Yacker Tracker* (shown in the preceding image)--a noise level monitor, which clearly indicates to the classroom when they have gone too far-too red.

It is interesting to note that thresholds for sounds are also contextual. A loud music performance may feel *okay* at a rock concert, but cause discomfort and agitation when it blasts through a neighbor's window.

Appliance designers use sound to alert users. For example, when the water in the kettle is boiling, when the temperature level of an oven has reached a desired temperature, or when the baking time set by the user has ended. In these cases, the designers must balance the need to sound an alert that will spring the user to action, without causing unnecessary stress: piercing beeps may cause frequent and needless disruption, while soft beeps might be too low to register if no one is in the kitchen. Sounding a progressively louder alarm is a good solution.

Habituation is the term for decreasing response to a repeated stimulus. Without habituation, we would all go mad. We are blissfully saved from constant awareness of all the sounds around us because the brain "gets used" to sounds and ignores them. We can sleep in a building near the train tracks, read in a coffee shop, and pay attention to our boss in a long meeting thanks to habituation.

But just as with thresholds, there are individual differences in this ability. Extreme cases of poor auditory filtering of environmental sounds can be a seriously disabling condition. Most people, however, habituate to sounds enough to carry on with their daily activities. Experience designers consider habituation when the goal is to overcome it or to use it to reinforce a specific experience--emergency vehicle sirens use rising and falling sounds to ensure continued alertness on the part of drivers, whose default is to ignore the sounds surrounding them on the road.

More than anything else, however, individual differences in how auditory information impacts experience, is in the emotional associations elicited by sounds. Sounds can generate a wide range of emotional responses.

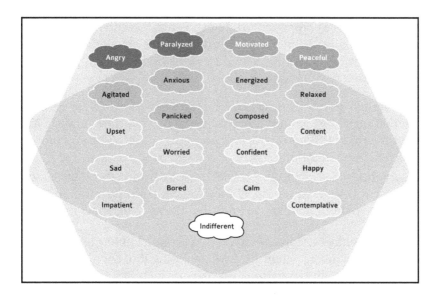

Sounds have a large emotive potential. Sounds from nature, sounds from man-made instruments, as well as the sound of the human voice, can be pleasant, irritating, stimulating, or relaxing. Sounds can change our mood and influence our activities.

Individual differences in emotional responses to sounds may be a matter of what we can call "taste"--preferences that do not have specific or exact explanations, but are weaved into the fabric of personal histories and characteristics, as well as cultural and aesthetic norms. From the experience design point of view, individuals' likes and dislikes of certain sounds invite serious consideration, and not only in connection to products or situations where sound is the main feature of the experience.

For products in which sound is a central feature, offering selection is a good approach:

- Doorbells come in various shapes and more importantly, with various sounds from the classic buzz to a birdsong, there are options for the customer's ears.
- Personal GPS systems offer a selection of voices, including the option to record a favorite voice to guide one's road adventures.

In other situations, sound is a component, but not a central feature of the experience. Background music is a good example. Background music is developed through research on how various sounds/music impact people in different situations. The goal is to identify sound patterns that promote situational success.

- The proverbial elevator music is intended to reduce stress for people enclosed in a crowded metal box hanging on wires, while supermarket music is indented to slow us down, uplift our mood, and hopefully purchase many more items than those listed in our shopping list.
- Auditory input that includes recorded sounds from nature (birds, sea waves, and so on), music or spoken words, is used to help children and adults go through scary and/or painful medical procedures, like the MRI machine or dental work.

The *Mozart effect* was a widely-embraced marketing gimmick that claimed that listening to Mozart and other classical music enhances the development of cognitive skills in young children. For a while, it was almost unthinkable to raise a child without a CD, video cassette, or DVD of the Mozart effect--much to the delight of the company that produced them. The Mozart effect failed to withstand the scrutiny of research, and a direct link between Mozart's music and cognitive enhancement, has not been established.

Nonetheless, the idea that certain music or other auditory stimulation can help people learn and improve skills such as memory, attention, and spatial orientation, has substantial anecdotal evidence and continues to interest researchers as well as experience designers in various areas of practice.

At the opposite end of the response to sound spectrum, experience designers tackle the challenge of eliminating unwanted, unpleasant, and annoying sounds with product in categories such as:

- Sound proofing technologies and designs for home and office
- Personal and environmental noise-cancelling and/or masking devices such as noise-cancellation headphones, or products like Sono, noise-cancelling gadgets that selectively convert an annoying background noise into a more pleasant sound

The power of sound

We discussed various facets of the power of sounds, and they all trigger emotions: Sounds can be alerting, calming, annoying, pleasing, bringing joy or sadness, putting us to sleep, or making us jump and dance. Many experiences are associated with sounds, and sounds play an important role in people's routines and habits: For hundreds of years, bell towers have kept time, sounded alarms, and announced weddings and funerals. Nowadays, the timer of the toaster-oven alerts us that our food is ready.

But sounds affect more than habitual actions. Do you have a special tune that triggers a special memory every time you hear it? Couples often have "their song". Music and sounds often take us back to places like our childhood home or college dorm, with vivid memories of events and a sensation of being flooded by the emotions of that time and place.

The power of sound to evoke strong emotions and emotional memories can be a rich source of creative ingenuity for experience designers.

Of course, we do not only hear sounds--we make a lot of sounds too. With the advancement of voice recognition technologies, designers are working hard on making the experience of having a dialog with machines effective and pleasant. Apple's Siri, Google's Assistant, Amazon's Echo, and Microsoft Cortana are competing artificial intelligence systems that introduce voice and sound interaction, as an integral part of the user experience. Humor has proven to be one of the successful design strategies in this context (as seen in the preceding snapshot).

Finally, auditory and visual information blend when sound is made into an image. Musical notation is a great example, and you can see the development of such notations from antiquity, to our times in the image below.

Touch - The tactile sense

The tactile sense is primary-it is the first to emerge in the developing fetus at about eight weeks. It is a crucial defense mechanism and therefore essential to survival. The tactile sense helps distinguish between multiple distinctive perceptions, each of which can be experienced on a range, such as deep versus light touch, soft versus hard, sharp versus dull touch, as well as the sensations of heat and pain.

Each one of these components affects our experience of the environment and protects us from the dangers in it. Touch sensation is pleasant or annoying, comforting or irritating, reassuring or anxiety-provoking. It makes us want to linger in an experience or to move away from it as quickly as possible. Meret Oppenheim's 'Object', below, is a wonderful illustration of the suggestive power of touch.

Touch and texture

Individuals tend to have definite preferences when it comes to the sensations fabrics on their bodies: flannel or silk pajamas? Exercising in tightly-fitting stretch fabric or in loosely-fitting oversized cotton training gear? The difference between deep and light touch is one of the central parameters that define the role of tactile input in various experiences.

An overly strong squeeze, or a heavy book landing on your foot is painful. But most of the time, the sensation of deep pressure on the skin is processed in our brains as pleasant and calming. Deep tactile input can improve experience in a variety of daily situations.

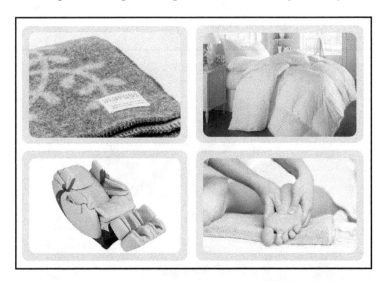

Consider the case of the winter comforter. A light fluffy down-filled comforter can feel wonderfully warm on a winter night. But for some users, its light weight may not feel cozy enough. Many people need a weightier sensation to anchor their body, which helps them relax into sleep. Feeling good under the blanket, it turns out, is not only a question of temperature. Often, the perceived sensation of comfort comes from a combination of warmth and deeper tactile input, which sends information to the brain letting you know: "I'm warm and cozy."

Light touch results in a very different sensation on the skin. A mosquito softly landing on your arm produces a barely detectable tactile stimulus, and yet the swat in response is swift. How about that strand of hair repeatedly falling on your forehead?--it is driving you crazy! Light touch is alerting and sometimes irritating, yet it can also be a pleasant, even pleasurable experience. Just think of the sensual touch of silk or the pleasant sensation of bubbles lightly touching your skin in the bathtub.

Although individual differences in sensitivity to deep versus light touch can be significant, each person usually has a wide sensory spectrum that ranges from "feels wonderful" to an absolute "Aghh!!!". Moreover, in many cases it is not even necessary to be in actual physical contact with an object or a surface, to categorize sensation they produce on the skin.

The processing of tactile input has a long memory-as evidenced by the incredibly strong attachments people have to specific fabrics, upholsteries, or the food textures. In the design of objects, it may be impossible to please everyone's tactile preferences, but it is plausible to highlight tactile properties in a manner that emphasizes potentially positive tactile associations.

The chairs in the image above are made of materials with vastly different tactile properties: Leather, wood, mesh, metal, plastic and upholstery. Responses to these chairs are influenced by an individual's tactile memories of each texture. For some, a leather chair suggests a pleasant and smooth sensation that is associated with comfort. For others, leather evokes a tight, sweaty, and sticky sensation, and a desire to stay away. Some people may feel neutral when it comes to leather surfaces, but most are likely to experience the "oh yes!" and "no!" responses when exposed physically or imaginatively to various textures touching their skin. These knee-jerk responses permeate our interactions with the objects of daily life, often underlying our material habits and consumer choices.

Think of a wooden dining table versus one made of steel and glass. Various characteristics of the table would influence potential consumers looking to update their dining room. Shape, size, color schemes, and price--all play an important role, and may be subject to negotiation among the purchasing decision makers. However, people are unlikely to buy a table that has a surface they do not enjoy looking at, or touching.

The dense fibers and natural colors of a wooden table bring to mind a homely feeling, while the smooth, cool, and shiny appearance of glass and steel are evocative of modernity and cleanliness.

Whatever we do, wherever we are, we are always experiencing touch. For the most part, our tactile sensation goes unnoticed-as it should. Who wants to expend precious neurological energy on constantly feeling the shirt on their back or the pen in their hand? However, if we approach the end range of our tactile comfort zone, either the pleasant or the agitating sensation of it, touch springs into our awareness with immediacy and force. Our response to pleasant or repulsive touch dims other sensory information, especially when we touch something hot, sharp or slimy.

Discrimination of hot/cold and sharp/dull as well as the sensation of pain, are part of a defense mechanism built into the tactile sense. These sensations are as ubiquitous in our daily lives as deep and light touch. Anyone who ever picked up a hot pot from the stove thinking that the handle does not conduct heat, remembers the pain and what they thought about the design of that pot. We need the objects in our lives to be safe and we need clear indication of danger where it exists.

To alert the user to the potential danger of touching certain objects under certain conditions, experience designers resort to communication via the other senses, by providing audible or visual alerts such as those represented in the image below.

We touch the world and the world touches us. Every object or environment, physical or virtual, has a tactile aspect, which sometimes draws or repels us. The sensations sent from tactile receptors in our skin to the brain can easily overtake other messages when danger is involved, but in many cases, the magnitude and character of these sensations can be manipulated in the design of experiences.

Visual, auditory, and tactile senses that influence and shape experience are joined by smell, taste, a sense of our body in space (proprioceptive sense) and a sense of our body versus gravity (vestibular sense) -- all play an important role in how we respond to objects and environments.

Furthermore, many objects, and certainly--most experiences, engage multiple senses and require an integrated processing of sensory data. Watching a movie, buying new shoes, pushing a child on a swing-we are constantly process inputs from numerous sources through our sensory system, interpret the data, and respond in thought, feeling, and action.

These are the raw materials experience design is made of, and designers have been thinking and shaping them throughout the history of civilization. Next, an exploration of mental processes, such as time perception, planning, and changes in effect.

Time

Experience always occurs in time. We can measure objectively the duration of an event or action-minutes, hours, seconds, and so on. But to measure the length of an experience, we should consider subjective time. Time perception is influenced by several conditions:

- The individual's state of mind
- The events that are taking place
- The environment and the context within which the experience occurs

These, and other factors, affect how a person experiences the passage of time. Time passes fast when we are having fun, and drags on when we are bored. When we wait for an exciting event such as a vacation abroad, the time seems to stretch forever before we get on the airplane, but then, the trip is over in what seems as an instant.

Time is slow when we are tired, fast when our mind is engaged, rushing when we want to accomplish more than what we can, and crawling when we are waiting for a bus on a cold rainy day. Moreover, the perception of passing time operates simultaneously on two planes, as you may have observed if you ever felt like, "the days go slowly, but the years rush by." In our mind, time is elastic - it can be both fast-moving and slow-moving at the same time.

The terms Instant Gratification and **Planned Obsolescence** are rooted in the association of time and pleasurable reward. When technology and design are added to the product design mix, time becomes an important influence on the decision-making process of people. **Instant Gratification**--reducing to zero the time between desiring something and having it, creates a mindset that *fast is good* and *slow is bad*. To be fast, things need to be as simple as possible, or appear to look simple, hiding complexity under a beautiful design.

Products that rely heavily on the latest technology have a short life cycle, because within a couple of years, newer, more powerful versions are released, making the previous generation obsolete. Each new generation of smartphones, for example, features better, faster and more stunning design--typically--thinner and lighter, than its predecessors. To upgrade, one's previous device, which still functions just fine, will be replaced--but this is something most consumers seem to be interested in--either to stay trendy and to enjoy the benefits of the latest version.

Whereas the physical dimension of our world: width, length, and depth, are verifiably measurable, time, the fourth dimension, is both objective and subjective, measureable, and ephemeral. Experience designers are thus especially sensitive to the role of time in the product they design--the spectrum of creating a timeless experience, while reaching for the optimal duration for each interaction.

We live through time in a few ways:

- We orient events and ourselves in a continuous vector of time--behind us is the past, we are experiencing the present, and ahead of us, is the future.
- All languages have grammatical tenses, which is how people have expressed the passage of time throughout civilization.
- Physically, we live in the present, which makes some experiences special to us because they attempt to transcend time--we *forget* ourselves in the experience, and don't notice time passing by.
- Duration of events is another way we experience time. A slow website is viewed negatively, because we expect the response time to be near instantaneous.

Emotions and executive functions

There is no universal agreement on exactly what emotions are. The terms emotion and feeling are often used interchangeably.

Emotions are triggered involuntarily and involve physical reactions such as increased heart rate or elevated blood pressure when we get angry or become fearful.

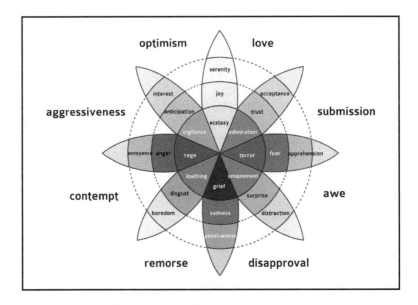

The *Wheel of Emotions*, illustrated in the image above, is a model developed by the psychologist Robert Pluchik. The model arranges 32 emotions by levels of intensity and positivity. The colorful depiction is misleading, and only a closer observation reveals that the number of negative emotions far surpasses the positive ones. The emotions that are important to good product experience are generally limited to: anticipation, interest, joy, serenity, and trust. Most of the other emotions are on the spectrum of negative experience.

Where time and emotional states connect, is in the length of the emotion and its intensity. For example, when one is in a state of rage, that state consumes that person's entire emotional bandwidth. On the other hand, it is possible to be in a state of anticipation towards an upcoming meeting with a loved one, or the arrival of a new gadget and at the same time fear snakes, be interested in the latest news on travel to Mars, and be annoyed by a person in front of you in the line who just purchased the last chocolate doughnut you were craving the whole afternoon.

The state of agreement on what exactly feelings are, is similar to that of emotions. Some argue that emotions are brief experiences that can be measured--change of heart rate, for example, whereas feelings are persistent and mostly mental states.

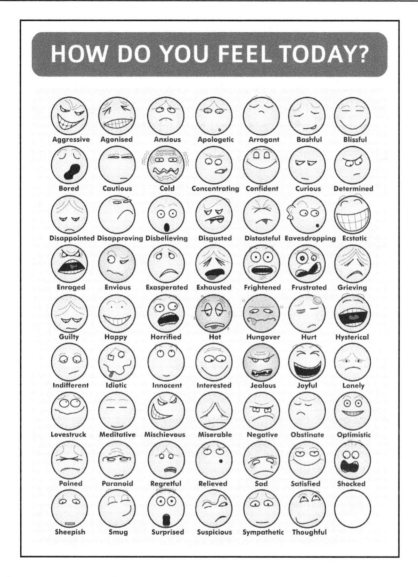

The image above shows visual representations of 62 feelings. But like the wheel of emotions, the majority of these feelings are negative, and only 11 or 12 could be considered positive, in the context of good product experience. It may appear that it is difficult to keep people happy! But experienced product designers find that the opposite is true: people respond positively to products that are designed with users in mind.

Mounting evidence from social psychology and behavioral economics research shows that people are irrational beings. Important decisions are often made on a whim, influenced by mood, unconscious biases, and strong but misguided beliefs. And yet, there is also plenty of strong evidence to demonstrate highly rational mindsets.

Our cognitive ability to control and plan our behavior, is handled by our *executive functions*. The following are a few of these functions, and product design examples:

- **Attention control**: Being able to focus on what's important while ignoring what is not (at least for the moment):
  - **Print and online content**: Fierce competition over the reader's attention is inherent to editorial and advertising content. Designers apply various techniques such as changes in typography, imagery, styling, and layout, to help readers distinguish between content or advertising, and conversely, get readers to shift their attention to the advertising.

- **Inhibitory control**: For example, being able to make the right choice which might not be fast nor easy, instead of falling back on the easiest, fastest, or familiar alternative, which may be satisfying in the immediate term, but wrong in the long run:
  - Driving and texting is proven to be extremely dangerous, and yet drivers can't resist the temptation. Designers are exploring a variety of solutions that will prevent texting while driving.

- **Working memory**: This gets us deep into structures and functions of the brain. Suffice it to say, we don't need to remember everything forever. Many things we need to keep in our mind for a short time, only while we are using them to do what we are trying to do:
  - Following recipes when cooking, workflow when completing a timesheet online.

- **Cognitive flexibility**: It is being able to see that going around the mountain is a viable option even if you planned to climb it. It is about managing several ideas at once in a way that gets you closer to where you want to be:
  - Changing the location of a meeting when faced with unexpected traffic on your route; or, quickly moving from one category to another like price versus utility of an object

When these executive functions work well, they enable the next level of cognitive controls: reasoning, problem solving, and planning.

Individual and social

We are social beings, and many of our preferences and experiences as individuals are shaped by our social interactions. The following image shows the expanding social circle that has the individual in its nucleus. As the distance from the core grows, the context that binds the individual to that circle, changes.

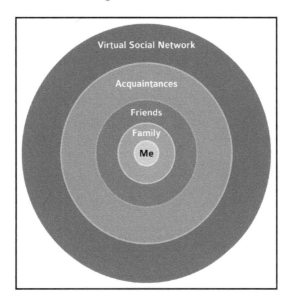

Proximity to the core of the circle, to the self, has only some influence on the quality of relationships, however. One can be estranged from their family, but have deep and meaningful relationships with friends. The emotional variability is wide. Another way to understand the preceding concentric circle, involves influence, a quality that experience designers are very interested in.

A competitive urge is another quality of an individual in a social context. It is a desire to do better than others, and the motivation may be a quest for internal fulfillment, or anticipation for external reward. Business, sports, and politics are the quintessential competitive arenas. The negative and positive aspects of racing to the top are in a constant battle that blends ethical and moral questions with pragmatic, number-driven realities.

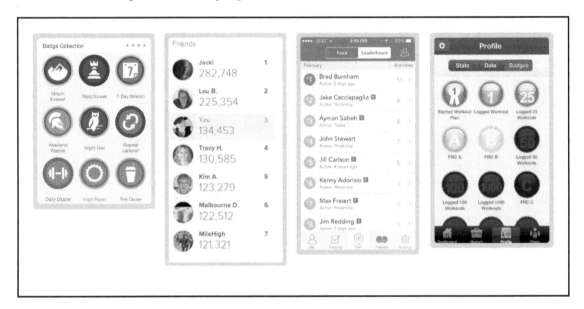

Experience designers have been using an aspect of competition, to motivate users who struggle with difficult challenges. Gamification is an approach to design that provides the user with rewards in the form of virtual badges or awards that function much like real badges and medals--they communicate to others the level of achievement, and motivate the user to work harder, reach higher goals, and be rewarded with a prize.

In the image above are a few examples of mobile apps that incorporate gamification in their experience--a perfect match for fitness and healthcare apps. For example, Fitbit, a company that manufactures activity trackers, encourages its individual customers to create or join a *circle of friends*, which serves as a motivational aid. The daily activity of all members is automatically posted, with most active people ranked on top. The game is meant to use a friendly competitive context as a healthy motivator to increase one's activity and improve fitness.

Summary

The efforts to understand how humans experience and perceive the world and themselves, has produced philosophies and theories, such as:

- Dualism, an ancient philosophy that sees a clear separation between body and mind, each, an independent entity to itself
- Behaviorism, an approach that explains all behaviors, emotions, and thoughts purely as a product of stimuli transmitted through the senses
- Functionalism, a recent theory, explains all human thought and behavior as if it was software that operates with inputs and outputs

"I see what you meant", "I was touched by this experience", "Smell the roses", "The taste of paradise", "Sound bites"--these are just a few examples of phrases that demonstrate the paradox of experience--while our five senses continuously feed objective data about the physical world, that data is being processed and reconstructed by the brain, and the result is subjective, a mix of thoughts and emotions.

Designers found that controlling the objective ingredients of the experience can lead to a reliable prediction of the subjective response to that experience. The careful curation and arrangement of shapes, materials, colors, textures, and other elements, can make an object desirable, usable and emotionally satisfying. But as mentioned before, finding the right blend is hard, with so many variables, and so many unknowns.

This chapter has been the first of three that make up the experience theme--a deep dive into the physical and psychological building blocks of human experience. Next, an exploration of disciplines that evolved the practice and theory of experience design.

6

Experience Design Disciplines

"In all matters, but particularly in architecture, there are these two points--the thing signified, and that which gives it its significance. That which is signified is the subject of which we may be speaking; and that which gives significance is a demonstration on scientific principle."

- Vitruvius

Design is not a monolithic domain, and so, this chapter addresses the following questions:

- What are the branches of design knowledge and practice?
- What are the shared design principles and challenges they address?

Marcus Vitruvius Pollio, better known as Vitruvius, addressed these questions 2000 years ago. While he focused on architecture, much of what he wrote about applies to the most advanced Experience Design technologies being developed today, and the ideas are as valid as they have been since he wrote them and throughout history.

Vitruvius was a Roman architect who is known as the author of *De architectura*, or *Ten Books on Architecture*, which he dedicated to Augustus Cesar. The book is the earliest written work on architecture we know about. It was a "best seller", although, at the time, the manuscript had to be hand-copied for additional copies to be distributed. At some point after its publication, awareness of the book faded, and it only resurfaced again in 1414. It has been in print ever since. You can easily get a printed copy of this ancient manuscript from the library, or download a digital copy online.

By the time Vitruvius wrote his book in the first century CE, the Romans, Greeks, and Egyptians of antiquity had already reached remarkable heights of technical and aesthetic achievements, so Vitruvius was able to draw on the body of knowledge accumulated over centuries.

Architecture was the first discipline to formalize a thought and practice process that combined practical engineering considerations with aspirational design objectives. In other words, architecture has emerged as the first multi-disciplinary domain of knowledge and practice. As such, it has completely transformed the experiential relationship between people and their landscape.

Today, many of the design disciplines mentioned in *Ten Books on Architecture* have evolved, and new ones have been created. The term architecture is now applied to many of the disciplines that are part of modern design, including software architecture, information architecture, experience architecture, and so on. Currently, the *Wikipedia* page for "Design" lists no less than 39 disciplines, but some might still find the list quite incomplete.

Experience Design is a multi-disciplinary practice and the outcomes of design fuse the product's function and meaning. Consequently, it is difficult to organize design disciples in neat hierarchical buckets because they blend in ways that make it impossible to discern any linear relationship. They all have a role in impacting our experience, senses, and thoughts.

This line of thinking is finally being fully embraced by companies and organizations, as well as academic departments and professional organizations involved in design teaching and research. This chapter is an introduction to the major design disciplines that literally shape our lives, an a homage to Vitruvius and the multi-disciplinary approach he advocated so long ago.

This is a journey that closely follows human evolution as a species and culture, going back thousands of years. Some disciplines preceded others, have a long, rich history and amazing artifacts that survive to this day, while others literally emerged a couple of decades ago and produce artifacts with a life span measurable in months.

Although each discipline uniquely contributes to the domain of Experience Design, many of the principles and methodologies of design are common, as are the debates around the theoretical and practical mission of design.

Mapping the disciplines

We are multi-sensory beings in a multi-dimensional world. Our senses and cognitive processes help us maintain a consistent orientation of our physical and mental input and outputs.

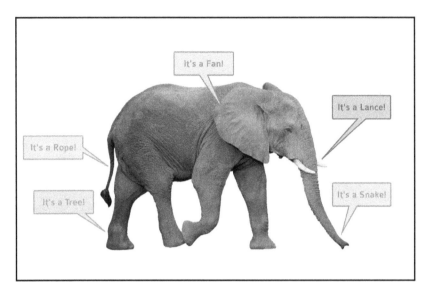

Many design disciplines, however, specialize in solving a specific problem, and sometimes, in the context of a specific dimension. Often, the outcome is that each design discipline only addresses part of the whole picture, as illustrated in the preceding image.

Trying to map out the various disciplines and how they relate is impossible, because their nature is fluid and because rapid changes lead to constant redrawing of domain boundaries. Core design disciplines can be wrestled into three major clusters--surface, space, and time-based experiences. Science and technology domains, which have always been tightly fused with design, include complementary disciplines.

The entire map is visualized in the figure present after the bullets:

- The disciplines of two-dimensional surfaces:
    - Graphic design
    - Typography
    - Web and software design
- The disciplines of three-dimensional spaces and objects:
    - Architecture
    - Fashion design
    - Product design
    - Vehicle design
- The disciplines of time:
    - Lighting design
    - Sound design
    - Film and video
    - Interaction design
    - Animation
    - Game design
    - Instructional design
- Engineering disciplines:
    - Architectural
    - Mechanical
    - Electrical
    - Software
    - Information design
- Scientific disciplines:
    - Anthropology
    - Sociology
    - Psychology
    - Linguistics
    - Mathematics
    - Physics

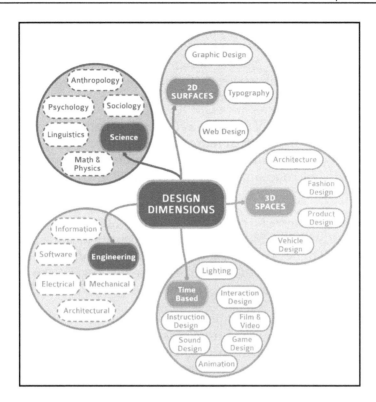

Throughout human evolution, people greatly changed our planet through waves of agricultural, industrial, and information revolutions, and in the process, exponentially expanded our sensory and cognitive.

The evolution of design has paralleled these revolutions, helping address new needs that emerged over time. Early on, our ancestors faced survival needs just like any other species. But unlike birds or beavers, for example, humans elevated the need for shelter, moving beyond satisfying their basic needs.

At some point in our development as a species, buildings and objects were assigned meaningful functions that reflected social and symbolic needs, and their design became essential to communicating their symbolic meaning. The value and symbolic significance of objects and structures began to extend well beyond the value of the raw materials or labor that went into producing them.

Human societies are hierarchical and the ability to express status and class differentiation through design became important, because most societies formed around the symbolic power of religious and aristocratic classes. Design helped elevate the notion that few people are chosen by divine intervention, making them special--endowed with heavenly powers that afforded them their position and rule.

Design became the pivotal means of communicating the abstract concepts of endowed power, through concrete means of visual representation of the sublime and precious. Buildings and artifacts were infused with beauty and meaning that were designed to communicate and justify the concentration of power and means, at the hands of a small, select group of a society.

The demand for skilled artisans who could build and decorate palaces, places of worship, furniture, and garments widened. Skills necessary to articulate meaning, have evolved into well-segmented artisanal trades--stonemasons, metalsmiths, goldsmiths, armorers, blacksmiths are just a few examples of domain expertise that began to be passed from generation to generation through systems of apprentices, guilds, and trade associations.

This is the origin of some of the design domains listed previously. For centuries, people in the design trades were not distinguished from artisans who mastered other trades, such as bakers, tanners or millers. They were respected, but generally poor and illiterate just like the majority of people at the time. The rate of change was very slow compared to our times, perhaps because science and technology evolved very slowly as well. For example, *Thales of Miletus*, the Greek philosopher, experimented with primitive forms of electricity in the 6th century BCE, but electricity became a common utility in industrial countries only during the first part of the 20th century. Industrialization, the big driver of change, was only possible once energy manufacturing and distribution became common.

While it is possible to place the various disciplines on a historical timeline, attempting to pinpoint their emergence has limited value because the boundaries of disciplines are so difficult to delineate. Instead, we will consider how various disciplines evolved to address specific challenges and opportunities.

Mapping common design themes

All Experience Design disciples share common themes that help drive the development of each individual discipline towards a unified and holistic experience approach.

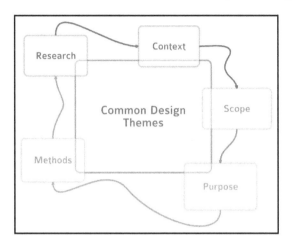

The following are themes that are common to all Experience Design disciplines:

- **Context**: Focus on creating a good, positive emotional experience that is intended for real people, as opposed to impersonal categories such as 'consumers', 'buyers' or 'customers'. Context involved an awareness of and adaptation to personal and social experiences, communities and cultures, global and local, public and private, biases and stereotypes.
- **Purpose & Scope**: How complex is the design problem we are looking to solve? Is it a global application meant to serve a wide and diverse audience, or a very targeted one? Does the design need to scale and grow?
- Efficiency: Balancing the needs of the experience, with environmental and sustainability concerns. How to create more with less? How to simplify without losing track of complexities that are important to the user? Often in design, 'less is more'.
- **Methods**: Multi-disciplinary collaboration, fast-paced iterative cycles of design, validation and refinement of concepts, anticipation of emerging trends and technologies and their incorporation into the evolving design.

- **Research**: The ethical means of knowing what people needs and wants from a product. Measuring the experiences of individuals without infringing on their dignity and privacy. Assessing the cascading effects of social media on the experiences of the individual.

Form and function

The first dimension we explore continues to be a topic of heated debates among designers, critics, and the public. The question at the center of the debate is how important is design to the overall experience? Or, in other words, which is more important--form or function?

This is of course a "chicken or egg" kind of a question, one for which right or wrong are contextual to each specific instance. But it is the process of trying to answer the question that is tremendously important, because the debate challenges accepted views of design's mission and principles, and fuels the advancement of theoretical and practical topics across all design disciplines. It is an interesting dilemma, but first, to some basic definitions:

- **Function**: It is about how well does a product perform what it is supposed to do. Experiencing a function is often associated with the gap between our expectations from the product, and its actual performance.
  For example, a phone is meant to enable a user to dial someone remotely and have a real-time conversation, or conversely, accept a call from someone and have a conversation. The expectation is to hear the conversation clearly, and to be clearly heard by the other person. If the quality is consistently poor, calls are often dropped and dialing is cumbersome and prone to input errors; we feel that the product has disappointed us, that the experience of using it for its primary function is poor.
- **Form**: It is about the aesthetics of the object. Experiencing form is evaluating the degree its use gives us pleasure beyond fulfilling its basic functions.
  Continuing the phone example, a brightly colored plastic case might appeal to younger users, or those who like bright colors more than polished aluminium cases, which might appeal to business users who want a more hi-tech look. Function-wise, both devices are identical, so technically the case could be made of either material.

When the focus is on making the phone looks and feels amazing, but the experience of phone calls is poor and important features are missing, it is an example of form taking over function.

Consider the peacock and the Lamborghini shown in the preceding image. Both are visually striking, and in both, form significantly appears to overshadow function--perhaps for a good reason.

Male peacocks have an amazingly beautiful tail, which they fan to attract female peacocks. The larger, more beautiful the fully-spread tail, the more successful the male may be in its amorous pursuits. In most species, male or female bodies have strong visual features as a means for attracting the opposite sex, but male peacocks seem to be way out there.

It is not difficult to find an analogy between the peacock and a Lamborghini--a symbol of the ultimate show-off. The Lamborghini and other super cars are meant to be seen by others and shine a glamorous light on its driver, as they are built to provide the excitement of cutting-edge automotive technology and design.

An elaborate tail can be a real liability for the peacock. The size and weight of the tail makes the bird less agile, and exposes it to more risk from predators. Likewise, Lamborghinis are expensive to purchase, own, and maintain, and they have very limited space for passengers and cargo.

But this is where the tail of the peacock and super car literally ends--the male peacock is born with its fancy tail, and uses it for a function, which involves form. Cars, on the other hand, are products--for some they are pure utility, the means for getting from point A to B, while for others they are a source of deep emotional experiences, a declaration of self, and a public expression of status, personality, and life style--a class and social statement.

Transportation has played a major role in shaping our emotional attachment to cars, and to product experiences in general: The domestication of animals and the invention of the wheel and axle combination, about 6000 years ago, led to robust commerce and exploration opportunities. Most people, however, did not travel much, because there has been few reasons to do so. For those who did, the experience must have been poor--trips took a long time since land crossing options were one's own feet, or the power of strong animals such as camels, horses, and such--an improvement, but still limited to low sustained speeds. The roads were unpaved trails and carriages exposed passengers to the elements. Roadside inns were of questionable quality and far and few along the path. Finally, the looming danger of occasional robbers further curbed the demand for long-distance travel.

The invention of the self-propelled automobile dramatically changed the experience of travel within a few decades, and also created new categories of emotional experiences. The sense of independence was primary--the notion of freedom afforded to the driver, the ability to cover long distances at speeds never imaginable before. Many desirable destinations became reachable within minutes or a few hours, as was the option to live in a quiet suburb and commute to work.

American society and culture, in particular, has been deeply shaped by the automobile experience, which was a catalyst for major social and economic changes. And in most countries, albeit often pushed by dictatorship regimes, the idea of a "people's car" ignited the imagination of, well, the people because a car really meant a new degree of personal freedom and independence, and the excitement of the potential to explore new places.

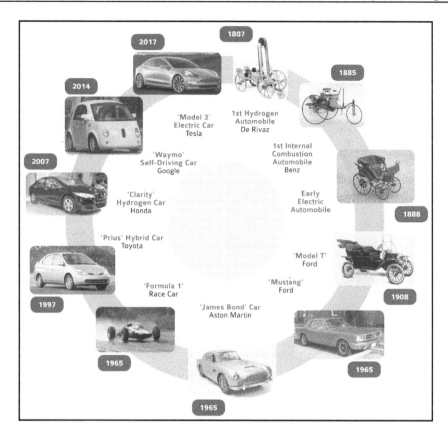

Car riding services such as Lyft, and the promise of self-driving cars, are leading a transition that marks the next phase in the emotional connection between people and their cars--the car as a smart appliance and entertainment center. The driving function, just like the voice phone call with smartphones, is becoming marginalized. Which is why Apple, Google, and other hi-tech giants are entering the car design and manufacturing space, in direct competition with traditional car manufacturers.

Needs, function, and form

It is only logical to assume that function was first to emerge, since we can't tell for sure when aesthetics and design got fused with the construction of dwellings and artifacts. The following diagram shows the intersection of **Form** and **Function**, in relation to the shift from use of found objects to modern manufactured products, which depends heavily on design (**Form**) as a competitive advantage.

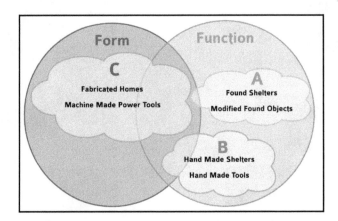

Early humans sought shelter from the elements and predators in caves and other types of nature-made dwellings, which could be used with little or no modifications. They also used found-objects such as rocks and sticks as utensils and weapons. It can be reasonably argued that in those early times, function topped form, because there was no other option --you need to use whatever works regardless of its look and feel. In the diagram, the bulk of found objects use (**A**) positioned within the **Function** circle.

With early use came experience, habit, familiarity, and the ability to recognize a functional fit in similar found objects--which was very important for a nomadic culture on the move. Over time, patterns of use assimilated in the way of life and customs of a culture, passing from generation to generation.

In the preceding diagram, the small part of **A** that is within the intersection of Function and Form, is an acknowledgement of the existence of some inherent ability or instinct, to recognize the potential of specific found objects to serve specific functions. In other words, some type of decision-making, of selectiveness, had to be applied by our ancestors to help them determine which rock would make a better weapon, or which cave will be more protective.

We share this ability with many other species and it seems especially evident in the use of found objects for the creation of dwellings, as we can see in birds, bees, ants, and beavers who create large and elaborate structures, as shown in the following image. These animals are selective when they collect the materials from which they assemble their shelter.

Selectiveness means recognizing the availability of choice. Choice, in turn, means having to decide which item, among similar items that fit a function, is better. If all options qualify on a functional level, there is an opportunity to use additional criteria, which is less objective, but rather a reflection of personal preference. The preference is an individual's response to sensory properties of the item, such as the material it is made of, shape, texture, and color.

We don't know for sure about animals, but we have all experienced the feeling that an item is "just right" for us. This confidence is often accompanied with a physical sensation of internal calm and comfort, which follows an evaluation phase of other options. The decision-making process, involves rational and emotional behavior.

The following diagram illustrates the two primary types of experience evaluations:

- Rational (function first)
- Emotional (form first)

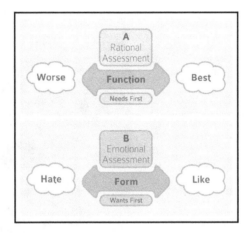

Science fiction reality

Experience Design disciplines today are facing old and new challenges. The new challenges potentially far surpass anything design disciplines have addressed so far.

Scientific and technological advancements are turning ideas that until recently were in the realm of science fiction, into reality. Virtual reality design, for example, is an emerging design specialty that is moving beyond games and entertainment, into areas such as education, medicine, and commerce:

- **Self-driving cars**: This introduces radical changes, not only to the way we are used to operating cars--driving them ourselves, but more importantly, what will this do to our emotional connection to our car, and to our sense of independence? Google has removed the steering wheel from its cars, and Uber is experimenting with a service model that makes owning a car a thing of the past.
- **The Internet of Things**: The notion that all devices are connected to the internet, passing data about the world and about us, constantly monitoring themselves, us, and the environment. What are the implications on experiences such as privacy, individualism, and creativity?
- **The connected home**: It is promising to let our dwelling run itself, taking over most tasks and decisions we currently perform in what we call home, tasks that to a great degree make us feel that we are in our home, will be performed by smart appliances and robots. Will the home become a sterile pod of existence controlled remotely by companies that manufacture intelligent products?

2D surfaces and meaning

Delivering experiences in two dimensions is the principal realm of graphic design, typography, and software user interfaces for the web and mobile apps.

The origin of the word "graphic" is from the ancient Greek, "graphe", meaning writing and drawing--two means of communication that are executed on and are experienced via surfaces--may they be pages of a magazine, the screen of a smartphone, or the fabric of a dress. The brain is capable of making sense out of the markings on those surfaces, and a common cultural agreement on the meaning of the various markings, makes it possible to distribute compact messages that can be understood by wide audiences.

Tradition is extremely important to the development of typography and graphic design. Until 200-300 years ago, most people were illiterate. Reading and writing were limited to a relatively few people, mostly men who were members of the upper classes or clergy. And so there has been a gap between written and verbal language.

Verbal language was much more informal, variable, and flexible, while written language was used in formal domains such as laws, literature, and scripture. Before the invention of print, reproduction of manuscripts was by hand copying--a slow and time-consuming task. Ink and parchment were expensive, and not so easy to work with, although, perhaps not so when compared to etching on stone, as some cultures did.

Typography has evolved then as a craft of high importance and an aura of sacredness. The preceding image has a few examples of ancient typography in Japanese, Muslim, Christian, and Jewish manuscripts. Because manuscripts were often copied by scribes who could not understand the text they copied, they copied methodically the shapes of the typefaces, and the illustrations that accompanied them. Traditions and meaning thus persisted for centuries and well after the invention of the printing press and the movable type.

As readers, we experience the meaning of a page well before we finish reading it. The layout, typeface, and size of the type, spacing, illustrations if any, size of the page--all are coded with expressive meaning.

Like typography, graphic design is a powerful medium of expressive content in a very compact way--icons, logos, posters, and billboards are prime examples of concentrated communication that bridges the interpretation of content to form a unified understanding.

You can tell the meaning of the random items in the image above despite the fact that they have nothing in common with the content of this book--their significance is embedded in them.

How is it possible to communicate so much meaning and emotion in a compact form of delivery, such as an icon or logo? The secret is in understanding the effectiveness of visual design's primary ingredients and how they can be blended:

- Shape
- Contrast
- Color
- Transparency
- Alignment

- Perspective
- Patterns
- Background and foreground
- Emphasis

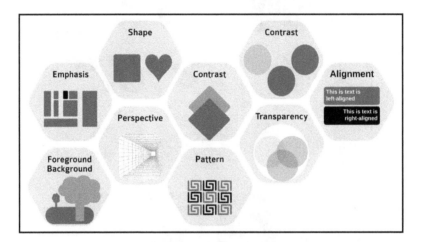

These ingredients, some of which are visualized in the preceding image, must be harmonized to create a visual representation of specific content and then evoke an emotion--regardless of where the graphic is seen. Other aspects of graphic design involve the creation of forms and documents, various web and print artifices, packaging, and numerous other applications. In many of these applications, the guiding visual principles need to work within the confines of given surface--be it a page, a street-sign, a shampoo bottle, large-screen TV, or a small phone.

Exterior and interior spaces - architecture

Delivering experiences in three-dimensional spaces is the domain of architecture, product design, vehicle design, and fashion design, to name a few key disciplines.

Vitruvius defines three qualities of a "good" building, which are as relevant today as they were thousands of years ago, and they can be applied to all products:

- **Durability**: The notion that a building or a product should last. When it comes to buildings, there are several wonderful examples that not only survived time, but some are still functional, such as the Pantheon in Rome. But how does durability reconcile with rapid technological changes?

- **Utility**: It should be suitable for the purposes for which it is used.
- **Beauty**: It should be aesthetically pleasing.

Architecture has a unique dimension of experience that few other design domains can practice--the awe of sheer scale--very large structures and spaces that tower over their landscape like artificial mountains. The preceding image includes a few ancient architectural treasures which survived--examples of durability, utility, and beauty.

The experience of walking in streets of a modern metropolis has been compared to hiking in canyons--the pedestrians at street-level dwarfed by towering skyscrapers' facades. Experiencing scale and proportion is an innate quality--we can easily compare ourselves, in size, to everything around us.

For thousands of years, nature had no competitor when it came to size--oceans, desserts, mountain ranges, and canyons. The emergence of monumental architecture, manifesting the ingenuity, inventiveness, and skills of people, introduced symbolic adoration and awe, which were reserved to nature, to the rulers, institution, organizations, and designers who made these structures possible.

Architecture covers the deepest range of human emotional experiences. It is about designing shelters from nature and its rough elements on the one hand, and a defiance of nature expressed in amazing structures, on the other. Additionally, architecture is the only experience domain that is effective in design at a very large scale, such as urban planning, to the minute scale of personal furniture, as illustrated in the following figure.

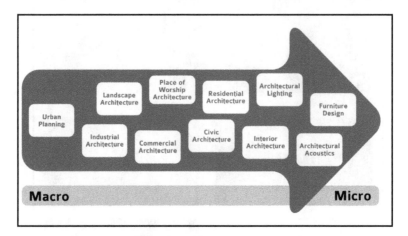

Clothes, fabrics, and fashion

It can be argued that clothes are the most complex of all product categories. From personal, to official, to ceremonial uses, clothes are encoded with historical and cultural significance. In the biblical story, the first thing Adam and Eve do after eating from the forbidden tree of knowledge, is covering their nakedness with fig leaves that they sewed together. Adam and Eve can be considered as the first fashion designers, sewing--as the first technique for manufacturing cloths, and fig leaves--as the first materials to fashion clothes from. While the scientific community is still debating when people started wearing clothes, the range is between 50,000 to 540,000 years ago.

The image above illustrates some of the ceremonial uses of uniforms by royalty, clergy, physicians, justices, and soldiers. The use of special fitted garments and uniforms to distinguish the wearer by their special role cuts across all societies and cultures. The saying "You are what you wear", still holds today, as an effective means to communicate the authority of the wearer, and depending on the context, exact obedience, and respect from those in the wearer's immediate vicinity.

And of course, the design of clothes has also specialized over the years to address gender, age, and function differences. Additionally, social and religious norms have influenced strict codes that dictate--to this date, what one should or shouldn't wear in certain contexts.

From a domain expertise perspective, the development of design professions in clothing parallels that of architecture. Like Adam and Eve, the majority of people were able to make their own clothes using available materials and basic sewing techniques to create covers that were effective to the climate and circumstances. Resources were very limited and so was the available technology. Techniques for processing raw materials such as leather, fur, and plants, in order to transform them into processed elements that could be used for the production of clothes, were refined and passed from generation to generation.

The constant refinement and adaptation naturally led to the adoption of design patterns and styles that were common to a specific culture, trade, social, or religious class, and to further specializations such as cobblers, milliners, tailors, wig-makers, and so on.

As societies stabilized, roles and organizations formed--rulers and royalty, clergy, soldiers, and so on, and this evolution too, contributed to the development of widely spread and familiar design patterns.

Uniformity and consistency of appearance became critical to the recognition of wearers and their role, as did the demand for skilled tradesmen who could produce the necessary items at the quality and consistency needed. As with architecture, clothes were handmade for most of human history; craftsmen and artisans gained their expertise as apprentices and gained their reputation over years of practice.

Practitioners in this domain have always been in the forefront of technology and improved manufacturing technologies, taking advantage of new materials, such as water and stain resistance fabrics, for example, the outcome of nanotechnology research. Because clothing is an essential artifact that protects humans in their endeavors, there are constant challenges posed by extreme needs such as those of the military, space programs, and healthcare.

We may be only a few decades before implants and bionic sensors become the enhancement norm for casual, non-medical consumption. Until then, Experience Design in the clothing domain continues to focus on growing opportunities to transform garments into active data hubs, changing our relationship with the clothes we wear.

Human factors (ergonomics)

Human factors, also known as **ergonomics** (the terms are interchangeable) emerged as the leading domain dedicated to adjusting the design of physical products to fit the human body and mental states. Over the years, the domain has contributed to significant understanding of the human physical and cognitive condition under stressful conditions.

Stressful conditions do not necessarily mean extreme conditions. On the contrary, often the circumstances appear on the surface to be relaxed and easy. Like using a computer's keyboard and mouse, for example, which, after an epidemic of Carpal Tunnel Syndrome in the 1990s, has led to research into the causes of the ailment, and product designs that attempted to eliminate or reduce the problem.

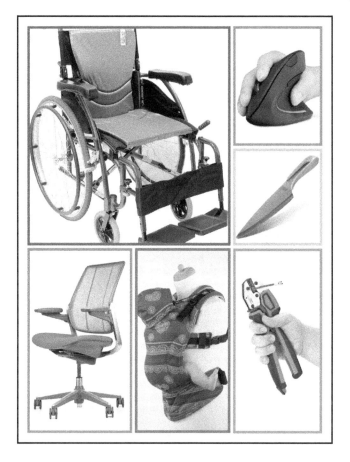

The term ergonomics first appeared in the 1950s, a mashup of the Greek word "ergon", which means "work", and the English word "economics". The latest definition of the term, according to the International Ergonomics Association, is:

> *"The scientific discipline concerned with the understanding of interactions among humans and other elements of a system, and the profession that applies theory, principles, data and methods to design in order to optimize human well-being and overall system performance."*

> *"Practitioners of ergonomics and ergonomists contribute to the design and evaluation of tasks, jobs, products, environments and systems in order to make them compatible with the needs, abilities and limitations of people."*

Examples of ergonomically designed products are numerous, and a few are presented in the preceding image. These include kitchen knives with non-slip handles, office chairs and desks, driver seats in trucks and buses, headsets, baby strollers, computer input devices such as keyboards, mice, backpacks, and wheelchairs. The list goes on to include many items in categories of products used at home, work, and leisure settings.

The list of items in these product categories that are not ergonomically designed is much, much longer. Ergonomic design is expensive and requires the skills of specialized practitioners, lengthy research and development before a product can come to the market and claim ergonomic benefits. And so, companies do not invest in ergonomic design unless they are pressured in to doing so, or, they realize that such an approach will give them a significant competitive edge.

Time-based design disciplines

The design of time-based experiences includes a number of disciplines that have roots in the arts and entertainment industry, such as animation, video, sound, and lighting design. The integration and commercial application of these artistic means in Product Experience Design, has been made possible through relatively recent breakthroughs in technology, such as high-speed networks and LED lights. The following section includes brief explorations of commercial time-based disciplines.

The two common themes to all time-based experiences are very distinct from each other:

- The first theme is handling the formation of stories and narratives, of guides and journeys that walk us through real or imaginary situations. Narratives are communication devices, meant for personal and social interaction. The ability to create narratives is an inherent human capability. It enables us to find or invent complex meaning in practically anything we want, including in products. This ability is the driving force of all artistic and design-driven creation and consumption.
  Narratives take time to unfold, although they do not require suspense or a surprising end. Products that deliver education, training, guidance, or entertainment content provide opportunities for multi-sensory interfaces that use video, audio, and touch to engage the user with the material in immersive, narrative-driven experiences. Content that might be otherwise dull and difficult to process becomes entertaining, easier to understand, retain, and apply.

- At the core of the second theme is survival. More broadly put, products that include features to alert the user of a change and need for action--timers, alarms, notifications, and so on. Our senses are fine-tuned to constantly monitor changes in ourselves, others, and our surroundings--physical changes in properties such as temperature, light, motion, noise, size, proximity, and so on, and emotional changes such as facial expressions and body gestures.
  Sweating, shivering, knee jerks, and eye blinks are examples of our body's involuntary physical responses to change. Other responses are learned from personal experience or from following the experience of others. Either way, given the constant stream of information fed from our sensory and nervous system, we learn to normalize inputs and distinguish "normal" changes from changes that require attention and possible action. In other words, we tend to tune out and ignore events.
  The challenge for product designers is how to alert the user of a current or impending change and trigger the appropriate response to the change--without causing the user to tune out of the experience.

Animation is a time-based discipline that is heavily used in Experience Design to address both narrative and alert content. It is being incorporated into the interaction experience of apps and web pages, lighting systems, car and appliance dashboards, and wearables.

In 1944, the psychologists Fritz Heider and Marianne Simmel created a short film for what is considered to be a landmark experiment in psychology. In the short film, a frame of which is shown in the following figure, and which you can view on the web, we observe the movement of three geometric shapes--a small circle, a small triangle, and a large triangle. The movie has no sound track and the shapes are two-dimensional, black, over a simple white background.

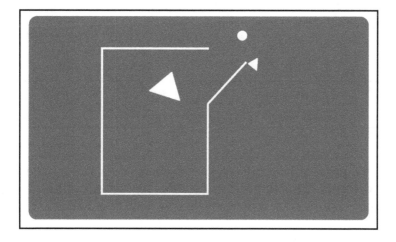

In other words, it should be quite clear to the viewer that the shapes on the screen are exactly what they appear to be--lifeless objects. And yet, the movie is full of suspense and emotion. It clearly appears that the large triangle is attacking the small triangle and circle, which are united in their brave fight against the evil attacker.

As viewers, we attribute human qualities, emotions, and intentions to still objects, visuals, sounds, and even abstract shapes--an inherent human trait called anthropomorphism-- which makes animation a fantastically engaging experience medium for delivering content. Similarly to video content, the user gets exposed to large amounts of information in a compact frame, and designers can organize graphics, charts, text, images, narration, music, sound effects, and user control to communicate content and deliver it as a multi-sensory experience.

As users, we take pleasure and delight from interactive interactions with products, such as gliding our hand over an object or a screen, and have the system respond, by either omitting a sequence of tones, conversation, changing colors, pulsing, glowing, shaking, and other effects. It is a basic form of dialog, using basic animation principles, which is extremely effective for creating engagement with products as alerts or confirmations of interaction.

Interaction design is a new time-based discipline that borrows heavily from animation, by integration timing principles, audio-visual effects, and narrative development concepts-- core animation concepts, with interactivity, to create more engaging and meaningful experiences.

Armed with a large engagement inventory of techniques, and a research-driven understanding of the interactions they are modeling, interaction designers help transform mundane experiences. For example, *wizards* are task-based interactions that guide the user through a complex set of sub-tasks, such as tax preparation, insurance applications, software installation, flight reservation, and many more. Moving one screen at a time, with each screen focused on a sub-task, the user has only to provide relevant information and preferences.

While wizards are a major improvement over non-wizard approaches that require expertise, they too often result in a bad experience--users zoom through the screens without paying attention to details, or, getting lost in a tedious sequence, ending up making the wrong choice despite confirmation screens, which are also ignored.

When viewed as a concentrated form of time-based narrative, wizards can become truly engaging, keeping the users focused on each of the sub-tasks, through audio-visual animation effects. Interaction designers can also figure out how to simplify the process and when possible, completely eliminate steps that the product can perform autonomously. The result, from the user's perspective, is effortless, positive, and error-free.

The importance of time-based disciplines such as interaction design is underscored, as artificial intelligence and machine-learning usher in a generation of products that are perpetually on, monitoring whatever it is they are meant to track and performing tasks autonomously. Smart appliances and self-driving cars are contemporary examples.

Lighting design is another example of a time-based discipline that emerged through applications in architecture, theatrical, and cinematographic settings, to widespread home and commercial use. The iridescent lightbulb is being phased out by advanced LED lights, which are significantly more energy efficient, have a wide and dynamically changeable color temperature, and can be controlled by the system or remotely through a mobile app, by the user.

Light can infuse a space with unique ambiance, which complements the overall exterior or interior experience of a structure, enhancing the effect of natural light, which changes throughout the day and night. Conversely, adjustment to the color and intensity of the light can improve health by helping the body adjust to time shifts and changing conditions, such as in the design of airplane cabins, homes, office spaces, venues, or the use of LED for street lighting, as shown in preceding image.

Lighting is used to provide feedback about the operational status of a product, such as kettles with indicators that change color from blue to red as the water get warmer.

The LG LMXC23796D 23 cu. ft. InstaView™ Door-in-Door® Counter-Depth Refrigerator, for example, has a long name, but it is also an example of an ingenuous application of light-design. Knocking on the appliance door twice makes the door transparent, and the content visible without having to open the door.

Ironically, in an age where increasingly people prefer to communicate with each other over texts and emojis, we are getting increasingly more conversational with our products. Conversational interfaces are sprouting everywhere, in cars, home appliances, mobile devices, robots, and toys.

Another discipline that shapes time-driven experiences is sound design. Unique to our species is the ability to create musical compositions that can be expressed through symbolic written notations, performed with musical instruments, recorded and played back on demand. These capabilities afford us the experiences of artistic performance and commercial communication.

It was Thomas Edison's invention of the phonograph in 1877, which made it possible to capture and reproduce sound and usher in a new wave of new experiences, which today is manifested in streaming music services, portable audio devices, conversational interfaces, and so on.

Sound is an incredibly important ingredient in immersive products or support systems. Companies increasingly turn to bots--algorithmic interfaces which are capable of handling independently interactive dialogs with people. To these interfaces, the tone, intensity, accent, and cadence of the artificial voice are becoming as important as the content of the conversation, because the experience of the human partner in the conversation is extremely sensitive to the slightest variances to voice quality

When Siri was first released, users had a blast trying to hold a stream of conversation with the virtual speaker, trying to trip it with nonsense questions, and delighting with smart and seemingly contextual results. But as artificial intelligence advances, the conversations are likely to become more substantial, as portrayed in Spike Jonze's 2013 movie 'Her', or Jacques Offenbach's 1880 opera 'The Tales of Hoffmann'

And so we will close this section with virtual reality design, a time-based discipline that folds into its practice all of the disciplines discussed previously, and others that the scope of this book could not let us cover.

The human imagination is the most powerful virtual machine that has ever existed. Wherever and whenever you are, you can imagine yourself and engage in any number of situations and environments that you invent, at any level of detail, regardless of whether the environment actually exists, or you have ever been there, and so on.

When combined with technology, the human imagination gives us devices such as fiction books, music, theatre, radio, movies, video games, theme parks, and other experiences. Some are more immersive than others, but the immersion is a partnership between the user and the technology--in other words, we generally allow ourselves to be swept into the virtual settings, and engage mentally with the situations.

In recent decades, the term virtual reality has become closely related to and associated with computer-generate environments that can be accessed through a special headset. The commercial promise is overwhelming, because of the ability to interact in virtual environments, but impact the real world.

For example, supermarket layouts are generally predictable, and when we frequent a particular store, location of various items become ingrained in our mind such that when we are in a hurry, we can be very efficient finding what we are after. And of course, we can identify items visually. We also know, based on the position of items, where other items might be, and so on. Shopping for produce online has been slow to pick up for a number of reasons, but among them is that the online shopping experience is much slower and inefficient than it is in the physical store.

The isles of the virtual supermarket are an example for an emerging type of immersive experience that lets the user shop a store from the comfort of their home. With a VR helmet, they can experience the physical aspects of walking the isles. For merchants and customers, virtual stores open many opportunities that are now limited by size and cost. Designers can turn shopping into an incredible adventure--why not include elements from movies, action games, and other narratives in the experience? Place the store on a tropical island or some remote universe with aliens busy shopping included.

Indeed, game designers have always been in the forefront of Experience Design. That's because when we play a game, be it a physical board game such as chess, or bubbles played on a phone, we forget about reality, as we are transformed into an imaginary space where only the game's special rules apply for the duration the game is being played. Like animation and audio-visual disciplines, game design has applications well beyond the entertainment industry in domains such as education, training, and healthcare.

Engineering and science in Experience Design

In approaching each other's disciplines, designers and engineers often fall victim to some of the stereotypes that define them in popular culture, expressed in the following joke:

> *Engineers:*
> *Go to school and learn a great deal about a very narrow subject area.*
> *They continue to learn more and more about less and less,*
> *Until they know everything about nothing.*

> *Designers:*
> *Go to school and learn a little bit about a great many subjects.*
> *They continue to learn less and less about more and more,*
> *Until they know nothing about everything.*

Stereotypes aside, engineers, were always integral to advancement of product design, and over the past few decades alone, have opened frontiers of experiences that were in the realm of science fiction not so long ago.

Take space tourism, for example. At companies such as Blue Origin, Virgin Galactic, and SpaceX, scientists and engineers collaborate with designers to develop an inspirational, intense experience for those who can afford it--the exclusive opportunity to satisfy deep emotional needs, fulfil a childhood dream of being an astronaut, or a yearning to see our blue planet from space.

A massive scientific and engineering effort will be required to make space travel a safe and ubiquitous experience product similar to commercial aviation. But, although the motivation is fueled by hopes for significant financial rewards to pioneers, the effort itself illuminates the essence of the human relentless quest for knowledge and exploration, and the desire to experience a range of emotions that extends any practical value.

Science and engineering thus make it possible to design the most powerful experiences, which, while delivered through ethereal hardware, satisfy ephemeral, emotional needs such as curiosity and excitement, which are hard-to-reproduce--and thus extremely valuable.

Scientific and engineering research often leads to applied solutions that sometimes change the course of human existence. Probably the most impactful to our current times is electricity. Pause here to consider life without it--most of the products discussed in this book would not have existed.

The quest to understand the nature of electricity was a scientific area of study that persisted for centuries, and pioneered by numerous scientists such as Alessandro Volta and Andre-Marie Ampere, whose names are eternalized in the electrical measurement units Volt and Ampere. Once understood, it was through the combined efforts of many engineers such as Pavel Yablochkov, who invented transformers, generators, and the rest of the infrastructure that made electricity a utility.

In recent decades, the science of understanding the human mind has opened new fronts for User Experience Design. Relatively new domains of research, such as cognitive, social organizational, and quantitative psychology, as well as behavioral economics, are having a tremendous impact on Product Experience Design.

For example, the *Hick-Hyman law*, named after the psychologists William Hicks and Ray Hyman, helps designers analyze the effectiveness of their design from a decision-making perspective, and simplify the design if necessary. The law expresses in mathematical formula the fact that increasing the number of choices a person has, increases the time it takes the person to make a decision.

Designers often interpret this law to mean that a long decision-making process due to the availability of many choices, is a bad thing, and thus reduces the number of choices the user has.

Related to the Hicks-Hyman law is "The Paradox of Choice", a term coined by psychologist Barry Schwartz, to argue the point that too many choices offered to consumers actually increase consumer anxiety due to the difficulty of making the right choice among the various options. The psychological value of many choices is further diminished by post-purchase regret due to the sense that selecting a different option might have been a better decision.

As a simple thought experiment, imagine two ice cream stores at a remote train station, on a very hot day. A train stops for a 10 minute break, and all the passengers are lining up in front of the stores, eager for a cone of delicious cold ice cream. The first store offers only two ice cream flavors--chocolate and vanilla, served in a sugar cone. The other store offers 24 flavors of ice cream. Now, estimate your chance of getting ice cream at any of those stores before the train departs.

Clearly, the flow of customers at the first store will be much faster and efficient. If you can't choose between vanilla or chocolate, you can just take both. The decision-making process at the other store is much longer, as customers first take in all the available options, and struggle to decide which of their favorite flavors to select. In the meantime, the pressure to choose is high, because time is running out and there are many people still waiting behind.

As designers, the lesson from such an example is that in some cases, a very limited set of options is superior to many options.

Summary

Design disciplines connect core aspects of experience, explored in Chapter 5, with the various design roles and practices which are covered next. Some design disciplines such as car design, are specialized while others, such as graphic design, have a wide variety of applications. But across the board, they share a focus on establishing meaningful and lasting emotional connections between people and product, be it a building, a car or an appliance. They also share some methodologies, tools and techniques. Similarly, practitioners you will meet in the next chapter have specialized skillsets, and shared visions about the role of design and designers.

7

The Design Team

"A designer knows he has achieved perfection not when there is nothing left to add, but when there is nothing left to take away."

- Antoine de Saint-Exupery

This chapter addresses the following questions:

- What is the composition of design teams?
- What are the settings of design teams?
- What is the contribution of each team member throughout the design process, from onset to realization?

People tend to associate designers with the Arts more than with the technical precision of engineering, despite the fact that design disciplines--from architecture to interaction design--require mastery of both domains in equal parts. In academic settings, design departments have been traditionally a part of the art schools, although ironically often viewed there as inferior trades, comparted to the pure artistic mission of the *real* arts--painting and sculpture.

Opposing this common view of design as somehow inferior to the arts, is the fact that designers since antiquity were expected to acquire a broad and deep education, as well as extensive practical training, in a wide-range of technical domains. Vitruvius wrote 2000 years ago that:

> *The architect should be equipped with knowledge of many branches of study and varied kinds of learning, for it is by his judgement that all work done by the other arts is put to the test. This knowledge is the child of practice and theory. Practice is the continuous and regular exercise of employment where manual work is done with any necessary material according to the design of a drawing. Theory, on the other hand, is the ability to demonstrate and explain the productions of dexterity on the principles of proportion.*

Architects were probably the first experience practitioners whose work required the coordination of multi-disciplinary teams to complete large complex projects. Architecture requires the blending of engineering and art into an outcome that to the user, the "experiencer", reflects only the art, and masks the engineering complexity of the framework that supports it.

In past centuries, the scope of knowledge to be mastered--science, engineering and design combined--was small enough for a single person to master. The architect did not have to do all the work, but after years of training that began in childhood, moving up from a starting position of lowly apprentice, he was very familiar with the details of each of the collaborating disciplines.

Today, the term "Renaissance Man", which used to describe polymaths - people who, several centuries ago, were thought to possess deep knowledge in all known areas of academic inquiry - has been replaced by the trendy "unicorn", meaning a person who is skilled in business, strategy, research, design, and development. Like the imaginary animal, such people don't exist, but the desire to fuse all this knowledge in a single person is still very strong.

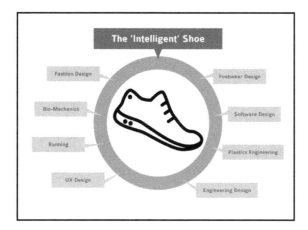

The blending of design and engineering disciplines applies to every aspect of life. As specialization became prevalent in all disciplines, companies that create every-day products needed to form multidisciplinary teams of specialists.

For example--back in 2004, Adidas, the global maker of Activeware, announced the *Adidas 1*, which was coined the first "intelligent shoe" . The product promised to change the experience of running in a profound way. Each shoe was equipped with sensors in the mid-sole that continuously monitored the runner's motion, and dynamically adjusted the firmness of the sole to the running conditions. The shoe even had a user interface that allowed the runner to adjust the settings manually.

The preceding image lists some of the domains of expertise that the design team had to include. Members of this team represented expertise in fashion, footwear, software and user experience design, engineering, bio-mechanics, and running. Although at the time, the Adidas 1 and the concept of an intelligent shoe fizzled, footwear companies continued to invest in improving the experience through high-tech and design.

This chapter features design practitioners from various design disciplines. These are the personal stories of real people, from all over the globe. Some are seasoned professionals with many years of experience, and others are making their initial steps in the field. Each is involved in some aspects of the design process and contributes to the collective effort of a team. They all share the passion to simplify complexity--beautifully and skillfully.

Role of the designer

Are designers just commercializing emerging trends and fashions, or do they set the trends? Do we need so many fonts, shoe styles, smartphone models, and breakfast cereal flavors?

Experience designers have always worked within the constraints and pressures of commercial settings, because their services are tied to the demands of individuals, companies, and organizations who pay for their services. And yet, for centuries, individual designers and design movements set important trends that supported or led to major shifts in industrial, social, and personal attitudes towards aesthetic and functional appreciation of experience.

The twentieth century marked a dramatic change in the role of the designer. It was a part of a shift to the *modern*--the notion that the world is turning a new page with the power of scientific and industrial breakthroughs. Influential movements in philosophy, art, architecture, and industrial design, brought forward the ideas of "total design".

Frank Lloyd Wright   **Walter Gropius**   **Steve Jobs**

At its core, "total design" places the individual designer at the front and center of creating, curating, and controlling the user experience--for the user. In other words, the designer knows best what's good for you.

In "total design", or "closed design", the designer controls and orchestrates the creation of all aspects of life--from the macro--the layout of a city, the design of buildings, parks, vehicles, street lamps, signage, and so on, to the micro of furniture, appliances, utensils, and clothes.

Total design went to the extreme of wanting the macro and micro to be governed by a total design system. Frank Lloyd Wright, for example, demanded that his clients use the furniture and fixtures he designed for each of the homes, and he did not allow any alteration. The owner lived in Wright's creation, and Wright believed that he knew better what the ultimate experience should be. A small sample of his interior and furniture design is featured in the following image.

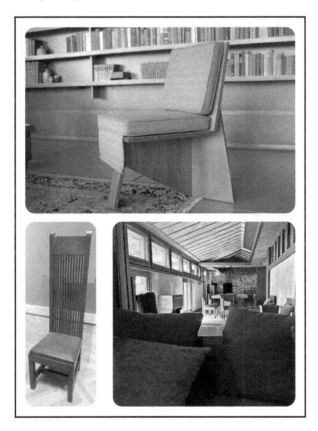

Decades later, Jonathan Ive of Apple, has implemented Steve Job's notion of a total design system. The attitude was that Apple must control every aspect of its hardware and software products, and minimize the user's customization possibilities--for the sake of a user experience that is much superior to the alternative "hodgepodge" of open design experience championed at the time by Microsoft and its Windows ecosystems.

Companies have been relatively slow to adopt "total design". There is an inherent gap between short-term business objectives that demand the fastest, cheapest path to market. Design is expensive, which is why bespoke design has been associated for many centuries with luxury and social class barriers.

And so, while movements such as Bauhaus enjoyed brief periods of influence, continuous industrialization and mass production rejected the idea of homogenization around some "ideal" design systems. Each industry considered its needs first, which made it possible for companies to move at their own pace and be more competitive.

For designers, the second part of the twentieth century has been a golden age of individualism and fame within the various vertical domains they practiced. Companies embraced unique, distinguishing designs for their products, and designers became famous for their experience creations.

We are seeing now the emergence of an era of "new total design"--one in which a handful of corporations--most visibly Google, Facebook, Amazon, Apple, and Microsoft--dominate product experience through a combination of proprietary data infrastructure, hardware, software, and global reach. These corporations continuously expand their control over the entire commercial, special, and personal landscapes, and to gain access to their billions of users, products must comply with one or all of these global ecosystems.

Individual designers who "know best" are being replaced by multi-disciplinary teams of designers who collaborate within the constraints of pre-defined experience patterns set by these few corporations. Can individual designers still thrive in an age of pre-defined patterns and data-driven experience flows governed by artificial intelligence?

The relationship designer

As mentioned previously, the pendulum has swung back towards total design at an escalated pace, due to the confluence of major technological advances--primary among them are:

- The internet
- Fast wireless networks
- Miniaturization of hardware
- Advances in logistics
- The mobile revolution
- Social media
- The Internet of Things
- Advances in artificial intelligence
- Advances in speech and image recognition, and text translation
- Cloud computing

These enabling technologies open the option to maintain a closer, continuous contact with the user. This is a major shift in relationship management that impacts how designers think about their role and about their design.

Suppose you purchase a watch. In the past, your relationship with the brand would have been limited. The company would use various advertising channels to build brand awareness, and sponsor various events to enhance its reputation. You might find the watch you need at a store or online and, generally, your purchase decision would tie to the look and price of the item.

The designer's primary goal was to make the watch attractive at the point of sale, often limited to a split of a second you spent browsing through cases full with other watches. The design was locked in time, figuratively and literally, and so was your experience.

Once you purchased the item, your experience would be limited to occasionally glancing at it for the time, and enjoying its looks.

With smart watches, and for that matter, with more and more products we use, such as vacuum cleaners, home thermostats, lightings, appliances, and other wearables, designers now think about an on-going relationship between the product and the user because:

- The user interface can be customized--a single smart watch can offer its owner tens of different face design options to fit each mood, time of day, or occasion
- The experience is being constantly updated--updates to the software provide enhancements to the user experience, with more customization options and refinements
- Usage data helps personalize the experience for each individual user

For designers, the two important implications of the continuous design approach are:

- **Broader design scope**: It requires an on-going involvement of designers in evolving their design system.
- **Multi-disciplinary collaboration**: Any successful collaboration requires that each individual designer brings an open-mind to the process. The flexibility to change, adapt the design to fit with the feedback from and the requirements that are related to the other disciplines.

Team configurations

Flow diagrams that model the typical design process depict a neat and orderly procession of boxes and arrows depicting the transition of the design process from phase to phase - start to end. In practice, the team often needs to constantly shift focus, improvise, and deal with stressful timelines and difficulties. The work can be very stressful at times, but it is interesting, challenging, and rewarding.

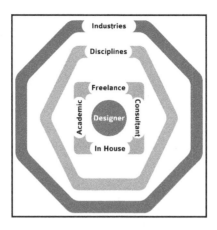

The size of teams varies with the size of the organization one works in. From a "team of one"--a single individual freelancer who offers their services on a temporary basis, to design departments within large organizations.

As an experience designer or developer, one typically works throughout their career--by choice, opportunity, or need--in one or more of the common settings:

- **Freelancer - a team of one**: Individual designers offer their services, typically on a project-by-project basis. Industries and projects change based on whatever work is available, or the designer specializes in a specific domain. This model used to be very common among architects as well as print and software designers, less so in product and industrial design--domains that often require expensive specialized hardware and software tools. Some people love this model; others might find it very stressful and lonely.

- **Agencies and consultancies**: These companies specialize in various forms of experience design and range in size from small boutiques employing a handful of designers, to global firms with hundreds of designers across multiple locations. Such companies can scale to meet the needs of much larger projects than an individual can ever be able to support. For the individual designer who works in a consultancy, there are colleagues to share ideas with, and less stress around finding the next assignment.

- **In-house teams**: This model is becoming common in business and organizations, as design has become an integral part of business. Depending on the company's product line, size, and emphasis on experience, internal design departments vary in size, hierarchical structure, and compartmentalization. In some companies, design is centralized; in others, autonomous design departments focus on a particular product line.

Meet an experience design practitioner

The following entries were written especially for this book by practitioners whom I asked to describe, in their own words, what drew them to their domains of experience design, who were their influences, their work, and some words of advice, in case you are considering a career in the field. Experience design is a wide-ranging, dynamic field with constant change, and so, the stories are presented in the alphabetical order of their last names, to randomize the domains and avoid the stagnation of grouping.

Each of these individuals tells a unique story that unfolds their journey in their respective domains. Some are self-taught and others acquired formal education, some were drawn to design early on, and some traversed through other careers. Some are experienced veterans who witnessed the emergence of experience design trends, while others were still children and are making their initial steps in the industry. They all, however, share limitless curiosity, self-drive for learning, and a passion to create better user experience.

Marlys Caceres - Visual Designer

My background as to how I became a designer is a pretty common one. I grew up with two entrepreneurs who used their art skills as a means to provide extra income. Both my parents liked doing things by hand and would spend long hours into the night knitting or painting. Growing up I knew I wanted to do something with art, but I also knew that I needed a career that I could profit from. Design gave me this option, and I couldn't be happier with my choice. Even though I spend most of my time designing on the computer, I also have the choice of doing things by hand.

I love how versatile my career is, and my generation (and the ones to come) is very lucky to have so many choices. Designers can choose to be in digital or print or be their own entrepreneur doing both; they can specialize or try many different outlets until finding their niche, all under one degree.

I earned my bachelor's in graphic design at *The Illinois Institute of Art - Chicago* in 2012, where I proceeded to work in both digital and print in the areas of public relations, UI design, and marketing. I then attended grad school where I earned my master's focusing on data from the *School of the Art Institute of Chicago* in 2016.

In school and in my everyday life I have been inclined to collect things and information. It would not be surprising to find the information I've collected and dissected it into categories, breaking it from its mundane form and placing it in different structures. I was able to play with as many forms of organizing information through my thesis, which showcased an abundance of AARP junk mail material in a made-up laboratory.

The project turned out to be so much more than just junk mail, a piece that talked about time, its passing, and its structure, leading me to create a calendar that, rather than offer structure, just marks days lived and days left to live based on my life expectancy.

Through my interest in collecting and the environment I have been influenced by artists such as Mark Dion, El Anatsui, Andy Warhol, and a number of self-taught artists who use unwanted materials as their medium. The research done by Annie Leonard, author of *Story of Stuff* has been critical to the knowledge I know today in the subject of environmentalism; I also really enjoy the way she showcases her research through interactive videos and info-graphics.

I believe it is important for a designer or artist to feed personal interests, to have a practice outside of client work and to be able to work on personal projects. I've found this helpful to learn new skills and stay interested in the field.

Marlys's LinkedIn profile is: https://www.linkedin.com/in/marlys-caceres-1420b033

Eddie Chen - UX Engagement Lead

I started out studying mechanical engineering. I always liked thinking about how people work with physical objects every day. I suppose that this was the closest an engineer can get to UX. Somewhere along the way, I realized I had a talent to explain things to people. They could be how things work, scientific theories that I got, or just explaining math homework to other classmates. In effect, I considered myself a translator, translating words from or for one audience into other terms that are well understood by a different audience. I didn't see myself as a communicator, although many told me that was what I could do. I saw communications as creating a message. I explained messages and, to me, that was more translation than communication.

So I thought, "how do I turn this into a profession?" I landed at a company in Massachusetts and tried out all sorts of different roles--technical writing, QA, development. I happened to like technical writing, and development was a lot of fun but, none were as interactive as I liked. And, so, when I got the offer to build out a new process and lead an integration team to deliver rapid fixes in short order, I took the chance to try something else. That role ended up turning me into one of the company's first agile program managers.

That role fit me well--I solved problems, worked with a team to do it, cultivated ideas, and cleared the way for us to make things happen. It was a great way of keeping your pulse on things and getting things done.

My most significant influencers are the ones that gave me the freedom to accomplish things the way I saw fit while providing the guidelines to not go off the rails. Being able to do that is, in itself, a fine art, to be sure. I've had a handful of people who influence me that way-- Steve, Dan, Karl, Sam, Rob. In terms of books, I am a huge fan of the Freakonomics series. To me, that is the written form of data science. These books popularized looking at data to find trends and make decisions.

About my work

I think that there are three things engagement leaders such as myself can do to make for a successful design. First, the designers have got to have the tools to clearly define the problem to solve. I sometimes see projects where designers are given a pen and then told what to draw with that pen. Or they are given a screenshot or even a PowerPoint diagram and instructed to design that layout. This may get you to your desired state, but it isn't designing.

To get maximum benefit from your UX designer, it's important to give them a problem statement and let them explore various possibilities and solutions. Iteration is really important here and iterating doesn't mean the design didn't work. It means that you've discovered that there are other elements that need further consideration, that you're refining what you have.

Just as iterating code to get to right functionality in software is important, iterating design is important, too. (By the way, in those cases where designers were told what to design, the final products either didn't succeed or were scrapped for a new design.)

Second, you have to make your designers part of the requirements process. I see a lot of projects where designers are treated as developers within a sprint. Designs and requirements should work hand-in-hand with product owners and designers working together to determine the best solutions for a given problem statement.

When this happens, you end up with much more thought out designs with much more detailed requirements along with the supporting wireframes or prototypes to communicate that solution to not just developers, but stakeholders and customers, too. All of a sudden, your requirements are in both written and interactive form. Ideas of how to interact with a component are easy to communicate, what the product owner is trying to accomplish becomes evident, and stakeholders and customers get excited seeing the feature come to life.

Third, product owners and engagement leads need to knowing when to tell designers when they've crossed the finish line. It's a tough thing to do, telling someone that we finished.

Designers, just like every other person who works really hard, like to get things just right. But, there are times when just right happened last week or just now. You need to have a relationship with your designer, judge everyone's feedback, look at everyone's body language, and listen to everyone's tone of voice to know that the design is complete.

That's not to say that designers don't know when done is done. But the entire team will feel good about done when everyone agrees when that is.

I think that the evolution of my role is one towards the use of visuals and data. Today, I see lots of people in my role take status or count hours or points and call it a day. I don't subscribe to that concept.

My role is to get things done and that means knowing what our starting point is, knowing what our finishing point is, and knowing what levers I can pull to successfully get to the finishing point. That means not just counting hours or measuring velocity and points, but also understanding the interpersonal nature of the role. Would stakeholders be responsive to this idea? Who will a change benefit and how does that impact the end goals everyone has? What is everyone's desired end result and how can we all get what we need and want?

My role will also involve more understanding of how things happen. Not only do I need to know the process, but I need to know how people accomplish that process. What tools do designers use? Who receives the output of their work, and how do they use that output? What inputs do designers need to be successful and how do I get that input to them?

I'll end with a question and answer on my philosophy.

Quickly, your team needs clarification on some outstanding sprint requirements, your client manager really needs a progress report, and your boss is screaming for a time to meet on budget. Who gets your attention first?

The answer is your team. Without them, it doesn't matter what your progress report or budget look like; you won't have either if you don't keep your team moving along.

Eddie's LinkedIn profile: `https://www.linkedin.com/in/edchin`

Dino Eliopulos - Design Leader

As a young person, my personal heroes were renaissance men like Da Vinci and Ben Franklin - people who were interdisciplinary, inventive and innovative thinkers, and who often crossed the lines outside the traditional areas of study.

I literally walked around high school wearing a tuxedo jacket like Ben Franklin because those were my heroes. So, with that in mind, I've always been kind of a polymath, interested in a lot of different disciplines--honing skills but mostly intent on learning from each discipline and applying it to the others. So, when I went to college, I took fine arts and science and engineering, but chose not to refine my area of interest even in terms of my degree. So, I obtained a set of certifications as a sound engineer and as an acoustical engineer, a minor in physics. I took fine art, did sculpting and painting and things like that.

Those things stayed with me in my professional experience. I always take the approach of drawing from different areas of inquiry and different inputs, and solving problems in ways that involve thinking creatively, laterally - combining technical and creative disciplines.

My jobs have been very varied as well. I think the first job was a children's book illustrator. I did sound engineering for a local Chicago theater. Later I broke into more of a corporate setting where I worked in product development, running prototypes in a lab setting. All the different jobs I had were a good match for somebody who has these kinds of broad interest areas and a multi-disciplinary approach.

I would occasionally flip back and forth between the business side and the technical side of the house - being a project leader or a lead architect, until I ended up in a situation where I could run a practice. Running a practice meant that I could bring together innovative teams and collaborate with folks who had deep specialization.

What was interesting about the direction my interests carried me--and I didn't have a strategy around where I would go and work--was that this nexus of design, implementation of design, tech and engineering coincided with the emergence of the Internet. As the Internet became an area of focus, design and engineering were the two components of successful transformation for companies. I had a passion for, and interest in both, as well as skills in both, which made me good at helping companies go through those kinds of transformations--Building teams that combine creative and engineering mindsets and abilities. It's been like a playground for me because that's been my love--being multi-disciplinary and combining creative and technical pursuits.

A couple of the people I worked for early on were very influential. Arnie Lund, who was at Microsoft and G.E., is one. Our paths crossed when we both worked in Telecom--one of the regional Bell companies, where he led the user experience practice there. He gave me an opportunity to run a four-billion-dollar lab; a massive installation of technology. I was a young person at the time and he said, "Help the teams with their experiments". And so, this person really gave me an opportunity to learn so many things, and to learn how to learn about new technologies. He went on to do marvelous things in his area of expertise and in user experience. So, I think it'll be worth the while tracking that guy down to see what he's done and published.

Advice to those who consider a career in design

I didn't go to school for design, but I met people who exhausted themselves while getting great education. And I think there's room for both options.

I think that there's a sensibility or a pattern of thinking, which is valuable to somebody who is in the design discipline: It's about keen observation and curiosity. It's about always probing and taking a deeper look at something; an inquisitive kind of mindset and trying to understand why something is the way it is.

When you turn that sensibility on, it becomes disruptive to your day to day life because you can no longer look at anything the same way again. You get in an elevator and you're analyzing the position of the buttons. You are looking at the dashboard of a rental car, and you're evaluating whether you know how design decisions for it were made, and why. And, of course, on any website--you're always evaluating.

I think that developing that sensibility and natural curiosity is the first most important part of going down this path: Not being afraid to ask questions, learn, experiment and fail. Sure, this is true of many different disciplines, but I think that design as a discipline is interesting because it is a clear outward representation of that type of thinking: Everyone sees it. And so if you think like that and apply that pattern of thinking, you're going to be very good as a designer, because you don't get locked into idea-driven processes that are insensitive to new information or learning.

Your thinking should be informed by a rigorous process--combining research with this constant asking and curiosity. Nothing is designed from scratch, and there are always inputs from other sources. This constant rethinking and improving is amplified in the extreme with a career in the design disciplines.

I had the fortune of working in an environment where I learned a lot on the job, but not everybody gets that opportunity. I've seen people come out of very strong programs with great toolkits, but if they lack that kind of natural curiosity, it's a problem.

I think that education can give a great start. Somebody coming out of education will have the toolkit for solving some real practical problems. They have some training to fall back on, but very quickly, when they get into a real-life scenario, that training will bump right up against the practical limits and the realities of what it takes to be successful. So, the training will only get's one an early advancement in one's career. The rest will be hard-won by applying experience.

How do you see the evolution of XD in general?

I don't want to say it quite like this, but you can edit out what you want. I don't want to say that we're in a post you UX world, but I will say that my mind it is drawing towards a new phase. At some point, everybody realized that user experience was necessary. You almost can't find anyone who just don't believe in user experience. But there are, of course, lots of variation in terms of what people do from that impulse. Everyone is aware of the big rise in the industry around UX, and I think there are some things that separate good design from bad design that will be true for a long time. It is sort of sad to see, but there are also some conventions that have really settled in--sites like Amazon and linked-in and Google's design standards. So, I think that the role of design now is to ask questions and struggle to break away from what's happening, to push past this kind of conventionality that has really invaded this space.

I remember an anecdote from a time we showed some examples of creative work we did for clients and they asked us, "Do you guys have a template that you're using for these designs? Because when I look at your portfolio and I look at your designs, they look like they come from the same toolkit, like you guys have this one design." Now, that wasn't true formally, but it was sad because the designs were all starting to look like they had come from the same place. So, I think this is a real risk right this minute.

And when I think about my own place in that, I'm kind of peeling the onion ongoing one level past that design into what inhabits the design. And what I mean by that is, what's actually being delivered-- what experiences being delivered through the design. That involves the content, understanding of the business transaction, the intent and the data that is required to drive that experience. When we talk about designing digital experiences, I know there's more to it than digital. More and more of these applications are not just responsive to your device. They are integrating information, analytics, algorithms and personal preferences, and they behave--and that's very hard to model as a designer.

But I think that's what we are dealing with--these AI -driven, machine learning or cognitive computing applications. That's where a new design process and a new design form must emerge and cover this gap, because these systems are very complex.

Designing applications has always been complex. But earlier, they have been procedural in a lot of ways. The next generation of interactions is not going to be so procedural. Applications are going to be a lot more dynamic and a lot more situational in the way they behave. I think that the evolution of the designer role is to understand how machine behavior interacts with human behavior, and the way these interfaces are a bidirectional kind of communication between the human and the machine. I think that's different from the portals, transactional shopping websites, knowledge bases and other things like that that we've been designing for a couple of decades now.

Dino's LinkedIn profile: https://www.linkedin.com/in/deliopulos

Jay Kaufmann - Design Manager

Design management career. I never envisioned those three words together until I hit 40 years old. It happened by chance and circumstance.

My first passion was words. As a teenager, I was reading Kafka, de Beauvoir, Woolf, Zola. I wanted to be a novelist.

Or so I thought. In hindsight, I simply always loved making stuff, whatever that may be--free-writing with my babysitter, photocopying a zine, hacking my Apple IIe, shooting abstract photos, designing an album cover for a progressive rock boy band, or staging off-the-wall straight-edge violin-plus-poetry performance art, influenced by the works of Laurie Anderson and John Cale.

In college, I studied literature, but my bias for making over reading and doing over thinking led me to become Editor in Chief of the student newspaper in my junior year. I took the job more seriously than my studies. Accustomed to excellent grades, I barely squeezed out an American D (a German 4) in a literature class I loved with my favorite professor, in order to put the bulk of my energy into my obsession of publishing provocative ideas, building a team, and growing the scope, quality, and impact of our publication, the Earlham Word.

The formative transformation, though, came next. I realized that what I found most fun was layout. So in my senior year I focused on redesigning the paper, curating artwork, and laying out the articles (I also swung back to a work-life balance that I look back to as ideal today--achieving good grades, political activism, and meaningful friendships).

This self-taught design work and my acquired skills in Quark XPress landed me a job after graduation at Seattle Weekly. I became a designer.

A career found me

But I never wanted a career. I simply wanted to do something enjoyable in order to make money so that I could support my true passions (making art and someday raising a family).

When the World Wide Web surfaced I was back in university studying art, and supporting myself as the secretary of a multi-media lab. I became interested in the internet as an artistic medium. So I taught myself the necessary tools.

Knowing web coding in early 1996 made you sought-after, and I landed my first start-up job through a friend. I was hired as an HTML programmer, and took it upon myself to look after the structure and layout and flow of the screens, since no one else did. I read About Face by Alan Cooper, signed up for Jakob Nielsen's Alertbox, and taught myself Interaction Design and Usability Engineering.

In Seattle, I worked for three startups, spending about 2 years at each company. Throughout, I made sure to balance my jobs and my art, working four days a week and spending the rest on art projects, such as Circus Contraption (`http://www.circuscontraption.com/home.html`), an avant-garde adult variety theater. No career yet. Work and art had equal weight. Though I loved both, I quit it all, to travel with my wife for eight months in Asia and move to Berlin.

It was only after I was settled in Berlin for some time, and while designing a dating website, that it dawned on me that I had been doing user-centered design of digital experiences for almost 10 years. Without aiming to, I had a career.

Management brought it together

Despite having a career, I had no desire to climb a career ladder. After my second kid was born, I had gone back to my old habit of working 32 hours/week--although now, parenting took the place of art. After some fun work building a social network from the ground up, I had another transformational moment.

I created a strategy deck around social commerce for my boss's boss. While in past projects I was fortunate to be involved at a strategic level, this time it triggered something new in me--I realized the power of channeling the creative passion that I had reserved for art, into my work life. I realized that my work could give me dramatically more satisfaction by bringing everything together--by not compartmentalizing work as separate from art and relationships.

My burst of enthusiasm led me to found and lead the first user experience team at Fox Mobile. I had stepped up in the organizational hierarchy. But the real step up was the personal satisfaction that came from leading people--while leading a strategic product design initiative focused on a new B2C brand stoked my ego, guiding, mentoring, and coaching employees stoked my soul. Today I try to bring my whole being to work--mental, emotional, artistic, spiritual. Human-centeredness starts here, in my own heart.

The work - designing design

Design is about creating effective solutions to human needs. Design builds the framework for dialog between brands and customers. For me, design is still very concretely about ideating, making, testing, and iterating human-computer interfaces.

However, I also work frequently on the meta level of design. Design leaders are responsible not only for the product design, but also for team culture, professional development, process and practice maturity, stakeholder education, hiring and employer branding, plus a myriad of administrative necessities.

Some examples of things on my agenda recently include:

- Designing a career matrix to help designers see where they stand and inspire growth
- Defining professional development as the intersection of personal goals and business needs, with concrete KPIs over a defined time period (*Tour of Mastery*)
- Assessing teams' practice maturity and identifying logical next steps
- Prototyping cultural fit checks early in the hiring process
- Identifying pain points and delight opportunities in the designer candidate journey
- Screening potential recruiters to find the best partners to work with
- Publishing career advice out to the wider design community
- Co-creating objectives and key results for a user research team

The artifacts I create now are more often whiteboard sketches, presentation slides, and spreadsheets than flowcharts or click dummies. But I find designing organizations and acting as a change agent just as fun as designing UIs and getting them built.

The profession - paying it forward

When I entered the profession, the world was very different. My story--on the surface--won't be much like the career path of any young designer today.

All the same, I would venture the following advice:

- **Start with yourself**: Figure out where you stand (values) and where you want to go (mission) before embarking on your job search (https://www.linkedin.com/pulse/start-your-job-search-within-5-simple-steps-orient-direct-kaufmann).
- **Look for overlap**: At the start you might not have much choice of employers, but you can always look for the intersection between your own goals and the goals of the company and devote your energy to that sweet spot of mutual benefit. Read *The Alliance* for more on this.
- **Follow your passion**: You need to do something frequently to get good at it. So do something you love.

Design will evolve. Designers are makers and disrupters, so we'll continue to reinvent ourselves.

But the demand for creativity and empathy in solving human needs will always exist, so-- no matter what else changes--designers will always be in demand. And designing will always be rewarding work.

Jay's LinkedIn profile: `https://www.linkedin.com/in/jaykaufmann`

Ritch Macefield, PhD - UX and IT Consultant

I graduated from the UK's Loughborough University of Technology in 1985 with a BA (Hons) in Creative Design (Technology). Of course, by definition, all design is creative. However, I think the three words in this title all say something important about the UX world. Surely, we are all creative and fascinated by technology. The good UX professionals I've met also have an excellent grounding in "design thinking". This is something re-emphasized by Jeff Gothelf in his excellent book "Lean UX" and includes things like-- defining constraints, using structured methods for generating and evaluating options, and iterating designs. I also did a Certificate in Education in parallel to my degree (allowing me to teach in schools around the world), and sharing what I'd learned would become a key aspect of my career.

By chance, my personal tutor at Loughborough turned out to be a genius called John Branson. He not only taught me to program in BASIC and Assembly language, he also instilled in me that good design is elegant, efficient, and progresses from existing best practice. I often see UX designers focused on "progressing" our discipline through their designs, but find many have not first visited the existing best practice, nor are their designs elegance and efficient!

The latter parts of my degree led me into FORTRAN programming and Computer Aided Design (CAD) systems, and I ended up teaching my tutors about CAD systems. This led me to my first job demonstrating advanced Computer Aided Engineering (CAE) systems at DeltaCAM (now owned by Autodesk). I then spent a brief time selling these systems. I did my sales quota but sales wasn't my thing so I moved to the Data General Corporation. But I didn't regret my time in sales--soon after I joined Data General, I was privileged to work for Manfred Wittler, another genius who, as well as having a PhD in interstellar space travel, explained to me the value of "living with a sales quota".

I ended up doing a whole bunch of things at Data General and ended up migrating applications to use a new technology called a "Graphical User Interface" (GUI), that the heroes at Xerox PARC had invented a few years back, to make computers accessible to the "average person". This constituted my first brush with Human Computer Interaction (HCI)--I even read a few books on this weird idea of studying how users and IT systems get on with each other.

HCI didn't stick with me immediately and I spent the late 90s as a self-employed IT strategy and Business Process Consultant. I also did some lecturing in those areas at a few universities around the world. The consulting required me to specify and procure a fair few IT systems for my clients and, like many before me, I noticed these systems never ended up being what I'd envisaged or what my clients really wanted.

I set out to fix this! I picked up some relevant dev tools, such as Visual Basic and Lotus notes, and started modeling the interfaces I wanted to see. I'd show them to some of the users and iterated them until I thought I'd got what they needed. I even encouraged the users to do this for themselves, or do it with me. Then I went to the IT vendors with the designs and said things like "make this work" and "put a backend on this". Some did, and it all seemed to work out quite well. Others said "we don't work like that, where's the requirements document and specs?", and their systems generally didn't work out too well. Hum! I thought that there must be something in this way of working.

It was the year 2000 now and I realized that I'd stumbled on something much bigger than me and my work--apparently it was something called **User Centered Design** (UCD), and it turned out that my old university (Loughborough) were a global player in this stuff. So I went back there to do a Masters degree in "IT Human Factors". It was a full-time course, but I was still running my own consulting business as well as lecturing around the world. This meant that, for logistical reasons, I ended up having to convert to a Masters degree in "IT (Computing)".

I passed with distinction; coming top of my class, but the computer science still didn't excite me as much as the human factors stuff. Why? Well, I'll start answering that with a short anecdote--at Data General, I was working with my mentor, Bruce Zimmerman, on a complex technical design problem as part of a huge global project. It was freaking me out until Bruce said: "Don't worry Ritch, I'll get it working, you need to remember--these things are just computers! It's true that Bruce relaxed by integrating Einstein's special theory of relativity with the second law of thermodynamics, and that hacking operating system kernels was a part of his day job, so we need to put his comments in context. However, as complex as computer systems are, whenever you throw people into the mix, things tend to get even more complex, and I've always been attracted to complexity and anyone who tells you that UX design is simple, really doesn't understand UX design.

Anyway, I'd managed to pick up enough human factors stuff by then to get a senior job in a digital agency who said they did UCD. Like many agencies, both then and now, I didn't think they really did do UCD and soon left! I wanted to really explore UCD and ran off down all kinds of seemingly relevant paths, from psychodynamics and learning theory to AI and rapid prototyping. Of course, I also studied the HCI gods such as Brian Shackel, Ben Shneiderman, Don Norman and, of course, the "Usability Pope"--Jackob Nielsen. I'm always dismayed when I meet UX people who are not familiar with their seminal works, much of which is as relevant today as the day they wrote it.

Although I kept my hand in with some UX consulting work, I planted myself in the academic world because I wanted to do a PhD in how usability can be improved by explicitly giving users conceptual information about the system's structure. I found out that passing a PhD in HCI is a tricky. Some research argues that the pass rate is just 13%, partly because many examiners simply don't understand the HCI field well enough. I was saved here by choosing the great Harrold Thimbleby to lead my examination. He really does know what he's talking about when it comes to HCI, as well as a whole bunch of other things.

The present

After my PhD I returned fulltime to the commercial world, spending the next few years leading and advising the UX function on complex enterprise scale IT projects. But again I was frustrated; both at the intrinsic inefficiency of the UX functions themselves and how poorly UX was integrated with the wider **System Development Life Cycle** (**SDLC**). Guess what, I set out to fix this!

Since 2012, I've been evolving an approach to the SDLC that blends elements of **Soft Systems Methodology** (**SSM**), UCD, Agile development methods, Agile UX, Lean Start-up and Lean UX. Key to this are what I call **CIDS** (**Collaborative Interface Design Systems**), such as Axure RP Pro.

I've used this approach several times now on large projects and the early indications are promising! Fortunately for me, helping organizations transition to this approach involves lots of training, coaching, and mentoring; not only on the methodology, but also on the specific tools and techniques--something I still find the most rewarding part of my work.

The future

Those who study IT system design are well are that we have a lot to learn about how to do this. There remain lots of potential for improvement, not just in terms of what we produce, but how we produce it. So methodology is key for me; in particular, how UX fits into the SDLC.

Of course, that means we need new people and new thinking. Like all professions, we need informed and educated UX professionals, not just people who have just decided they are a UX expert after doing a few short online courses or have a very narrow understanding of UX like many of the visual designers I meet. Any UX professional needs to rigorously learn the craft and stand on the shoulders of the giants that came before us by studying their work.

In my work, I'm particularly interested in working with those who's IT skills extend beyond UX--I think the future involves multi-skilled UX professionals who's expertise overlaps (greatly) with others involved in the SDLC.

Ritch's LinkedIn profile: `https://www.linkedin.com/in/dr-ritch-macefield-524b1b1`

Saikat Mandal - Architect, Experience Designer

As a child, I was very active and restless. I always needed new toys to keep myself engaged. When I got a toy, the first thing I would do is break it apart, to learn its mechanism. The next step would be to put it back together. Initially I failed miserably, and my parents would get mad at me.

They would not give me new toys as I broke them on the very first day. But as I was also good at studies, I would get rewarded with toys, when I got good grades. Eventually, I became a pro in deconstructing and rebuilding toys.

This habit of tinkering with toys made me the mechanic of my house. I could fix whatever broke down at my home--from a TV and VCR to refrigerators. Specialized tasks, of course, needed outside help.

I would often be done with my homework in an hour. This allowed me a lot of time to play. So, I graduated from toys to the playground. I would spend a lot of time playing soccer and other outdoor games. I lost the sense of time in the playground--play for hours that felt like minutes. I also lost sense of time when I was interested in a subject. At times, I could not stop until I finished a story book or graphic novel.

Indian summers are very hot and children are not allowed to play outdoors during the afternoons, as they are expected to take naps instead. I would never get sleep and it made me restless. And so, during one of these hot summers, while on vacation from middle school, I decided to pursue art classes because they were scheduled in the afternoon, which gave me an escape. During these art classes, I again lost the sense of time. It opened a new door for me--I could imagine anything and sketch and paint stuff from my imagination. It's like playing with whatever toy I envisioned.

Within 3 years, I had a diploma in painting, and in what seems like a dream, my high school days were over too. I was facing a decision of my lifetime--I had to choose a college and a degree to pursue. In India, anything that is non-STEM is for poor students. I had good grades but did not want to pursue a degree in computer science or electronics. And while mechanical engineering interested me as I get to tinker with machines, the thought of being limited to only sketching machines was not inspiring enough for a 16 year old teenager.

It was a big problem. I had to choose something that kept my interest as well as what was acceptable to my parents. My classmate's elder brother had taken up a course in architecture. He spoke highly about the degree. I researched a little and it felt like the best fit for me. It had a perfect balance of art and science. As an architect, I would be an independent professional such as a lawyer or doctor and I could open my own business or work for a firm. The flexibility architecture offered me was immense and I never wanted to be caged.

The only problem was that it was a 5-year professional program, which meant a year more than engineering programs. But once convinced, no obstacle was going to hold me back. I convinced my parents and finally got enrolled.

My basic understanding of design came from this degree in architecture. I learned the principles of design. I learned to empathize with the user. A house for a lawyer will be different than that of a writer or poet--even when the basic needs are similar. I learned the difference/interrelation between form and function. Construction management, urban design, and urban planning were other subjects that got my attention.

One book that influenced me a lot during my formative years was "Architecture--Form, Space and Order" by Francis D.K. Ching. I was influenced by the works of architects such as Frank Lloyd Wright, Paul Klee, Charles Eames, and others, who, on top of being great architects, also shared a passion for product design as well. Wright designed the furniture and even the spoons and knives for his clients. Paul and Charles forced me to see the smaller details, and I developed a liking for product design and industrial design.

At one point, I wanted to become a product designer. This was in line with my trait of not being boxed into a compartment. I am a designer and I believe that if I put my heart into something, I can design it.

I craved new challenges. Software design was very immature at this time. I remember, we had to use Auto Lisp, a programming language, to get AutoCAD to do certain things that the GUI of the software did not allow at that time. I thought designing a product is easy because it is tangible--I can model it out of it and keep sculpting it until it meets the needs of its function and form. However, doing the same with an intangible thing is much more difficult. A lot more imagination and craftsmanship is needed to get it right. This seemed more challenging and I craved it.

Interface design was in its infancy in India. However, two good design schools offered me a master's degree in this field. This led me to a masters in visual communication with specialization in interface design. I learned the principles of user centered design and usability. Product semantics and syntactics became important. I was totally engrossed in the details of interface and interaction design. I loved to create prototypes and iterate until I got the product right.

After my graduation, I worked for various big and small firms as an interaction designer. During that time I realized that my knowledge was incomplete. It was easy to pick between a good and bad design, but difficult to pick a better design from a bunch of carefully designed products. I needed to know more, which brought me to the USA for my PhD in design. Two years into the program, I realized that I had learned a lot, but was craving to practice what I learned--I am a craftsman at heart and like to "work with my hands". I got back to the industry and since then, I have solved a lot of challenges for my clients.

I love my work and feel very fortunate to be in this field. Things are changing rapidly and thus I too need to keep myself updated. Someday when I feel I don't know what I am doing, I will get back to school and finish my PhD. It's a roller-coaster ride every day and I don't want to miss this fun. What I love most about this field is that the challenges are varied. There are so many variables and so many unique solutions.

The best part of my work is to understand the problem and the user. This understanding heavily influences your end product. In many cases, the client knows there is a problem, whereas in other situations they have a solution in mind. I am that chief craftsmen that makes this journey with this user, from a problem to its solution. My contribution to this solution is so varied that it keeps my creative juices flowing. I am still the same kid that craves new challenges. If you are someone who craves new challenges, this is a goldmine for you. The journey can be hard but absolutely rewarding. You get to bring to life your imaginations. Your work touches the lives of millions of users. You get to make a positive difference in this world through your work.

Like any other profession, ours is changing as well. We have different people coming from different fields. There are different specialists and generalists. Whether you specialize or generalize will depend on individual traits. But one thing is for sure, you have to keep learning. New and better ways to do the same things are evolving. Voice over interface is replacing visual interface. In the future, we might interact by just thoughts in our brains. No matter how we interact with this world, someone needs to design these. Are you game for taking up these challenges?

Saikat's LinkedIn profile: `https://www.linkedin.com/in/mandalsaikat`

Christine Marriott, PhD - Architect

The steps toward architecture for me began at a very early age. Perhaps it sounds like an exaggeration, but I think it all started in the sandbox, a place where I spent a considerable amount of time as a toddler. I graduated to other childhood obsessions such as Lego. Later I would learn that was very common with architects of my generation. Making forms and spaces, arranging objects, and drawing are some of the foundational activities that filled my childhood and, undoubtedly, had an impact on my career decisions.

My "serious" interest in becoming an architect probably started around age 12. My parents enjoyed traveling, and so with them I was fortunate to see a lot of cities and buildings as a young person. Unlike some of my college classmates, I had no doubts about architecture as a profession. It was clear to me that there were no other options.

The first book that truly amazed me was a book on the work of Michael Graves. The book included his early house designs, which were minimal and abstract. His work from that period connected him with the New York Five, a group inspired by the work of Le Corbusier. Later, and to my great disappointment, Graves would veer into a post-modern revival of classicism, but his early work remains influential to me as a designer, as does the work of Le Corbusier.

While a student at Pratt Institute in Brooklyn, NY, I was fortunate to find jobs working for architects part-time during the school year and also during summers. I was employed by professors and friends of classmates, and in my fourth year of studies I acquired an internship with the firm Gwathmey Siegel & Associates. Charles Gwathmey was also one of the New York Five, and his work was also very foundational to me as a designer. Gwathmey acquired his early fame designing houses in Long Island. Like Graves's houses, Gwathmey's were minimal and abstract, but Gwathmey introduced a more tactile expression using vertical planks of wood. Gwathmey's Cogan, Cohn, Taft, and de Menil Houses are some of the most beautiful works of architecture that I know.

After graduating from Pratt, I continued working for Gwathmey Siegel & Associates. A few years later I continued my studies at the Southern California Institute of Architecture (SCI-Arc) where I earned a Master's degree. Los Angeles is a magical place, despite the many problems that the city endures. Unlike my undergraduate experience, studying in LA was more like an extended holiday. That brief period was about playing, exploring, wandering, and reflecting. The city of Los Angeles was simply an extension of the SCI-Arc sandbox.

Following my graduate studies, my husband and I returned to New York. During that time, I was able to earn my professional license. My husband and I also had our daughter. We stayed in New York juggling work and family life until she was three. A real turning point came when our little family left New York for Chicago in 2001.

Both my husband and I have our regrets about leaving New York, but I suppose we needed a change. I learned through that experience, though, just how difficult it is to enter a market where you have no connections, and you need to virtually recreate yourself. Satisfying my livelihood had been so easy previously. It took a while to meet architects and find continuous work. During those first few years in Chicago I slowly began to build a practice and do consulting for other architects. In an attempt to redefine myself I also reached out to a community college, and by a stroke of luck, I was offered an adjunct position teaching an architectural drawing course. That experience marked the next major chapter of my career. After a few years of doing small projects, consulting for architects and teaching a class or two, I acquired a tenured position with the college, and with the exception of a year spent as a visiting professor at Kansas State University, it is there that I have been since.

My enjoyment of teaching came as a surprise, and admittedly, it has become all consuming. The faculty is small at Wright College, and as a consequence, I have been compelled to wear many hats and teach a broad range of course subjects to a group of students in the early years of their design education. It has been a pleasure to watch them develop and prosper.

While teaching at Wright, I completed a PhD in Architecture at Illinois Institute of Technology. The focus of my doctoral research was architectural pedagogy and technology. The intention of my research was improving the learning process for aspiring architects by integrating new pedagogies with emerging technologies. Using my classrooms as a laboratory, I have continued to explore these issues.

My life of professional practice has become more of a hobby as my role as a professor has expanded to program coordinator and department chair. I have been involved with curricular work, writing new courses, rewriting syllabi, and realigning the first two semesters of design studio sequence so that objectives are comprehensive and appropriate for beginning designers. Seeing that I am making an impact on the lives of many students is the real reward to this work.

I do try to keep my foot in the door of professional practice because it helps me to make sure what I teach is appropriate and relevant. I am fortunate to have some time to do consulting and to have the support of an advisory board that makes program recommendations. These activities and connections provide me with a sense about the future direction of the profession. I don't anticipate substantial change to the process or structure of architectural practice. I do think that the required skillset will continue to be technology based. I also think that specializations within the profession will continue to increase. As the world becomes increasingly urban-centric, architecture must respond and tackle the problems of cities and population growth. More than ever before, architects will need to collaborate with a growing cast of stakeholders with more complex needs and demands.

My advice to someone considering architecture would be remain flexible. Anticipate that the circumstances in which you work will change. Also, I would recommend that a young architect take the time to enjoy being in school, and keep in mind that formal and informal education will be a part of one's entire career.

Christine's LinkedIn profile: https://www.linkedin.com/in/christine-marriott-28739212

Ross Riechardt - UX Designer

I'm 17. I'm not sure what I want to do when I grow up. I like building things. I really like being part of a team. I like solving problems. Should I become an architect? In high school, I won a few art competitions. Art and fashion is so beautiful, should I go to art school?

This artistic, creative side of me led me to the very obvious path of training to become a spy. Yep, four years studying crime theory and sociology at a Jesuit university. Art and fashion gave way to being a good guy trying to catch the bad guys. And you know what? I loved it.

I loved every second of it.

The first day of my internship I was handed a bulletproof vest. I barely took it off. It was such an exhilarating feeling. Even though I was sitting in the middle of an office complex behind a computer mapping data trying to discover patterns in drug trafficking in the Midwest, I was geared up for battle. I'll never forget the euphoria from being a part of something so dynamic.

Alas, good things don't last forever. I migrated back home and started a job at Xerox. A real paycheck! I was working on an insurance platform. It was my first taste of enterprise software. It was old, it was janky. But it worked! I realized I had this burgeoning interest in the intersection of enterprise productivity and the software provided to its employees.

But something was missing. I took a leap of faith. I started working for some start-ups for nothing. Free! Do you see a theme here? Every time I find something that gets my creative juices flowing, I can't get enough. I'm a passion junkie. These unpaid stints didn't come without any compensation.

I was dying to earn some experience with consumer technology and more specifically, design. Nights and weekends, spending time empathizing and creating with founders and users. Bridging the gap. Creating value with design. Building things. Being part of a team. Solving problems. I was absolutely hooked. After some time, I started throwing my name in the enterprise hat. I had experience in niche insurance products as well as a knack for design, which leads me to today.

Now I'm designing enterprise solutions for America's largest publically traded insurance company. Did I fulfill my original dream of being a spy? Not necessarily. But more often than not I feel that spirit of being back in my bulletproof vest.

How does this feed into my design philosophy? Just start. I never planned this career path. It's far from a linear path. But it worked. I've traveled the States studying users. I've traveled the globe building products.

Just start

When I start collaborating with a team, I always emphasize isolating the problem. In some instances, that means banning any discussion about a solution. *What is the problem?* Working with designers to find the solution is the easy part. Picking apart the problem is hard. Then, you start. In early product design stages, I find it helpful to strip away functionality and decide what the least amount of function a user would need. My credo, stolen from Jack Dorsey--"make every detail perfect and limit the number of details." I can attest--people get by using very stripped down products and create massive value.

The lessons I've learned building software mirrors my career path. It's incredibly difficult to predict a plan when designing and building software. Often there are unexpected bumps and mountains. Expect the unexpected. In traditional product development, there's a tremendous amount of project planning that goes in prior to execution. But careers and software don't work like that.

You'll never learn more than on the day you start. Months and months of planning can be rendered useless in one day. The day you start. So, my parting words to anyone looking into getting into software design, development, or a career change in general. Just start. You're never going to feel ready. There's never a day you wake up "ready". There's no one that walks up to your doorstep and deems you "ready". There's no "ready" wand. There not a book titled READY. Just start. And if you need a bulletproof vest for some inspiration, I have one lying around.

Ross's LinkedIn profile: https://www.linkedin.com/in/ross-reichardt-11048b88

Derik Schneider - UI/UX Artist/Designer/Developer

Growing up, I was fascinated by computers and video games. One of my first memories was learning how to load a tape cartridge into a Commodore computer, and playing the "spaceship game". I am old enough to have played the original Nintendo when it first came out, and, several generations of consoles since then.

I had a talent for drawing when I was younger; I paid attention to the details. So, drawing different frames of animation from the original Super Mario Bros. on graph paper in colored pencil with my older brothers led me into understanding computer graphics--it helped that one of them showed me the ropes in several computer programs as we grew up, particular BiNed and Electronic Arts' Deluxe Paint II--Yes, that EA! They made more than just video games back then. I was in awe of that wonderful program--it was a superb package. I animated several fights of the included martial artist against a palette swapped version of himself in backgrounds that I digitally painted by hand using my own custom color palettes. With every successive battle scenario, I grew more bold in my wordless stories, learning to animate effects, making lengthier scenes, and exploring the software to learn new tricks.

One game in particular influenced my art style more than any other in my life--Out of this World (or, Another World). The polygonal rotoscoped art was forever embedded into my mind. My brother helped from time to time, showing me new ideas, and encouraged my art. Over the years, this led to creating animated intros to the Dungeons & Dragons campaigns that I ran for my friends in the style of Out of this World.

Around the age of 16, we upgraded our computer and I stopped using that program. All in all, it was about 7 years of practice with CG, animation, and gaming on that old computer. It's where it all began, and, I wouldn't be who I am without that experience.

The next computer was a Pentium powered Compaq with a better monitor. Mom bought CorelDraw Suite, which led into my self-taught graphic design phase. I didn't know what Adobe Photoshop was at the time, but Corel Paint and Draw were great programs, so I got a leg up on vector art before I left high school. I took to it like a duck on water, creating art for clothes for my "raver" friends. I also silk-screened several Nine Inch Nails shirts that were pretty popular with the alternative crowd at school.

As I was using my newly found vector skills designing rave flyers, I began downloading free fonts from the web--I became inspired by creators such as Chank and Larabie fonts. After a short time, I decided to find out how to create fonts, and it turned out that CorelDraw could do just that; either through creating them directly in the program on a 720 pt grid, or, scanning intricate sketches and vectorizing them. My wildest creation was named "Villain" (heavily inspired by *Uck N Pretty* by Rick Valicenti), which features two layers that stack by placing the uppercase letters on top of the lowercase ones in different colors. Fontography is my favorite hobby, and, something I'm going to start to do more seriously. Two of my free unfinished fonts are being featured in commercial brands and products. ISL Andvari in the upcoming Despicable Me 3 movie. ISL Jupiter has been used by *Ralph Lauren* for the new *Polo Sport* brand, in *Pacific Rim Uprising* as background/set dressing, and, in video game interfaces.

Young professional lone wolf

At the age of 18, I dropped out of Minneapolis College of Art + Design in only a few months--it was a low point. It didn't work for me for several reasons, so I moved back home feeling defeated. Soon after, however, I ran into a high school friend who said he wanted to start a web design business. He knew of my design skills and thought I'd make a valuable team member--I didn't qualify as a web designer yet, but I'd damn sure try. We worked together for a couple years--it didn't work out. But it was worth it--I had gained skills in UI art for the web, Macromedia Flash, and Actionscript--those were the hot new things. From that experience, I learned that if I wanted to make it as a web designer, I was going to have to rely on myself. I grew up self-taught and had all these skills and talent, so I could do it, right?

The unfortunate timing was such that my mom was fed up with me not having a real job for so long, especially after the fallout of my web design partnership, that she kicked me out. My always supportive brother said I could move in with him. He probably saved my life to some degree, maybe not from death, but possibly something worse--the edge of despair that I had made the wrong choices in life, and, would not be able to correct them. I needed support, and he always believed in me. He worked in video games and I admired how hard he had worked to get where he was. At that time I didn't want to work in the games industry; I didn't think my skills were up to snuff, and, I figured it'd be easier to get into professional web design since I had a couple years under my belt, and, I was passionate about it. There was time to get into video games later.

While living with him and playing tons of Metal Gear Solid, I taught myself HTML and CSS from online resources. I soon pushed out my website, applied to jobs on Monster, and after 6 months I was living in Newark, Delaware, working for one of the Big 3 U.S. car companies designing touchscreen interfaces, and earning a pretty penny as a contractor. The night I moved out of a hotel room I had been staying in for a couple weeks, and into my first studio apartment to live all on my own, I cried before falling asleep on the floor because I had no furniture. Have you ever had to talk and hype yourself up, like people do in the movies? I had that moment.

I was 21 at the time. It was my first dose of working with "customers" in this new role. I wasn't supposed to have to do that, I thought, because I work on computers and I design interfaces. In this role, however, I learned about that the factory workers who were on the floor that needed these touchscreens, and that there was no better way to get an understanding of their job, what their needs were, and how to build something that would work for them, unless I went and talked to them. I had never heard of user experience or user centered design, but, I was on that path of my own volition. Also, I was the youngest member of this contractor team, and I was in charge of a few others. I had the most years in CorelDraw, the program of choice, so I taught them everything I knew. No one else had a clue how to design these interfaces except me, so I started showing them by example, and coaching my team members in person. All those self-taught years had paid off, and I'm still teaching people to this day. It was my first experience in developing a style guide of sorts, without formerly putting it into documentation--I had to develop a design system that everyone could use. Never underestimate a former self-taught web designer with vast knowledge of paint and vector programs, and, the UI production pipeline.

Solid foundations and learning experiences

Over the next 6 years, I met my future wife, worked in and out of Philadelphia and its suburbs in the web design industry doing all sorts of work, and in Web/UI/UX roles you could find on my LinkedIn profile. Some good and not-so-great experiences, but all were valuable. My wife was accepted into a school in Canada, so I moved up there with her, and found it impossible to find a job as a spouse of a visiting student. I was desperate for work. Once more, you guessed it; my brother pulled through for me and suggested I apply for a User Interface Artist job at a different studio he started working for a few years back. I felt confident enough in my abilities and background to apply. It was my Flash skills that landed me the job--I had prepared a demo of an interactive UI prototype that conveyed some user-centered designs for a hypothetical third-person shooter.

So far, all of my self-taught skills, talent, and experience in UI/UX design had proven that skipping college to focus on my career was the right choice. I worked at two studios in the game industry for almost 6 years and shipped a few AAA titles, and contributed to a fourth. My family's living situation wasn't so great, however, with us having jobs 3 hours away from each other, living in between, with commuting 1.5 hours each way twice a day. It became untenable, so I left the game industry to work in the city where she held a job she would have for the foreseeable future, and went back to my roots.

Things have changed

Web design had dramatically changed during the time I was out of the industry--HTML5, CSS3, and JavaScript frameworks were new fundamental skills that you had to have. There was a lot to catch up on. So after finishing up a 7 month contract as a UX/UI designer for a boss that let me spend time on the slow days to beef up those skills, I got a more permanent contract job working at an insurance company through a contracting company. I had no idea exactly what it was they were going to have me do; the role sounded like a UX/UI Designer, but they called it a Business Analyst, a term I had become acquainted with in my last job that didn't have much to do with UX/UI as I understood it.

What the role was called didn't matter, because as I suspected, I was going to do UI/UX work, but in the capacity as a web developer. Titles are funny, they change over time. I didn't know it at the time, but the work did too. I was so used to doing whatever was needed; I figured all former web designers went through this evolution. It didn't quite work like that.

Our team lead had the vision for the software we created. It was something that had never been built before, and it soon went through the patent process. I co-developed the frontend and backend, which was sparked by my colleague teaching me about MySQL databases. I was familiar with how they worked, but had never set one up myself or made any connections before. It was one of the most useful skills someone had ever taught me. Over the course of slightly more than 2 years, I held a few "lead" roles without formerly being granted the title--I broke what it meant to be called a UX Designer in my division; I handled many areas beyond what that role was meant to do, leading other UX Designers in prototype development, setting up their development environments, installing software on the servers we used and working with IT to manage them, web security, managing databases, and writing pseudo APIs for our frontend. I was essentially a full-stack developer and dev-ops, but not in the manner that people in those roles would traditionally like to think of themselves. We winged it, and it worked. Our lone-wolf team was an anomaly, and I loved working that way. The contractor I worked for awarded me *Employee of the Month*, for July 2014.

The degrees

A couple of months after that award I learned that my wife was going to be bringing new life into this world. Working an hour away from home and realizing I couldn't sustain that job when I became a father meant I had to find something close to home.

Over the next several months, my co-developer had left, and so did our team lead. My baby was coming soon, so I decided to use my leverage to get a raise. So for a few months I was making significant money, which was good, because I knew I wouldn't make nearly as much working a full-time job back home.

The problem was, finding a job in this capacity without a degree in a university town known for its computer science, meant I was fighting an uphill battle. Some institutions and businesses won't even look at your resume if that box isn't checked "Yes, I have a Bachelor's or Master's degree". Years of experience and die-hard determination didn't count for anything to them.

Luckily, I landed a full-time job only 5 minutes away from where I lived, 3 weeks before my son was to be born, and at a startup that pays well for this area. In comparison to the money I was making as a contractor, the offer was a pay cut, to be sure, but a welcome one.

My current role is officially titled as a Frontend Developer. It is a bit removed from where I started--I have never had my coding skills challenged so much. I work among an amazingly talented and educated team--everyone I work with has, or, is working on a degree or PhD. I've probably written more code in this job than I have in my entire life, even in the game industry. My time isn't spent building mockups, art, or animations (yet); however, with my background in graphic/web/UI/UX design, I provide insight across a holistic spectrum of issues that may be missed by others, or come to solutions in different ways.

Wrap up

This wasn't your normal path to a frontend developer by any means. Back in 1998, I wasn't thinking I'd be in this exact role. Paths in life might take you to unexpected places. You can plan ahead if you know exactly what you want to do--so if frontend development sounds like a great career for you, I would highly suggest going to college or university in an area known for its technology sector. As a norm, having prior experience and a Bachelor's degree seems to be the minimum to find a full-time position in this role, with a Master's degree being preferable. Of course that is not completely necessary, as you've learned from my experience.

If you apply yourself well in school or on your own, participate in hack-a-thon events, develop projects on the side, then you might easily end up as an intern or junior developer at some tech giant, or, fast-moving start-up as your first career move.

In those environments, it's likely you'll need to be familiar with agile development, learning to be flexible, and develop solutions that may be out of your comfort zone. Prepare for the future by staying up to date with the latest technologies. Frontend development may change to mean your job is to handle app development, databases, APIs, micro-services, and so on. It might not be soon, or take those paths where you work, but you should keep in tune with technology. Expanding your skills will guarantee you'll always have a job somewhere that leads to other amazing opportunities.

Derik's LinkedIn profile: `https://www.linkedin.com/in/derikschneider`

Ginger Shepard - Product Manager

I have always had a penchant for problem solving. *Encyclopedia Brown* was my favorite book series as a kid, and I admired detectives and any job that gathered evidence to find a solution. But rather than follow the criminal justice path, I loved immersing myself in classic literature and the worlds I painted in my mind.

I graduated from college with degrees in English and Humanities, where I spent most of my Humanities coursework analyzing foreign films and the political commentaries embedded in the stories. After I graduated, I didn't have any clear career path, but I did have a curious and analytical mind.

I began my career in marketing for a large real estate company. At the time, real estate was just gaining an online presence. We still had a web master, but I noticed that he made choices based on code trends rather than experience (remember websites that had 10 different fonts and colors?). I coerced him into teaching me how to code and reimagined our digital presence as collections of virtual tours that helped home shoppers save time.

After a little over a year in real estate, I became an editor at a legal publishing company. A few months later, the technology attorney left the company. With technical support calls rolling in, and nobody on staff to fix the applications, I used my web development background to jump in and help. That is the moment that changed my career trajectory:

Talking with customers, in this case frustrated attorneys--inspired me to not just get the problem solved for the short-term, but to solve for the root cause. Peeling back the layers of the experience revealed that it wasn't just a poorly designed application--it was the documentation, the onboarding, the service, it was the total end-to-end experience.

I then started immersing myself in the lives of attorneys, I went to their offices, houses, court appearances, commuted with them, had lunch with them, wherever and whenever I could watch them in action. Mapping out their habits and their unique needs inspired me to go back and create technology products that would easily fit into their busy lives.

Don Norman and Jakob Nielsen were early muses for me, and I enjoyed early mobile first inspiration from Luke Wroblewski. I received my Masters in Communication with a focus on Interaction Design, and then I moved on in my career to support digital customer experiences in the insurance and financial services field. I really enjoyed working for smaller companies that could be more nimble and deliver experiences quickly, but I also loved the challenges of large, established companies as well.

In fact, large companies may be even more fulfilling because it begins with frustration, and lots of it, but in the end, when you get an area to look at things differently, they gain a skill that not only helps them operate at a different level at work, but makes them more aware of the world and diversity around them each and every day. What we do at work can impact the greater good, and experience design is the key.

Key activities

The most important part of the design process is to get into the action. Observe real customers, and always remember YOU are not the customer. It is fine to bring industry trends and common sense to the design process, but never ever design based on your opinion alone. Some people have great intuition when it comes to designing a great customer experience, but rarely does one person have all of the knowledge needed.

A key to the success of taking your design decisions all the way to production is to get your leadership or other decision makers exposed to what the real experience looks like from the customer's perspective. Have your executives sit in the call center, try to use their own products, or even just watch a customer using a product.

A lot of people think they are customer centric and design through the outside-in lens, but you really need to listen to your customers to truly understand the perspective and gather the data that will unlock a new level of design expertise. Here is my process in a nutshell:

1. **Know the vision and the strategy**: What are the outcomes you are trying to achieve?
2. **Understand the current state (if it exists)**: What are the pain points? Where are the missed opportunities?
3. **Get deep into the data**: Are you prioritizing the right things?
4. **Create personas**: Who are your target users? What are their expectations?
5. **Map out the journey**: Are there moments of truth that will make or break the experience?
6. **Understand the end-to-end experience**: What other factors or channels could impact the success of your journey? Would a poor call center experience negate your wins in the digital channel?
7. **Design with context in mind**: What outside factors could impact on focus? Can you achieve your outcome by finding a relevant context in another journey?
8. **Don't forget about accessibility**: Are all users able to complete their tasks easily?
9. **Test, iterate, repeat**: Can you get your working code in the hands of users quickly?
10. **Measure your success**: Did you achieve your outcome? Did you stay true to the vision and strategy? Are your users happy? What did you learn along the way?

Experience design is one of the most engaging careers you could imagine. It is filled with constant problem solving, adapting to new ways rules of engagement, and shifting demographics. It is one of the most satisfying and joyful moments in life to truly feel like you are making a difference in a company, and experience design is the key. A lot of leadership will focus on operational goals, but what they don't realize, is that an optimized experience will naturally improve their operational goals, and your customers will be happy and loyal for years to come.

This is a career for someone who has true empathy for people, who wants to make a customer's life easier, and is willing to challenge doing things "the way it has always been done". This isn't a career for people who just want to fade into the cubicle; this is for the people who have the passion and fire to speak up for the customer.

Ginger's LinkedIn profile: `https://www.linkedin.com/in/ginger-shepard-aa450019`

Courtney Skulley - Visual Designer

I studied Fine Art and Painting, and after college went immediately into three-dimensional environmental exhibit design. It was sort of a natural transition although I never studied Design. I worked on interactive science and history museums--permanent and temporary exhibits, for a few years. In the late 90's the internet sort of happened, and I just started designing websites for the company I was working for, and got hooked. I was tired of exhibit design, very slow-moving projects that stretch over 6 or 7 years. So I moved into web design quickly and never looked back.

I had to teach myself 2D pretty quickly and the internet was a whole new medium, so I was kind of learning it along with everybody else. The timing was just brilliant because otherwise I would have probably struggled. I always relied on looking at Swiss design, that's where I take almost all my inspiration from. I think like any graphic designer would say--the international type style, grids, spare color palette, all that stuff. I still go back to Josef Muller-Brockmann, Joseph Hoffmann, Van Krowl. Swiss and Danish is where my main influence came from.

I feel like I get to use my eyes and my hands as much as I do my brain. I get to go into my design bubble and stay there for quite a significant amount of time during a work week. I like that, and in digital design specifically, I like working with people who are coming to interface design from a different perspective. That has been my favorite part of doing UI work.

Key activities

As a visual designer doing UX, you have to understand the needs of multiple stakeholders, such as marketing people, who consider the brand and user constituencies, and others who have other priorities. You also try to sift through stakeholders who understand design, and those who have a more limited perspective. Early on in the project, you try to understand those dynamics and then work hard at being considered an important part of the team from the get go, which is sometimes a struggle. For example, when requirements are being established from the business and user perspectives, the visual designers are sometimes not seen as essential to that phase on the project, although they should be.

It really depends on the team's culture and environment. When you work at a more visually focused agency, the visual designers are the people who are spearheading the project. In the context of design for transactional data-driven applications, it's been more of a struggle, but it's gotten a lot better because visual design has become a key part of interaction design.

Artifacts

First I spend a lot of time looking at analogous kinds of work. I create folders of inspiration and mood boards for myself and other designers I'm working with. I often set up on my wall a creative brief that outlines the business constituencies, the personas and user groups that have been defined, and some of their key requirements and design considerations. This serves as a constant cheat sheet and I might go back and check to make sure that I'm looking at it from the perspective of a user through a new guy into a business requirement-- kind of like, I am representing them.

And also I think the one thing that is for me the most important thing is to constantly simplify--make the design as simple as possible. As I do that, so I constantly look back at my board and consider--can I simplify this for this persona, in this context, using this approach--is this as simple as it can be?

I recently began to use Sketch. It changed the way I work and has been a real incredible uplift to me. Compared to Photoshop, this tool promotes lots of iterations and different explorations--at one time. I do more obvious visual explorations at the beginning, which take the form of many screens on a canvas. I found that showing those to clients and having them react to seeing lots of subtle variations at once and getting a sense of real options--it's a lot more collaborative and effective. It opens up opportunities to working "on the fly" with clients, moving things around to better reflect the experience--compared to Photoshop, where comps are painstakingly massaged and then shown as a "one off". I feel such a collaborative approach is a great move in the right direction.

Once I get past visual exploration, details start to emerge. I am constantly looking at design systems, so it's thinking about patterns and components, looking for consistencies and reuse in patterns, and creating the building blocks of a design system, basically--using an atomic approach to design. I have to do so in almost every project I work on.

Advice to those who consider a career in visual design

I didn't go to school for design, but I studied painting, so I feel like I got an education. I developed an eye and a hand at some point, but I don't know how different it would be if I had gone to design school--perhaps everything would have been easier, perhaps not. Still, there are very practical ways to learn design that don't involve an expensive academic setting. I think that design is the kind of career that you could just jump into.

I see it with my daughter. She's a digital native and she's designing all the time on the computer, playing around with tools. She's developing an aesthetic already--and she's 11 years old. Go to school and then learn to use self-talk and your early success.

Design today is much more about the technology and the possibilities of interaction and motion, and so, I wish I knew how to code more hands on and have the ability to create little prototypes on a daily basis. Although there are so many tools out there that help with that, I feel like understanding the basics of frontend technology and being able to dabble in it, would be the key to moving forward.

The future to me seems a little bit scary because everything has become so integrated fast-moving that it's hard to keep up. So it is important to stay viable from an aesthetic perspective--avoid chasing trends while not letting your aesthetic get stuck.

I get concerned about AI and conversational interfaces, wondering if they might take away from the visual experience, or at least the amount of work opportunities for visual designers, and I'm hoping not. I don't really know what's going to happen, so I try stay flexible and nimble, and being prepared to keep running.

Courtney's LinkedIn profile: `https://www.linkedin.com/in/cskulley`

Ken Stern, PhD - User Research Practice Lead

Psychology was my major when I applied to college, but I had no idea what I wanted to do. I liked statistics, philosophy, and liberal arts, but what could you do with a Psychology degree? My first 'Aha moment' came when I took a year-long 'Experimental Psychology' course in my second year in college. The course introduced me to the scientific method, establishing hypotheses, and creating and executing a research plan.

I learned the fundamentals of how to plan, conduct, and document research related to vision, memory, and various behavioral principles.

That year-long course introduced me to the importance of conducting valid, reliable, and repeatable research and to avoid bias and confounding in designing and executing studies. My professor liked what I was doing and asked me to become a lab assistant to conduct research in the field of visual perception. I accepted. That job was the reason that I started to explore Cognitive Psychology as a career.

I conducted research in the Psychology lab while I completed my BA, and met my wife in the lab (she had a part-time job scheduling and coordinating research studies). I went on to graduate school to continue my focus on depth and motion perception. My graduate advisor offered me jobs as his research assistant and his teaching assistant for Experimental Design courses. I co-authored a few research studies, published in a psychology journal, and served as a reviewer for a "Depth Perception through Motion" book that my thesis advisor was writing. Another grad student and I tag-teamed teaching continuing education courses at a local community college, focusing on visual illusions, decision-making, and parapsychology (I did not teach that module). Good stuff, I thought – I'm going to be a college professor!!

I'm about to start my dissertation research in perceptual psychology) and I see this posting for a year-long research fellowship in Minneapolis, focusing on conducting APPLIED research. I'd be applying cognition and research skills to address problems in the real world. Success!! I was one of three graduate students awarded a fellowship in "Man-Machine Sciences". My wife and I packed the car with all our worldly possessions and we left the comfort and security of grad school in California for a year of real-world experience in the upper Midwest. The year was another 'Aha moment'. I met applied psychologists for the first time and conducted some interesting research. I conducted studies exploring options for optimizing keyboard design for typing speed and accuracy. I conducted interviews with physicians to aid in developing algorithms for diagnosing breast cancer using thermography. (Thermograms detect infrared rays to show patterns of body temperature.)

The research fellowship got me thinking about a career in "Human Factors". I became interested in designing and testing intuitive and easy to use hardware instead of conducting "pure" research to understand the physiology and psychology of vision. I returned to my final year of grad school to conduct my dissertation and I taught an undergraduate course called "Introduction to Human Factors." (I later learned that two students continued to grad school and ended up in user experience careers.)

I loved teaching, but chose a career in Industry where I could apply research methodologies to real-world problems. I liked research that resulted in interfaces that could be seen, felt and used. I accepted a job with a multinational technology company to design and conduct research related to the usability of hardware used in banking. Because of my background in vision, I conducted research on the readability, legibility, and privacy of displays used in banks and in walk-up and drive-up ATMs. I tested a pen that recognized and authenticated individuals based on the biometric properties of their signature. I provided design recommendations to more easily replace components in printers and client servers that previously required a call to a technician. Fun stuff, but we generally could not evaluate the final product until they were designed, 'hard tooled', and nearly ready for release. This was frustrating – as usability problems had to be pretty big to stop a product from release. We wanted to get ahead of the curve and test earlier in the design process. Thirty years ago, printers displayed their status using a two character LCD display. Users had to remember – or look up – what the code meant. We wanted a larger 16 character display so that words could be displayed. More expensive – but more effective and usable. Prototyping was coming into vogue, so we started prototyping printer panels for display on a touch panel to test concepts BEFORE they were built. The developers had never seen this approach and were surprised. The resultant test results documented the improved usability. Getting involved in design and prototyping, along with the introduction of iterative usability testing, was another "Aha moment" and career highlight.

Usability started to become a key differentiating factor in the industry and began to be measured and integrated into the development cycle. At the same time, the economy was taking a downturn, and internal funding for design and testing specialized software began to decline. One of our banking clients approached my department for usability support of a large-scale evolutionary design effort. I agreed to assist and flew to a bank in Boston weekly to work with business leads, designers, and developers. The collaborative design and research effort resulted in the release of a large and easy to use software platform used by Customer Service Representatives – one of the first GUI banking platforms!! This year-long client-facing engagement positioned me for a career as an industry consultant, just as consulting services began to take off. (Another highlight.)

I became part of a new consulting services organization (still with my original employer) and our department grew with the industry. Initially, our services were requested by companies when system usability was very poor and customers in the field were complaining loud enough to draw attention. We conducted heuristics reviews to identify the potential causes of problems, provided design recommendations, and tested the interface as the designs were updated. Our role and influence expanded when we crafted capabilities to focus on earlier stages of design, including requirements gathering, needs analysis, and contextual inquiries of how work was conducted to better understand the needs of the user.

We created iterative design, prototyping, and usability evaluation techniques to more rapidly evolve and validate the design.

As the Practice grew, I took on a management role, tasked with providing career and skills development guidance, along with engagement and performance oversight. I accepted the role under the condition that I continue to maintain a client-facing consulting services role. I did not want to lose touch with technology and industry trends. I have since become the Practice lead of this Research and Insights Practice, supporting research needs to clients in various industries and sectors across the country. Development is increasingly incorporating methodologies such as agile software development to drive flexible and continuous improvement. Design teams are using solution-focused and user-centered methodologies such as Design Thinking to match people's needs with what is technically feasible. User research is integrated in these methodologies and continues to be a differentiator and a critical path to success. I still enjoy the hands-on research and the discovery and insights that help guide the incorporation of ever-changing technology in new and novel ways (and still with my original employer).

Some books that have been influencers:

- Don't make Me think (Steve Krug)
- Cost justifying Usability (Bias & Mayhew)
- Jakob Nielsen – Designing Web Usability
- The World is Flat - Thomas L. Friedman
- Steve Jobs (Walter Isaacson)
- Quantifying the User Experience: Practical Statistics for User Research (Jeff Sauro & James R Lewis)

Advice to someone who considers a career in experience design

I've been in the field of user design, experience and research for over 35 years and have seen a lot of growth in the industry. The field has grown from usability validation late in the design cycle to becoming a collaborative partner in identifying user needs and a design direction. User experience research has become a differentiating factor and an influencer. Companies request user research in their proposal requests, and look for user research to support design and development. We continue to expand our involvement earlier in the design lifecycle, focusing on knowing the user and their needs before the design solution has been conceived. Technology is evolving very rapidly.

The emergence of virtual assistants and chatbots, natural language processing, artificial intelligence technologies that integrate cognitive computing, natural language processing, voice recognition, business analytics, and sentiment analysis provide a glimpse of what's ahead. User research will play a large role in the emergence and adoption of these technologies. User research will play a large role in the emergence and adoption of these technologies.

There are multiple paths to entry to user experience research. Researchers come from backgrounds in web design, ethnography, cognitive psychology, engineering psychology, Information Technology (IT), and anthropological research. An understanding of the principles of human behavior and the scientific method, the ability to adopt and adapt varied methodologies, being able to communicate well, and applying data collection and analytic methods to results are key to success. Being a forward thinker, well organized, willing to seek out challenges, being inquisitive, and demonstrating innovation doesn't hurt.

User researchers have to understand behavior and methodologies to study, describe and measure it. You have to listen to, and communicate with, people – not role play the part of a user. You need to focus on evidence-based research – not your experiences. You need to be a trusted partner. You need to handle and consolidate a wide variety of data – ranging from market research to research studies conducted in a lab or in the field. You'll be conducting qualitative exploratory research with small samples to form an understanding of patterns, trends, and user expectations. You'll be conducting larger quantitative summative tests to establish usability benchmarks and validate designs. This requires an awareness of the factors that can introduce bias and confounding into your data. You need to understand how to create objective tasks to study and create objective questions to ask in surveys. You'll need to handle data effectively and efficiently, synthesize the results and deliver them in a simple and meaningful format that is consumable by the intended audience. You'll need to be organized and be a planner. You'll need to document what you will be doing and document what you did.

IT skills are an important aspect of user research. These skills can range from an understanding of statistical and analytical tools for organizing and working with data, to using modeling and prototyping tools used by the design team. The analytical skills are important for planning and conducting research efforts, organizing test data and web analytics. The modeling skills are important to communicate insights and recommendations in a format that can be applied to the design. Many researchers that I work with have skills both as a researcher and designer. Some have designed their own tools. Some have built their own web sites. Some have taken on information architecture and user experience design roles.

You need to be relevant to your internal teams and to the end users of the products being developed. You need to understand the needs of the market, the users, and the business. You need to produce results that are relevant to your audience. Results are useless if you did not focus on the problems at hand – or delivered results in a format that nobody wants or understands. You need to have an inquisitive mind and be a good communicator. You need to be a good listener and have passion. You need to be a team player and collaborator, and you need to be humble. As researchers in a consulting services environment, the focus of your efforts should be on making your clients successful.

If you are considering a career as a user experience researcher, become acquainted with the field. If you are still in college, take some research methodology classes and see if you can assist a professor or graduate student in conducting their research. Learn a prototyping tool and research and design a web site, tool, or app. Attend a user experience conference to become exposed to the range of topics, industries, and research methodologies presented. Consider joining a user experience organization so you can be exposed to journals, newsletters, and articles.

Some additional thoughts for success:

- Understand your user - who they are – or may be, what they think, what motivates them, what excites them, and what they need to succeed.
- Have enthusiasm and passion for teaching.
- Think about people: their thoughts, actions, and motivations. Take a holistic view at what defines user interaction. What you think will happen in 3-5 years will happen in half that time.
- Look at customer and technology trends across industries and in our daily experiences. A user's best experience anywhere is their expectation of a user experience everywhere.
- If you are a researcher, get involved with design – understand the principles of user experience, usability principles, and industry requirements.
- If you are a designer, value the insights that can come from research.

Ken's LinkedIn profile: `https://www.linkedin.com/in/ken-stern-b4b6442`

John Tinman - UX Designer

I became aware of user experience design while working my first job out of college at an independent publishing company and book distributor in Chicago. I handled quality assurance of our eBook conversions and ran this arduous process of packaging and delivering hundreds of digital files to vendors such as Amazon and Apple each week. The process was mindless, time-consuming, and it absolutely needed improvement.

Fortunately for me though, I was working under a Director who had a background in **Human-Computer Interaction** (**HCI**). I went to him to learn more about what HCI was since it seemed similar to what I had studied in undergrad (which was market research, journalism, and web design). Because I expressed interest, he agreed to let me take on the redesign of what was a wildly inefficient delivery process. The result; I had my first wireframes under my belt; we sent the designs off to developers, and today a role that was once mine has been replaced by a content delivery tool that I designed.

What I took from this experience is that you don't need to be at some Fortune 50 tech company with massive name recognition to get anywhere in the design world. Start small. Look at your current situation, and if you see ways to improve an existing process, do it. Being at a small company with supportive leadership allowed me to get my start, and by the time I entered my HCI grad program, I had a leg up on other students because I had some experience in solving problems through design.

I decided to pursue a masters of Human-Computer Interaction from Depaul University. If you're considering a career in the user experience field, graduate school is one means to that end, but it's not the only option. I'm glad I went back to school, but HCI programs are very much what you make of them. There are so many routes to becoming a user experience practitioner. For me having a Masters in HCI taught me how to be more strategic in my approach. I have a deep pool of information and resources that I regularly reference in my work. For instance, I was also able to take a Design Ethnography course with a remarkable professor, Dr. Sheena, Erete, and while I'm not conducting ethnographic research in my day-to-day work, it gave me perspective and knowledge of a new approach to problem solving that has helped me with each new project I take on.

My design process and key activities

My current role is a **User Experience Architect** (**UXA**). I'm responsible for conducting user experience research, designing and testing information architecture, building wireframes, interactions patterns, and building prototypes for testing and demonstrations with business leaders. I work and sit directly next to my project manager, so I'm also involved in project planning, strategizing how we communicate and work with stakeholders.

My team uses the Double Diamond Model of product development, and we work in an Agile **XP** (**Extreme Programming**) environment. That means pairs of product designers and developers sit together for the entire work day cranking out designs, testing on live code, and rapidly iterating. I should mention that paired designing is not for everyone and roles like mine do not require sharing a screen with someone all day. It's an interesting environment in which to work though, and you get to witness the benefit of truly iterative design.

Research in this environment can also be a challenge as the fast pace of the XP model leaves less time for comprehensive upfront research. We handle that by leveraging UX strategists and researchers who are part of a core team to conduct exploratory research and develop strategy. That work is then passed to product designers who design, test, and iterate based on the "blueprint" that's been established by said core team.

My advice and where I see this profession evolving

A year ago, I had never heard of Agile XP, and that's why you must always be learning and developing. It's no shock that the design world is ever-changing and technology is rapidly advancing. As a designer, continuing education is practically a job requirement. One of the best places to start is on social media. Start following people who inspire you or who regularly contribute to and challenge existing patterns and paradigms, such as Luke Wroblewski (@lukew). You should also regularly check sites such as Smashing Magazine (https://www.smashingmagazine.com/) and Boxes and Arrows (http://boxesandarrows.com/).

During my morning and evening commutes, I listen to podcasts. There are so many great design podcasts, but some of my favorites are *99% Invisible* by Roman Mars and *How I Built This* by Guy Raz. *99% Invisible* is about designed artifacts in the world around you, and How I Built This tells the stories of some of the biggest companies around and the entrepreneurs who founded them. It's a nice reminder that design isn't always about screens.

For a good read, I would suggest Nudge by Richard Thaler and Cass Sunstein. For anyone interested in influencing human decision-making, Nudge is a great intro to the field of behavioral economics.

I would also recommend *The Goal* by Eliyahu M. Goldratt. Yes, it's an accounting book about the Theory of Constraints, but it's actually really entertaining, and even though I read it in undergrad, I still think about the implications this book has on design in my work today.

In addition to tracking the day-to-day trends in the design world, it's equally important for designers to look at where their industry and the careers in that industry are heading. On an organizational level, I see design, business, and technology relying on each other more than ever. Businesses are placing a new focus on user experience with some companies even hiring chief experience officers. It's not enough to just speak intelligently about usability and interaction; designers need to know how to communicate with MBAs. *The Mobile MBA* by Jo Owen is a book that was recommended to me by a peer. It's basically a guide to sounding intelligent when you're dealing with business stakeholders, and it's full of great advice.

The other trend that seems obvious, but is none the less important to understand, is that interactions and experiences will start to move off the screen and into voice interfaces, appliances, and everyday objects. The future of design will be less about point and click and more about natural conversation, and user experience professionals will be leveraged to understand and improve upon more robust customer experiences outside of phones. It's an exciting time to be in this profession. It can also be overwhelming if you're just getting a start, but never be afraid to ask questions, reach out to those in the industry, and don't be afraid to take on new challenges because you never know where they'll take your career.

John's LinkedIn profile: `https://www.linkedin.com/in/jon-tinman-33856633`

Richard Tsai - UX Architect

My first job was a programmer, working with a team of colleagues to develop a database management system. In 1998 I accepted a job opportunity in the advertising/marketing industry and over several years moved up from a role of a junior AE to be the marketing team leader.

As an IT professional, I learned how to develop software and applications and as a marketing professional, I learned about product promotions, branding, and mass communication. However, I became increasingly interested in figuring out how to design good products and services, skills neither which my IT nor marketing experience provided answers for. I felt this was very important and tried to figure out the answers, until I realized UX is the domain I'm looking for. In the process I was inspired by the work of Adaptive Path and JJG, and books such as:

- *Information Architecture* by Peter Moville and Louis Rosenfeld
- *Usability* by Jakob Nielsen
- *The Design of Everyday Things* by Donald Norman

I focused on three areas that helped me unlock the door to UX--information architecture, usability, and rapid prototyping. Evolving my knowledge and skills in these, helped me to build up the design knowledge and practice.

Today I'm a UX architect and evangelist leading a small UX consulting firm in Taiwan. Through the use of various qualitative and quantitative research methods, I gain insights into the motivations and issues of the users. Each time I interview users and listen to their stories, I learn a lot, and I find that interacting directly with users makes me feel good. After the research phase, I often build a prototype that helps test our ideas and assumptions, and finalize the design so that the product can be coded.

I think that curiosity is a very important trait and I also believe that you don't have to have an official job title, such as "UX designer", to do experience design work. You have to be curious and care about designing good product experiences.

The world is getting more complex than ever before, and I think that to be viable in the future it will be essential to possess a range of skills and knowledge in various domains. So I'm eager to learn new things, and work in a variety of different areas. In addition, it is important for me to be active in the design community, and so I have a very active role in establishing HPX, which is probably the largest community of training and support for junior designers or researchers. We hold over a hundred monthly events to discuss design, marketing, management, and so on, and share design experience with each other.

Richard's LinkedIn profile: `https://www.linkedin.com/in/richardtsai`

Summary

Design is creativity on demand--people get paid to invent and deliver experiences, and design teams operate in the context of specific business settings. Just like anyone else, they have a job to do, and this job is important to the success of the company that employs the team, and to the product the team works on.

Companies and organizations realize that design is an integral part of product development and are switching their approach to hiring design talent. From a nearly exclusive reliance on external design expertise from consultancies, organizations are establishing their own in-house teams. Some of the influencing trends are:

- The demonstrated value of user experience in e-commerce and other domains
- The business case for strong design focus made by brands such as Apple and Tesla
- The fast pace of technological innovation

As in any field, experience helps in dealing with change and its associated complications. It is common for designers to work in different settings throughout their career, and be exposed to various team configurations, industries, methodologies, tools, and points of views.

This chapter closes the foundations theme that covered an overview of what experience is, from physiological and psychological perspectives (in Chapter 5, *Experience - Perception, Emotions, and Cognition*), the various design disciplines that align with experience types (Chapter 6, *Experience Design Disciplines*), and in this chapter, the various professions within the disciplines, and their contribution to the design process.

Next we are moving to the "realization" theme, in which we combine your familiarity with design foundations and processes, to explore how designers create experiences. Chapter 8, *Delight and Engagement*, is a journey through the various techniques that designers employ to proven and new ideas and techniques to develop new and exciting user experiences.

8

Delight and Engagement

"Everything you can imagine is real."

- Pablo Picasso

This chapter addresses the following questions:

- What makes an experience with a product successful?
- What are the characteristics of great experience, and how do these characteristics maximize a product's desirability, engagement, conversion, retention, and reputation?

We will explore several dimensions, including localization, customization, and personalization, of the process that tailors an experience to a single user. We will look at how this outcome is achieved by creating engagement and infusing a sense of joy, marvel, and fun through visual effects, animation, gamification, and data visualization. While new technologies continuously expand the spectrum of possible product experiences, each design discipline has its proven methods for creating compelling engagement experiences, which are often technology agnostic.

This chapter includes an assortment of examples and instances that demonstrate what makes an experience with a product pleasing, and why. It will be like learning how to pull a rabbit out of a hat. Not that design is magic, but that it can feel like magic to those experiencing it.

Overview

Suppose you are in the market for a new winter coat. You do the research and end up with a great choice from a fashionable imported brand. The coat you purchased is very light and very warm, you love the material and the color, it fits you well. Additionally, the price was very reasonable, and significantly cheaper compared to coats by other brands with similar features. Everyone compliments you on your purchase, which was hassle-free in a well-designed store owned by the brand on the most expensive shopping street in the city. The entire purchase experience has been positive. You feel very good about the brand and congratulate yourself on a good choice.

And then, about a month into winter, the front zipper breaks and you end up walking home in brutal cold, tightening the coat around your chest with your gloveless hand.

As you walk home, you recall that when you were at the store, you thought that the zipper was flimsy. But at the time, you convinced yourself that, surely, the zipper will be fine, it just looks flimsy. Even now, finally thawing in a hot shower, you are thinking that perhaps the broken zipper was somehow your responsibility. Perhaps you pulled it too hard. And so on.

When you take the coat to the store for repair, you are told that they cannot repair the zipper, and because you wore it for over a month, they will be happy to give you a new coat at 50 percent discount. Now you are upset at the company, and at yourself.

The good experience turned sour because the experience has not been consistent throughout--some aspects of the product were great, but quality issues and poor customer service experience overshadowed the positive.

While this chapter is focused entirely on techniques designers use to create experiences, it should not come as a surprise that good user experience depends not only on the product's look and feel, but also on its quality and reliability.

Attractive design is powerful. It can be used explicitly to manipulate customers to purchase a product. And so, experience designers sometimes find themselves faced with ethical dilemmas:

- Is the experience they create honest, or does it serve as "smoke and mirror" to mask a known, fundamental deficiency in the product? For example, early in the history of user experience for software, it was not uncommon to hear dismissive references to design as "eye candy" and "dressing a pig". What these expressions mean is that design can help make the product look good, despite the fact that the product is difficult, deficient, and frustrating to use.

- Is it ethical to design perfect "mousetraps"? By mousetraps, I refer to products that appear to offer compelling user experiences, while collecting detailed data on private users and their behaviors, which is then used or sold by the company for purposes that might eventually harm the user. For example, think about fitness, health, and diet applications that constantly collect and monitor one's physical activity, vitals, and dietary intake. The data is highly personal and intimate, yet it is being collected, analyzed, used, and resold for commercial purposes over which users of such applications have no control.

Functional and emotional design

Design serves two primary roles--functional and emotional.

The separation between these two roles used to be distinct. Engineers dealt with the product's functional design, primarily the *backend* aspects. Product designers focused on crafting the desired emotional outcome associated with the product's attractiveness features, the *customer facing* aspects.

Technological advances have narrowed the gaps between the functional and the emotional to the point that they complement each other, and to the degree that they are sometimes difficult to differentiate. As long as the distinction between the roles of engineers and designers was maintained, there were negative implications on the product's user experience.

Let's use "buttons" as an example:

- Have you ever pressed a button on a device without knowing what the button does, or knowing what to expect?
- Have you ever wondered if a button indicates an *On* or *Off* state?
- Have you ever searched, unsuccessfully, for a button to turn the device on or off?

It is highly likely that you had such experiences with various products, such as home appliances, projectors, remote controls, digital watches, and many others. Why?

Products don't need buttons, but people do. Buttons allow the user to trigger an action that makes the product perform a certain function. The experience of using the product truly depends on the lowly button. The clarity of its position, label, or purpose can determine whether the overall experience would be satisfying or frustrating.

Buttons are everywhere. Their potential to unify engagement and delight for the user cannot be underestimated, yet the design of buttons is often neglected. Ironically, one of the primary reasons for this is designers' insistence on "clean" and minimalist designs, which end up being obscure and less functional.

Physical and digital buttons co-exist on numerous products, and designers have many options for buttons, such as shape, position, material, color, texture, and labels.

In physical products, little thought was given in the past to the experiential aspect of buttons. When button design was considered, the focus typically was on the on-off switch, which was relegated to the mundane and functional. Shapes used to be curiously limited to circles or squares, with the possible exception of buttons on children's toys. Since buttons equated functionality, little consideration has been given to the usability of button overload:

| Toolbars, MS Word Circa 2003 | The Flight-Deck of a Boeing 747 |

Increasingly, however, designers are re-imagining the use of buttons and their contributions to rich user experiences. These days, almost anything can be designed to function as a button, as the surfaces of products and screens can be engineered to respond to a user's voice, touch, gesture, or motion. As part of the re-imagining process, designers simplify the product experience by reducing the number of buttons with which users need to interact. Fewer buttons--sometimes just a single one--perform multiple functions in response to different types of user input, such as a single tap, double tap, and so on. Fewer buttons allow for streamlined and elegant designs, and the buttons themselves are designed to be points of engagement--glowing, pulsing, changing colors, and other visual effects.

In the physical world, we don't think much about the experiential dimension of buttons until we notice they exist. For example, in the case of the car ignition experience, consider the following image:

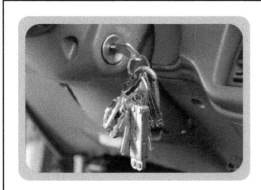

Until recently, the experience of many drivers included the rattling sound of a heavy keychain loaded with an assortment of keys, the car's remote, a charm or a small utility item, all hanging off the ring that also held the car key placed in the ignition switch. The ignition key is being replaced by a large single button. The following are several benefits of this transition:

- The old keys had a double function--they unlocked the car doors, and turned on the engine. Drivers who forgot the key in the ignition, sometimes locked themselves out, requiring assistance to break into the car, if a spare key was not around. This cannot happen with the electronic button, since the doors are controlled by a fob that the driver can keep in their pocket.
- Turning the car on and off feels more like interacting with an appliance or a personal device. It is very easy. The old key had three states, and the driver had to turn the key all the way to turn the car on or off. Not a difficult operation, but sometimes drivers had to try multiple times, or the key got stuck.
- When pressing the new type of ignition button on or off, it omits a pleasant and welcoming lighting and sound effect that greets the driver and adds to a sense of anticipation and comfort before the start of the trip, even if it is only to the grocery store.

Expressions such as "one click away" or "in a click of a button" represent a promise of ease and speed. Buttons have always held this promise, but as they became more common, we stopped noticing them. Like the example of the car ignition button that transforms a mundane action into a pleasant audio-visual experience, buttons on physical and digital products provide renewed opportunities to engage the user, and be fun.

And yet, just as car keys and keys in general, are slowly giving way to biometric authentication, there is also a trend of transitioning interaction and control of products from human manual actions to autonomic, automatic, self-learning devices that anticipate user needs.

This applications can offer a great user experience, but do you know what the companies behind such products do with the enormous quantities of intimate information they constantly collect from their individual users? The long-term risks for misuse cannot be ignored.

Is it ethical to design great experiences for unhealthy or dangerous products such as junk food, questionable food supplements, pornographic websites, or websites for extreme fundamentalist groups, firearms and other weapons? Like any other person, when it comes to ethical decisions, each designer decides on their zone of comfort, so we will leave it at that.

Visual and auditory experiences

On a cold winter evening, you find yourself waiting for the bus. It is a windy day, and the snow is blowing hard. Traffic is slow and the bus is very delayed. Fortunately, the bus shelter provides some protection from the gusts of wind and snow. You are cold, tired, and hungry. The bus shelter has a large illuminated panel with large, colorful photos that change every few seconds.

In the following image, the photos are advertisements, and on each, there is a QR code that you can scan with your phone for more details about the promoted product. Product **A** features an image of a lush tropical beach. Product **B**, an image of a hot beverage next to a fireplace. Which of the products will engage you to scan its QR code?

Visual design plays a major role in the customer's engagement with a product. It begins with the awareness phase. The awareness phase covers the time period from the moment a person becomes aware for the first time that a particular product exists to the time of the eventual purchase of the product.

Products that are advertised with eye-grabbing and emotion-triggering visuals in print publication, public signage, internet advertisement, television commercials, and packaging. The ads bring the products to our attention and sprout emotions of curiosity and desire. These visual imagery is also more likely to be imprinted in our memory so that it it easy to recall the products we saw in images that leave strong impressions.

Visual design can be presented on any surface, at sizes that scale from a tiny watch display to buses and buildings. The effectiveness of the experience evoked by visual design, independent of its shape and size, depends on the right blend of white space, typography, and imagery, to trigger an emotional composite of sensations and memories of people, places, smells, and tastes.

The preceding image includes images of lit fireplaces, each depicting a different setting, each meant to trigger emotions and set moods that might connect a viewer from a target-audience with some product or service (not shown here). When looking at the image **A1**, for example, the designer knows that the viewer is not likely to analyze each individual component in the composition--the wine glass, the grapes, the plate or the flames in the fireplace. Instead, the entire scene will be consumed as a whole and trigger an interpretation of intimacy and romance.

While image **A1** is as effective as image **A2** in communicating a romantic atmosphere, despite the fact that it does not include people, the differences in details suggest nuanced interpretations of the two scenes. Image **A2**, has a composition that includes two pairs of feet in socks, one of the persons wearing jeans, and a fireplace as a backdrop, may suggest a younger couple. The composition of **A1** on the other hand, with its sleek wine glasses, may suggest more sophistication and an older couple.

The single cup of coffee in image **B1**, and the single pair of legs in warm and cozy winter boots in image **B2**, create a wholly different association. These two compositions share some attributes with images **A1** and **A2**. All images include a fireplace and have a warm orange-brown color palate; all of them trigger associations with a contemplative calm and meditative relaxation. All images include a fireplace and have a warm orange-brown color palate; all of them trigger associations with a contemplative calm and meditative relaxation.

Similarly, the food compositions in the preceding images are intended to trigger a craving for food, or anticipatory thoughts about a delicious meal. These images might also remind us of a particular time, place, or person that are somehow associated with the food, and so on.

Where art and design differ, however, is that the designer must be fully aware of

- The experience that the visual design is meant to create in support of the product represents
- The cultural context of the target audience

The use of inappropriate colors or imagery as elements of the visual design might backfire. For example, for vegetarians or health conscientious consumers such as parents concerned about the nutrition intake of their young children, an image of a deep-fried sandwich with a side of fries might be a turn off and result in a negative experience.

Visual design trends

Visual, fashion, or automotive design, are prone to waves of trends that tend to sweep the market, dominate it for some time, fade out in favor of new trends, just to return at some point later on as retro fashion, and join the spectrum of general design patterns and vocabulary available to designers.

For example, flat design is in full vogue these days as the style of choice in digital user experience. It is very effective in mobile computing, and its origins can be traced back to the early 2000s.

The attributes of flat design include:

- Two-dimensional illustrations
- Bright colors
- Contrasts and simple geometric shapes
- Large typeface
- Simplified content

The overall effect can be stunning and attract user's attention. Images **A1** and **A2** are screenshots of award-winning websites that implemented flat design. The imagery is bright, simplified, and contemporary-looking. For some, however, this style of design brings to mind children books illustrations due to the use of similar stylistic motifs, simplified compositions, large types and flat illustrations that don't use perspective.

The popularity of flat design can be traced back to early technical constraints of mobile computing. By the end of the twentieth century, the rapid spread of smartphones, tablets, and other mobile devices required companies to rethink their mobile web presence. Since the mid-1990s, companies have invested in creating engaging web-based experiences for desktop and laptop computers, which now had to fit the small screens of mobile devices.

Visual designers turned to flat design as a technical solution to bandwidth and device size limitations. The file size of flat design graphic images requires significantly less bandwidth than more complex visual imagery, which includes shadings and intricate color gradation. Flat design images also scale well to a smaller screen size because they have fewer details and higher color contrasts. The approach has been so successful that Google, Apple, and Microsoft launched operating systems featuring flat design (see the following image **C**).

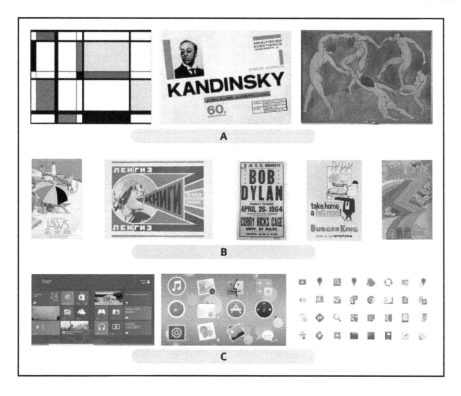

The origins of flat design can be traced back to the turn of the 20th century and the emergence of the *Modern*, a period of great leaps in science, technology, communications, and commerce, which included the spread of electricity, the telephone, radio, airplanes, cars, skyscrapers, and many other engineering feats. All these development allowed people to experience the world as never before. It was a social cultural generational mindset that sprouted new artistic expressions (see the preceding image **A**).

The *modern* sensibility permeated visual design and contemporary posters, which were the primary channel of public communications, well before television and radio broadcast became wide-spread. Graphic designers created visual experiences for purposes as diverse as social movements and movie advertisements (see the preceding image **B**)

The flat design we see these days on operating systems, websites, apps, and printed materials across the board has a long history.

Skeuomorphic design

Contemporary architects and designers sometimes choose to draw on elements of style that reference the work of ancient builders, dating back thousands of years ago, such as the stone and marble remains of Greek and Roman structures. In turn, those remains preserve the references that ancient architects made to their own heritage.

The triglyph depicted in the previous image is a common design pattern that you could easily identify on many public and private buildings in your area. This pattern of three vertical posts separated by grooves, is an example of a skeuomorphic expression--a stylistic, but otherwise non-essential element that stands for an original element, which was functionally essential to the structure. In the case of the triglyph, the stone depiction serves as an ornamental reference to the endings of long, massive wooden beams that used to support the roofs of buildings.

Early architypes of the triglyph pattern can be found in the remains of Greek temples and Roman structures dating 2000 years ago. The builders of those ancient buildings used stone and marble as the primary construction material, but they wanted to preserve the glory and symbolic essence of wooden religious and cultural structures that were perhaps lost to war and fire (see the following images **A** and **B**).

Skeuomorphism, then, is a purely visual, non-functional form of design that is used as a means to preserve the meaning and experience of an earlier function. Steve Jobs was really fond of skeuomorphic design. In his opinion, software objects that resembled objects in the real world were easier and more intuitive for people to interact with.

Skeuomorphic design used to be popular in user interfaces of audio-visual editing software that referenced analog mixing consoles. The latter, such as the one depicted in the preceding image **A**, had rows upon rows of buttons controlling the mix of each sound channel.

When editing software became available, user experience designers attempted to provide sound technicians and musicians with a familiar look and feel, which they could do with the skeuomorphic representation in **B**. This experience was important because the users who transitioned from analog to digital, brought with them a wealth of expertise, and skeuomorphic design made the transition to new tools faster and more efficient because interface elements were easily recognizable.

In skeuomorphic design, we find a tension between a desire to preserve old experiences in new technologies, and an opportunity to create entirely new ones. These days, most musicians and sound engineers start editing directly in software products, using their computers or smartphones. Such users no longer have the need for or the experiential connection to the giant original analog consoles. For them it is no longer important to preserve any visual references to that equipment.

The implication is that there are opportunities to simplify the user interface and make the experience of editing simpler and more productive. Similarly, the interface of many analog products reflects design decisions that solved physical hardware needs no longer relevant in the digital domain. The rotary phone in image **A** above, is a good example of a common user experience that virtually disappeared when the dial was replaced with buttons that improved the speed of inputting the phone number.

Turning a full circle, however, product designers sometimes use skeuomorphism as a means to introduce fun and delight to the user experience by incorporating options that let users select a *retro* look for their user interface, such as the phone app in image **B**.

Sequencing and directions

You just got back from a visit to the store, where you purchased a brand new home theater system. You can't wait to unbox the equipment, hook it up, and enjoy an immersive screening of a new movie with your friends, who will be envious of your new purchase.

A few hours later you are still attempting to install the system that includes a large-screen smart **high-definition television** (HDTV), multiple speakers, and some lighting fixtures. The instructions are cryptic and your attempts to follow the assembly process fail. You spend many minutes on the phone attempting to get some help from the manufacturer, but the recommendation is to hire the services of a technician who will assemble the system for you. In the end, you need to call your friends and cancel the planned screening.

From toys to self-assembly furniture, most people are likely to find themselves setting up a product at some point in their lives. The setup, moreover, is often required not only during the first use of the product. Some products are used infrequently, and each use might require some setting up process. Other products are shared among several users, and each needs to set up the product to match their needs.

Technologically and culturally, we live in an age that conditions us for instant gratification--elimination of the wait between feeling and need or desire for something and fulfilling that desire. A good example is Amazon's **1-Click** shopping button.

However, many products require assembly or initial setup. Some are more involved than others, but all can dampen the experience of enjoying a new product either because the user is unable to complete the initial setup, or because the user does the setup incorrectly. Either way, positive emotions towards the product, such as excitement and anticipation, are replaced with negative emotions such as dismay, frustration, disappointment, and even anger towards the company and the product.

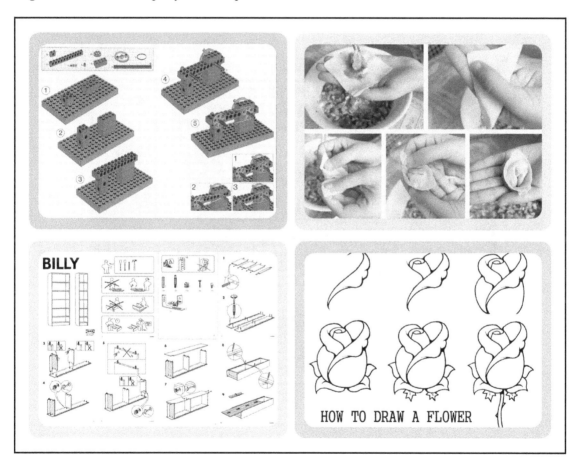

Compelling setup guides, when relevant, are essential to a satisfying experience, including the pre-use experience of shopping and un-packaging. The preceding image includes some examples of design principles for step-by-step guides. The construction steps are illustrated rather that written, and the user can see the product's gradual transformation. Illustrations make the instructions universal because they are language and age independent. Language can be a barrier even to native speakers when the guide uses technical words and terminology.

Another type of products that provide guidance experience is navigation systems. Highways can be terrifying to new and inexperienced drivers, and are often challenging for experienced drivers too. Generally speaking, though, most drivers can easily perform a complex task such as changing lanes in order to merge to an exit ramp, despite driving at high-speeds on a busy multi-lane highway.

The navigation challenge is greater in a complex downtown intersection in an unfamiliar location. In addition to reading printed instructions, a paper map or a GPS screen, the driver must look at street signs, keep the car in the right lane and track the proximity of pedestrians, cyclists, and motorists. This is a complex set of interactions with multiple sources of input data streaming in real time.

The growing demand for the services of ride-sharing services such as Lyft has expanded the number of drivers driving in unfamiliar locations. They are dependent on the user experience of navigation systems, which are essentially advanced interactive data visualization systems.

The software's visualization feature predicts the driver's needs and reduces the mental effort necessary to handle the stress of driving in unfamiliar neighborhoods. The features, some of which are shown in the preceding image, include the ability to view the map at different zoom levels, display the map in 2D or 3D and in perspective, adapt its colors to day or night driving, and automatically zoom to show the appropriate lane to take prior to entering an intersection. A clear and constant cursor indicates the location of the car on the map, and the direction to take.

Most smartphones are now equipped with powerful computing powers, dedicated GPS chips, and large, high-resolution displays. Navigation software are more accurate, providing real-time traffic data, audio prompts, weather conditions and road hazards, and many other details about the area.

The latest generation of navigation software such as Waze delivers real-time advertising, alerting the driver to local businesses and promotions. Waze also combines aspects of social engagement, allowing members to alert other drivers to common traffic issues such as accidents or speed traps. Navigation software evolves to become a platform for social and geo-content discovery, which is compelling to both local and passing drivers.

In future generations of navigation software, experience designers face the interesting challenge of balancing the basics of step-by-step driving guidance through visualization with the extra content, which is not essential to the driving task.

Grabbing attention

We filter out a lot of sensory information about which we don't need to care. While our eyes transmit a great deal of visual data in a continuous feed, we can only focus on a single item at any given moment. Only the item in focus is the subject of engagement, although unconsciously, we keep monitoring our surroundings for changes that might require a shift in our focus or attention.

Similar filtering happens with products and information:. There are so many products, services, and information, that it is impossible to keep track of it all. Experience designers create content that must engage potential customers, pass through their filtering, and make the product stand out from all other options.

An effective experience can imprint the existence of particular products in our consciousness by evoking emotions such as desire, craving, enablement, and joy. Earlier in this chapter the effect was mentioned in the context of instant gratification. Here, the intent is to make us aware that a product exists and, when the time of actual need comes, a specific brand or product would surface in our memory.

The preceding image includes a couple of examples that demonstrate how designers create interest and engagement using non-commercial visuals. A goldfish in a fishbowl might be a banal image. But when the goldfish is the only color element in the otherwise grayscale image **A**, our eyes pay closer attention to the photo, and we notice the dripping faucet connected to the fishbowl. Our brain expects the entire image to be either in color or grayscale, and it does not expect to see a faucet connected to the fishbowl. The entire composition creates a brief moment of visual dissonance and surprise.

We need to stop, focus, and think about the message. We are engaged. The combination of visual effects underscores the importance of saving water, and makes the message more memorable--to keep the fish alive (represented in image **A** by its life-like color appearance), we need to prevent water waste as represented by the ominous appearance of the grey faucet.

Image **B** is another example of a water-saving campaign. Here, the designer engages the viewer through a realistic-looking image of a metal faucet, but this time the faucet is tied in a knot, a metaphor for stopping the drip. Again, the visual effect creates a mental surprise that builds on the contrast between the hard, solid nature of metal, and the plasticity in which the faucet has been tied.

The image is engaging and also fun--the important message is communicated to the viewer, who is most likely to take moment to look closer at the ad, while leafing through the pages of a magazine or browsing through web pages.

In the preceding images we can see examples of another visual engagement technique--the use of empty space. The Latin phrase "Horror vacui" means "fear of the empty", and refers to a trend in antiquity to fill the entire visual composition with ornaments and details. In such images, many intricate patterns blend together and it is difficult for the viewer to isolate specific elements.

Painters and visual designers found that organizing fewer elements on the page, so that many areas in the composition are left empty, can create stunningly engaging images. The viewer's eyes are much more attuned to the contrast between the foreground and the elements.

The power of minimalistic design helps focus the viewer's attention on specific elements in the surface, and controls the flow of viewing. This technique is well suited for commercial engagement, where competition over fleeting customer attention can be aided by fewer yet more memorable details.

Animation is another technique experience designers use to draw attention to products and services. Most people love animation. The novelty effect of seeing inanimate objects come to life is irresistible. From the experience designer's perspective, animation offers many ways to engage the user by bringing to life situations that are impossible in reality yet illustrate reality better than a documentary:

- Visual and sound effects such as exaggeration, special effects, and interesting camera angles
- Visual style of characters in drawings or three-dimensional puppets

- Delivery of content through humor or dramatization

Early adoption of animation in product design has been in education and training materials. The image above is a frame from a short instructional clip about airline safety is included.

The inherent power of animation is used increasingly in high-tech products. Brief sequences of animated effects accompany the initialization sequences of many products such as cars and mobile devices. These very brief sequences provide a visual cue that the system is operational, and also create an emotional effect of personality and a welcoming gesture.

Data visualization

Raw data becomes valuable and impactful when it is transformed into meaningful insights that help us understand the past and predict the future. Data visualization is a fusion of technology, scientific, and experience design disciplines that make it possible to process monumental quantities of data very quickly, and present in a compact, beautiful easy to engage visual format.

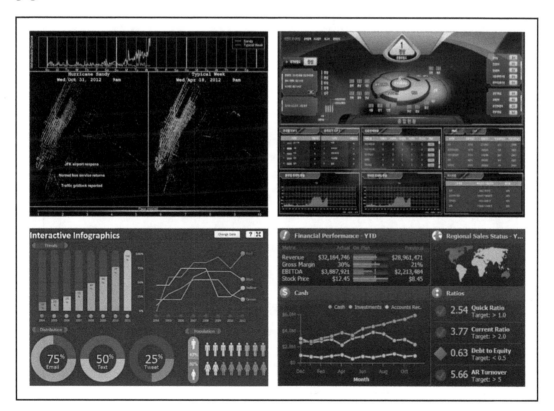

The preceding image contains visualization samples of scientific, financial, and population data dashboards. Each of the panels is an engaging interactive representation of information--massive datasets are expressed as charts, graphs, maps, and graphics. These representations are compact in size but highly versatile in use. Users of visualization dashboards can quickly and easily form insights and support their decision-making process.

Data visualization software greatly improves the efficiency and analysis quality of people who need to analyze very large datasets in domains such as research, finance, or economics, compared to the use of Microsoft Excel.

Data presented in charts and graphs is fast and easy to scan and interact with. Visually, the user receives an initial understanding of the story the data is telling--the size, color, and concentration of clusters superimposed on a geographic map can tell a story of demographics or public-health issues; the direction of a trend line can indicate the positive or negative projection of financial investments. The user can click on elements of the visualization to filter or drill in for more details.

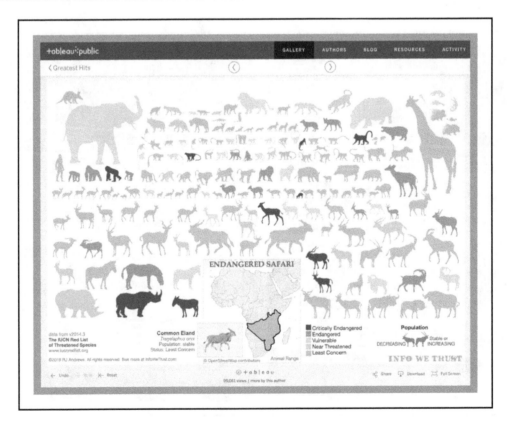

In the example shown in the preceding image, the user can click any of the African countries outlined on the map to see all the wildlife in that country, to see a visual depiction of all the endangered species there. Conversely, the user can click any of the animals and see its endangerment status across the continent. Such data can be presented in a spreadsheet, but the speed, flexibility, and beauty of the visualization would be replaced by tables of numbers, and a need to perform various time-consuming calculations in order to obtain some of the information-- of course, without the images and the engagement.

Data visualization helps us see ourselves in new ways, literally, as the representation of data-points collected by our phone in apps that track our activity. Biometric tracking devices such as headbands that track brain wave activity, smart watches and activity bands collect our body's data constantly--body temperature, blood pressure, heart rate, sleep patterns, calories consumed and burned, number of daily steps, and so on.

The self becomes the center of our attention--we *are* the experience, and experience designers naturally use data visualization to provide us with the best picture of ourselves.

These are wholly new experiences--most people tend to notice their body in extreme situations, in the context of key life moments, athletic effort, or when something is wrong. During an illness or following an accident, however, medical professionals in medical settings are responsible for collecting, analyzing, and interpreting vitals and other physical data.

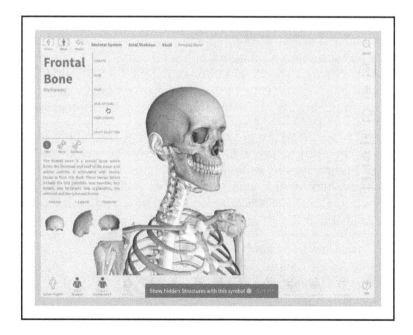

Finally, data visualization provides enticing learning environments such as medical and allied health training. The visualization above is a great example of a how learning can be enhanced by three dimensional models of the human body, which the user can rotate, zoom in and out, or filter out to get a better look at deeper layers or systems. The simulations are significantly more effective as a learning tool for healthcare students than what was ever possible with books or videos.

Shaping experiences

The last topic in this brief survey of visual engagement experiences is the materials used to produce products. Materials shape the user experience physically and have an enormous impact on a product's attractiveness and desirability. People's relationship with various materials is elemental and often charged with strong preferences and biases.

For example, basic "natural" materials, such as wood, cotton, and leather are considered by some to be more durable, wholesome, and pure. In a world of dwindling natural raw materials such materials are often more expensive, and the products made from them more exclusive.

We first experience products through sight, and our impression of a product is often established within milli-seconds of looking at it, well before we touch or use it. E-commerce websites provide a better experience than their forerunners, the mail-order catalogues because they offer a superior visualization. There are photos of the products in various angles, 360 degree rotation, a zooming option to take a closer look at the details of the material, videos and animated simulations of use--all are some of the experiences that respond to customer needs for a visual inspection of the product. By sight, we can assess whether the product is hard or soft, smooth or course, heavy or light, new or worn-out, and form an independent--if not always accurate-- impression of the product's quality.

The development and widespread use of synthetic polymers, commonly known as plastics, throughout the twentieth century, has revolutionized product experiences. It can be argued that plastics changed human society, exponentially expanding the availability of consumer and commercial products world-wide at large quantities and low cost. The following dialog, from the movie *The Graduate (1967)*, reflects how the promise and possibilities of this new material were seen at that time.

> **Mr. McGuire**: *I want to say one word to you. Just one word.*
> **Benjamin**: *Yes, sir.*
> **Mr. McGuire**: *Are you listening?*
> **Benjamin**: *Yes, I am.*
> **Mr. McGuire**: *Plastics.*
> **Benjamin**: *Exactly how do you mean?*

Mr. McGuire: *There's a great future in plastics. Think about it. Will you think about it?*

Lightweight, strong, easy to mold and inexpensive compared to natural materials, plastic was the first modern material that enabled designers to dream up new visual experiences of physical products. The following image shows some of those products:

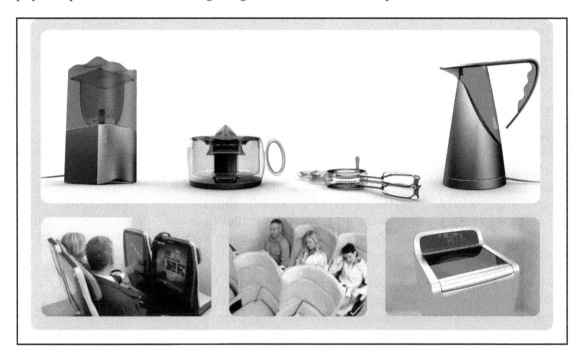

Using plastics, products like the ones in the picture above, can be produced in any colors, be translucent or opaque, soft or hard, smooth or rough, and most interestingly, they can look like natural materials such as wood, metal, leather, or glass. The ability to simulate natural materials can backfire when customers perceive the substitution as inferior. Apple's hardware products, such as iPhones and MacBook Pro laptops, are encased in aluminum shells to differentiate them from competing products encased in plastic that appears to look like aluminum.

Constant advances in science and manufacturing, such as nano-technology and 3D printing, introduce "smart" materials with specialized properties. Examples are materials that are resistant to water, heat, or radiation, self-healing materials, and materials that feature adhesiveness and conductivity.

Conversational experiences

One of the first things I did with my first GPS unit was to replace the default voice with the voice of John Cleese as he sounds in *Monty Python.* I also got the voice of Homer Simpson, and a few other favorites. The tediousness of long drives was softened with navigation instructions dispensed by Cleese's wry humor or Homer's shrieks of delight.

This customization feature was a nice novelty, but the experience was limited overall. GPS systems have a small vocabulary and after a while the effect wears out. But what if I could hold a conversation with John Cleese and get his recommendation for the nearest family restaurant, gas station, or movie theatre, and then have him make a reservation, purchase tickets, and arrange for parking?

Conversational interactions with computers has been a common theme in science fiction. The idea swept the popular imagination in Stanley Kubrick's film *2001: A Space Odyssey,* in which a spacecraft's computer, HAL 9000, a machine with high intellectual reasoning and communications capabilities, kills all but one of the crew because it feels that they threaten the craft's mission. HAL maintains a highly emotional, "human" like conversation with the remaining scientist, pleading for its life, until it is eventually powered down. More recently, in the 2013 movie *Her*, a man falls in love with his computer's operating system, personified by a female voice.

The compelling promise of conversational interfaces lies in their uncanny resemblance to interaction with people. Traditional interfaces such as keyboards and screens clearly differentiate people from computers, but now we are at the dawn of a new experience era. Tremendous advancements in artificial intelligence and machine learning usher in auditory product experiences that offer natural conversation with a product in place of the physical interaction facilitated by touchscreens and keyboards.

The shaping of the speech-driven user experience is complex.

As speakers, we can modulate our voice dynamically during a conversation to communicate our message. Generally speaking, speech fuses two primary layers of information:

- The first layer involves information communicated by the elements of the language, such as sounds that make up words, vocabulary, grammatical structures, word order, and sentences. Additionally, our linguistic choices embed the social and personal contexts of the conversation. In a conversation, this aspect of speech is delivered by voice, but it could be delivered in writing as well.

- The second layer of information is passed by the dynamic quality of our voice--tone, pitch, volume, speed, etc. The second layer of information is crucial to social and personal communication. It allows accurate interpretation what is being said within the overall experience of a conversation.

Here is a simple often-used example. In a meeting, if I said, "It is a pleasure to meet you," and you relied on the words in the sentence, you would understand that I have positive feelings about meeting you. But how I say the sentence impacts your accurate interpretation of my real feelings. If I use a flat, low tone, my words come across as a formality and imply that I'm not really happy to see you. I my tone is abrupt, you may think that I'm being sarcastic. I can modulate my voice to form the sentence in an infinite range of subtle meaning variations, as a question, declaration, or ambiguous statement--and each of these variations creates a different flavor to what I say and how you interpret it.

Use of speech for interaction design has been fairly limited until recently, because it has been difficult for computers to manage the complex range of implicit and explicit meaning communicated in regular, day-to-day speech. The challenge is still significant.

Early on, most common examples of use began as a one-sided messaging, with the product alerting the user about incoming mail, calls, news and weather alerts, and so on. This made a lot of sense and was intended to alert the user to time-sensitive events. These auditory messages came in addition to or as a substitute for visual notifications. The flip side of this development is a cacophony of audible alerts from multiple apps, which can cause experiential overload and be disruptive to both the individual user and anyone within hearing range.

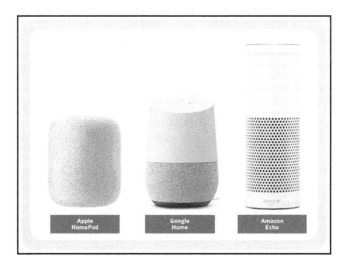

Apple's Siri, Amazon's Alexa, Microsoft's Cortana, and Google's Assistant are conversational interfaces, also known as conversational bots.

The underlying promise of the technology is products that understand us. On the most superficial level, the understanding is basic and functional--I have a dialog, an interactive conversation with the product instead of talking with a real person. The software knows me, it has access to massive amounts of data that it can process and filter to identify my needs in real time. It can help me book a flight, find the best deal on a vacation package, do my shopping, and so on. This can be done while I'm engaging in activities that prevent me from using my phone or computer, such as driving. And also, there is no need to wait on hold for the next available customer support representative, when such support is needed. The bot can handle this.

The latest versions of these products are getting better at handling environmental noise. The bots are available on the phone, car, and home appliances. People use them in the office, car, public spaces, outdoors, and at home with the radio and television on and family members around. In such potentially noisy circumstances, the system must be able to interpret correctly the user's intentions and to prevent unintentional or dangerous outcomes.

To do this, the system must first isolate the user's voice from other voices. The harder task is perhaps ensuring that the user is actually addressing the product and not a person. At minimum, the experience requirements are:

- **Accuracy**: The product should understand the meaning of what is said. This is the most challenging of all the inputs processed by the system--just think about the variability of speech, and the multitude of accents, dialects, intonations, inflection, tone, and volume.
- **Responsiveness**: The speed with which the interface confirms the input's accuracy and performs the desired action. We don't expect our conversation partner to repeat constantly what we say, and we are not expected to repeat what we had just heard. But with conversational interfaces, there is a need to validate that the product correctly interprets the user's message, by repeating verbatim or by rephrasing, which slows the interaction and leads to a frustrating experience.

It can be argued that conversational interfaces will have a profound influence not only on product experience, but also on the evolution of personal and social interaction norms. An increasing number of products can be set to a permanent stand-by mode, waiting and ready to engage with us and fulfil our needs. In other words, smartphones, Amazon's Alexa, Google's Home, Apple's HomePod, and many other products that are being launched, are listening to everything we say, everything that is going on in our home, office, or car.

The power of context

The user experience of most content-dependent products relies heavily on translation and adaptation to the local language, units of measure, regulations, patterns of use, price, and other relevant cultural aspects.

For example, the world-renowned **New York Times** (**NYT**) is a daily newspaper with a global readership of several millions, but the web edition of the paper is available only in English, Spanish, and Chinese (see the preceding image). These are, after all, the three most common languages on Earth. In contrast, Facebook, with over a billion and a half users, has an interface that is nearing a universal support for all languages.

The difference between the New York Times and Facebook is that the first provides content, and the latter relies on users and advertisers to generate content. Both relay on Unicode, the computing industry standard for text, which was designed to handle most of the world's written languages. Unicode is a remarkable invention, of which most people are not aware, but it is the underlying technology that makes possible experiences such as the New York Times and Facebook at a fraction of time and cost.

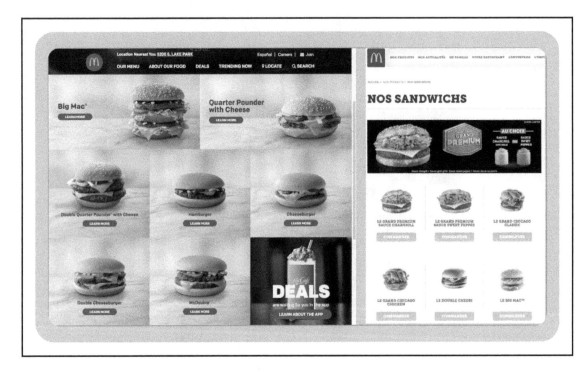

Making content available in the customers' native language is of major significance to their experience. Some products also require cultural adaptation. The image above shows examples of McDonald's menus from France, Russia, Japan, and the USA. In all locations, the menus include the iconic "Big Mac" and fries, which are universal, but each of the menus also features items with ingredients popular in the local market, such as ginger baked burgers in Japan, or rolls with cottage cheese in Russia.

Even when the product is language independent or available in your native language, it is difficult to make the right choice when there are many available options. Which of McDonald's 10 hamburger options should I pick? Or perhaps, I should have the chicken instead?! Then, which of the 10 chicken sandwich options? Perhaps one of their three salads? And should I also add small, medium, or large fries? Each of the choices is visualized in appetizing photos. With so many choices and combinations, it can be hard to decide.

The *Paradox of Choice*, a term coined by the psychologist Barry Schwartz, describes the cognitive and emotional state of having too many choices. It addresses difficulty in decision-making and post-purchase regret--thinking that I should have gotten the salad instead of the Big Mac. The dilemma faced by experience designers is, should the experience include even more choices by allowing personalization and customization of the product. The other option is to do the opposite and limit the number of choices because there are so many options available already.

We take for granted personal and cultural preferences for food and fashion. A preference is a consistent choice of one option over an alternative options. For example, when asked to choose between chocolate or vanilla ice cream, if you like chocolate and always ask for chocolate, then this is your ice cream preference. Product customization and personalization feature are layers of options that go beyond the simple choice. Do you want your chocolate ice-cream with any of 20 possible toppings? In a chocolate cone, waffle cone, or plastic cup? In a world of many choices, choice design is a challenging task.

The terms personalization and customization are somewhat ambiguous and often used interchangeably. In the context of experience design, customization is initiated by the customer, while personalization is a dynamic adaptation of the product to the user.

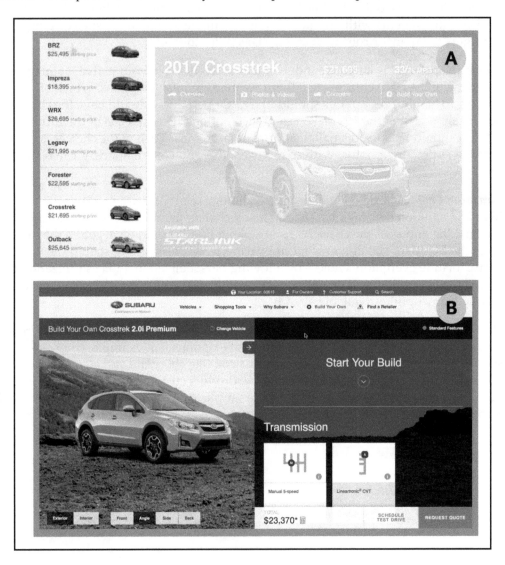

Customization options are typically offered by the manufacturer after the customer makes the initial selection of the product. Take for example the experience of customizing a new car. Purchasing a new car is a significant investment. For most, it is the second largest expense after their home purchase. The pressure of making the right decision is high--even when the tag price is not a concern--and a company that can help a customer feel good about the process and the final choice, can gain reputation and loyalty.

The initial selection does not involve customization, but it does reflect one's needs and preferences. It begins with the selection of a car model from a relatively small set of models, each with some distinct characteristics (see preceding image **A**), such as:

- **Body style**: A wagon or a sedan
- **Size**: Full size or compact
- **Use**: City, off-road, or performance driving conditions
- **Color**: Exterior and interior colors

For each model, the manufacturer offers additional options, typically:

- **Transmission**: Manual or automatic. This choice option is of course irrelevant if the person does not know how to use manual transmission.
- **Trim**: Often built-in options that create variations of the selected model, and require a decision at the point of purchase. For example, with or without a sunroof.

Image **B** above shows a screen from Subaru's car builder, a common feature on most car manufacturers' websites. The feature allows the potential buyer to add various options to their selected model and trim. These may include bike and or kayak racks, better audio equipment, and so on. Many of these items can be purchased later on, so it is an opportunity for the car maker to help the customer imagine fun activities they might do with the new car--even if they end up never going white-water rafting.

As the user adds accessories to customize their car, the price tag goes up --a serious downer, morphing a fun activity into an unpleasant surprise.

A customized product is also a personalized product, because changes to the base offering were driven by the customer. However, it is important to understand that the customer is in fact passive here: All customization options come from the product--the company or website know nothing about the individual user who makes the various options based on what is offered.

Customization and personalization are tied to social class, culture, and sub-culture. In an age of advanced mass manufacturing, hand-made items, made to order based on the customer's specifications--from designer suites to luxury cars, still represent the top-most quality consumers aspire to.

The most significant advances in experience design involve the ability of a product to identify a specific individual user, change on the fly to fit the needs of this person, and contextualize the experience to the needs of that specific individual.

Some car manufacturers offer cars that remember the seat configuration settings of several drivers, and adjust the seat to each. For people who share a car, but vary significantly in body size, this is a major improvement to the car experience. It can be frustrating to re-adjust four to eight different seat options manually, each time one uses the car after the previous driver had changed all the settings.

Another example of personalized experiences is provided by some websites. After login, a website identifies the user, and adapts its look and feel, as well as content and messaging. On a site selling athletic shoes, the site can default to known values that reflect past purchases--shoe type, size, width, running style, colors, and materials for the different parts of the shoe.

Increasingly, products are no longer mass produced and stocked in anticipation for potential demand. Rather, they are made to order and manufactured only after an order has been placed. Advances in material science and manufacturing technology make it possible to offer customers a sort of bespoke product made to order--which is highly desirable.

As companies collect more data about the behavior and consumption patterns of individual customers, they can develop more nuanced ways to predict their customers' context of need, and offer the appropriate product experience at the right time and price. This resolves the choice paradox by giving the customers exactly what they need, since it was made just for them.

Motivation

Doing something hard is an experience many people naturally try to avoid. The level of difficulty is often very subjective, and a task that appears trivial to one person, is an insurmountable challenge to another person. Often, the reward for completing a difficult task is sufficient, but for tasks that require a prolonged effort, the reward may be too distant.

Saving for retirement or college, losing and maintaining body weight, quitting smoking, and maintaining a regular exercise routine, are examples of major objectives with which people struggle and for which they seek motivational help.

Until recently motivational experiences revolved around *gurus* and their "proven" methods for success, which often required the purchase of a multi-step program. From live motivational events, to self-help books and videos, a multi-billion motivational experience industry has evolved over the years, and for the most part, has proven to be very successful for those who sell such products, less so to the customers who purchase them.

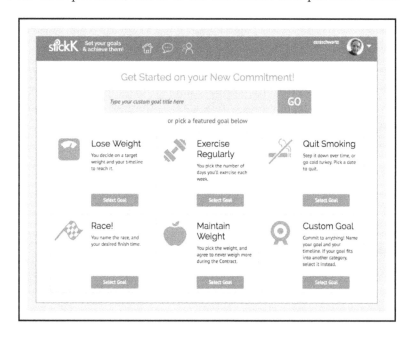

There are numerous products and services that attempt to help people stay motivated and achieve their goals, and many do not deliver on their promise. However, advances in neuroscience, psychology, and behavioral economics, coupled with the latest technologies and tools such as wearable and mobile devices, are changing the landscape of motivational experiences. We have seen the introduction of new and truly effective products with applications in healthcare, education, and finance.

For example, **stickK** (see image above) is an application that allows members set goals, stick to them, and eventually achieve them. This is accomplished by asking the user to sign a **Commitment Contract** that defines their goal--whatever it may be, describe what is needed to accomplish the goals, and finally, put money (optional) that would be lost unless the goal is met. At the time of writing, the application is free for use and has over $30 million on the line--referring to people who are using the application and have to accomplish their goals.

Experience designers who work in this space need to create experiences that anticipate the user's psychological barriers by enforcing known motivational aspects such as competitiveness, desire to excel, desire for a reward, desire to relax and enjoy, social recognition, being part of a group, and so on. Some of these elements are inherent to games. **Gamification** is an experience strategy that transforms mundane tasks into an engaging experience.

By incorporating play into experiences that are otherwise not too exciting, designers can motivate users to persist and achieve their goals. Learning is a good example. In a classroom environment, competition among students is often natural, and success is reflected in grades. Like in competitive sports, the distinction between successful and unsuccessful students can be as clear as a ballgame scoreboard.

Designers of educational and training materials regularly incorporate gamification into their products. Learning can take on the positive aspects of play. Characteristics like team spirit, collaboration, and mutual support can be part of the game, as well as desirable values such as clear objectives, benefits of practice, hard work, the desire to win. Above all--it is also fun.

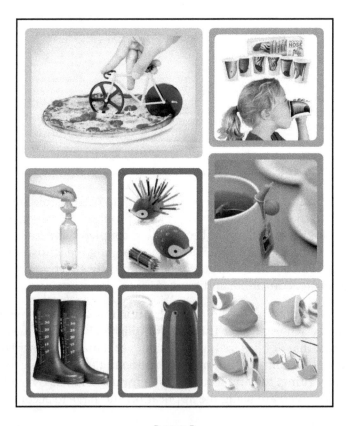

The closing example of experience design elements that contribute to engagement and fun is humor. The popular belief that laughter is good for health is now supported by scientific evidence that shows the effectiveness of laughter as a stress reliever. Certainly, humor can add a great deal to a positive user experience because it helps the user relax in stressful circumstances. The image above includes several examples of products that are clever, joyful, funny, and capable of evoking a smile. These can cheer up a person even in difficult moments.

Humor has to be approached carefully and considered within the context of its use. It has to be appropriate for the target audience. There are considerations of gender, social, and cultural taboos that should not be crossed, or, if they are meant to be crossed, there should be a good justification for doing that. A maxim to remember is the users should feel that they are laughing with the message communicated by the product, never that the product makes fun of them.

Summary

In this chapter, we looked at effective techniques designers use to harmonize surfaces, spaces, objects, sounds, and motion to support engagement, interaction, and delight--the outcomes most companies and designers aspire to have in their products.

Blending the various ingredients that make up an engaging, positive experience is complex, because multiple independent variables must integrate consistently and predictably at the right moment to deliver the desired outcome. Many of the techniques explored here have been acquired over centuries of continuous tweaking and evolution of products and design.

Delight is joyful satisfaction that results from continuous, consistent engagement with a product. It is a reproducible emotional state, an experience that does not wear off easily despite frequent use. Engagement and delight depend on functional execution of the product. It is critical that the product not only looks good and feels good but it must be good.

In the next chapter, we look at concept development and design, the phases during which designers assemble everything they know about the product's target audience, users, the company's competitive objectives, business and technical requirements, and come up with a unified design framework that ties together all the elements necessary for guiding the creation of the final product.

9

Tying It All Together - From Concept to Design

"Logic will get you from A to B. Imagination will take you anywhere."

- Albert Einstein

This chapter addresses the following questions:

- How do abstract ideas transformed to actual products that generate the envisioned experiences?
- What are the underlying design philosophies and principles that drive designers' approaches?
- What are the methods that help keep design processes consistent throughout product development?

To simplify our discussion here, the term *concept* refers to a phase in the design process which focuses on forming a design approach for the product. Also, let's assume that the idea for the product and its purpose, precede this phase. Finally, the term "design" will be used to encamps all the activities that transform an initial experience concept into detailed design specification.

In general, developing the design concept for product design is approached first at a high level and with an "everything possible" attitude. The designer should have sufficient background information about the product space to support thinking about solving design challenges, while maximizing experience opportunities and minimizing overall costs. The primary audience for concept work is internal: company stakeholders and decision-makers.

Design concepts tend to be bold, visionary, and, occasionally, somewhat removed from business or technical constraints. For designers, this is an exciting part of the project. Once the concept is approved, work commences on the more mundane phase of evolving the concept into a fully detailed design, which must take into account the realities of business and technical constraints.

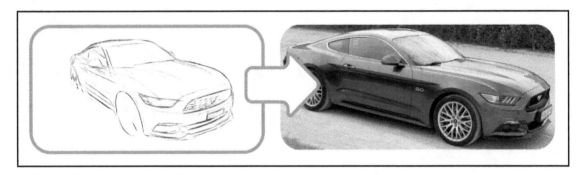

The sketch and photo in the image above represent the far ends of the concept development process, which often begins with a rough sketch, and ends with the final product. The car is Ford's iconic Mustang, a model that gained many fans since its introduction in the early 1960s. Every few years, the car receives a design refresh. The experience design challenge is significant because of the strong emotional ties that bind this particular car to its fans and loyal customers. The success of the Mustang, in terms of sales and profit, rests primarily on a redesign that communicates to potential buyers the continuity between what they are buying and the design of the automotive legend.

Mustang owners enjoy experiences that extend far beyond mere driving. Owning a Mustang allows them to communicate to the world something personal and important about themselves. The personification of one's personality and identity in what is essentially a competitively priced mass-produced product is the true essence of commercial Experience Design.

A successful design often needs to bridge gaps between experience attributes, which have originally endeared the product to its customers, and changes brought about by technology advances, shifts in customers preferences, and evolving aesthetic sensibilities. Change means evolving the competitive landscape and customers' expectations, so a new design needs to be fresh and bold, while referencing the product's experience heritage.

Projecting a desired image of the brand is an important factor that influences the approach to concept design. For example, designers of established luxury items, while often benefiting from full creative license and access to the best materials and latest manufacturing technologies, must fuse innovation with references to established patterns. A couple of common approaches to doing that are as follows:

- The "understatement" design philosophy is guided by the idea of exclusivity. Only those "in the know", usually also the ones who can actually afford the product, appreciate that the clean, unpretentious, and often old-fashioned looking design cloaks the finest materials, technology, and craftsmanship, with no compromise on quality and full attention to the smallest of details. These products are typically very expensive, and the essence of the brand experience they deliver is the exclusive sense of ultimate quality and reliability, a self-confidence that supposedly matches the budgets and sensibilities of the target customers.
- The "bold" statement design, as its name suggests, seeks a complete departure from tradition and flair in favor of emotions such as awe, excitement, envy, and desire. Designers are asked to take full advantage of the finest materials, technology, and craftsmanship, and come up with a unique yet exclusive experience, which is totally new.

Once an experience concept has been approved, the shift to pragmatics is rapid; the transition is not always smooth, and occasionally, the gap between the concept and final product is frustrating. Designers are expected to be creative despite budget and schedule pressures, stakeholders who constantly change their mind about key aspects of the product, technical limitations, and other unexpected challenges.

This is the nature of design--a constant balancing act aimed at minimizing the gap between an aspirational concept and the product that ends up being delivered. There is no set formula to reach an optimal balance because designers operate under a wide spectrum of parameters:

- Processes that worked well in the past do not guarantee future success. Times and circumstances change, the nature of experience objectives changes, as do the people who are involved in the project.

- Processes don't always apply to all industries and all types of design disciplines
- Designers operate on a spectrum that ranges from having complete control over the final product outcome, to having little influence over established processes in the organization
- Designers' personalities and design philosophy guide the methods and activities that make them successful

Design has been evolving for thousands of years, and throughout practitioners developed and successfully used techniques, such as sketching and prototyping, to transform their ideas into artifacts that communicate experience concepts to their clients. Today, digital design tools provide designers with a much extended array of exploration options--such as 3D printing--that enable the rapid evaluation of ideas at lower costs.

As design has become dependent on multi-disciplinary team collaboration, we see a shift in the process of idea generation. In contrast to the designer as the primary source of concepts, the use of ideation and design workshops has gained popularity as an effective generator of valid experience ideas in a team context. One of the designer's responsibilities is therefore to guide the experience creation process by blending the set of available activities in a way that best fits the design project's context.

Design philosophy

June 1922 was an exciting month in the period known as Modernism. News about daring adventures and innovations fueled the imagination and aspirations of people, regardless of their class, religion, or country. The Norwegian explorer, Roald Amundsen set out on an expedition to the North Pole, the aviation pioneer Henry Berliner demonstrated a helicopter prototype, and the American President Harding became the first president to use radio broadcasts.

During that time, in Chicago, a competition was announced by the Chicago Tribune corporation, a newspaper publisher, for architects to submit proposals for "The world's most beautiful office building."

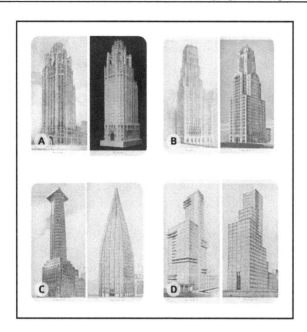

To this day, the Tribune's bold call for proposals is striking in its daring attempt to qualify a winning submission using a subjective measure. "Beauty" is after all, in the eye of the beholder. The image above includes some of the submissions to the competition. The wide range of approaches reflects all the major design philosophies of the time, philosophies that are still relevant today:

- **Proposal A:** The skyscraper is inspired by Gothic architecture dating centuries back, a style which was used to construct some of the largest cathedrals ever built, such as the Notre Dame in Paris.
  This is a juxtaposition of the traditional and the modern--an intricate brick layering, flying buttresses, and other traditional design elements, all for show. None of them actually perform weight bearing or support role unlike the original elements in giant medieval cathedrals. An invisible, state-of-the-art steel skeleton takes care of that. Instead, these elements support a design that aims to transpose the symbolic meaning and magnificence of those towering cathedrals to a commercial skyscraper. Elements so closely associated with religious settings are conjured to grace the secular, yielding an association that equates the two.
- **Proposal B**: While somewhat similar to A, the proposal provides a very different experience. The tapered shape and flat surfaces extenuate the structure's broad shoulders and the building's projection of modernity, confidence, and stability. This is very much the image that the city of Chicago has adopted for itself.

- **Proposal C**: Two very different approaches sharing a daring, out-of-the-box concept that generates a strong response even today. In the first, a giant Greek column, the design strips out all elements of ancient Greek and Roman architecture and leaves a single motif in the form of a giant, ridiculously massive Doric style column. The second concept, inspired by the contemporary excitement about rocketry is shaped like a giant cone that is reminiscent of a rocket.

- **Proposal D**: This concept was conceived by architect-designers who spear-headed the very influential Bauhaus movement. This was perhaps the only proposal that was driven by a very strong, ideologically infused philosophy of design and of the role of design in the lives of people.

In the end, proposal A won, and the building has been gracing Chicago's skyline since the completion of its construction in 1925. Thinking about these proposals, an interesting question to ask today, nearly a century after the competition, is which of these proposals has actually withstood the test of time, and has the winner indeed been the most beautiful building in the world?

Modernism was a turning point in the approach to the role of design in creating an experience of the *new* in buildings, products, and wearables. Modernism was a philosophy and a movement that swept the world with the excitement of endless possibilities. Paul Klee's work, *Tweeting Machine*, shown in Figure 2, hints at the more sinister implications of experience in a design-heavy technological age. It is as relevant today as when it was painted in 1922

People have been creating amazing artifacts of great design value, and thinking about design philosophy and process for thousands of years. In recent centuries, industrialization, technological breakthroughs, and mass production have greatly popularized design thinking and philosophy, restoring the interest in questions such as:

- Should the designers believe in, stick to, and apply a single design philosophy to guide their entire design work, regardless of what they are asked to design?
- Should the designers be agnostic to design-philosophy and use any design approach that best fits the product they are asked to design?

Few designers are in a position that allows them to practice the first option, but the philosophical debate among practitioners is still lively. Naturally, designers are drawn to design approaches that fit with their personal preferences.

The past and future

The following image illustrates four contrasting design approaches to furniture design. Each of the four designs reflects a distinctive aesthetic approach and intended to generate a very different experience.

- **Approach A**: This is a sample of a design philosophy and style known as Scandinavian Design. It embodies the ideas of minimalism, expressed in clean lines, smooth surfaces, and the composition of shapes, originally inspired by Nordic settings. It values natural materials and high-quality production. Simplicity and functionality are the promise of timeless experience, afforded by comfort and quality. Similar approaches were taken without any relationship to Scandinavia, in Japan, China, Africa, and America.

- **Approach B**: This design takes its cues from aristocratic high style. Known as Retro Design. This is a philosophy that aims to associate historical symbols of high-class with quality and aesthetics. In this case, the armchair echoes furniture used in the royal courts of Europe. As opposed to the classless Scandinavian Design, Retro Design is often meant to invoke an experience of a high class.

- **Approach C**: This colorful, imaginative, and fun design represents an approach to Experience Design that yields a unique product. The chair is attention-grabbing and it promises to provide a comfortable seating experience. It will certainly not blend into a room, and that is fine.

- **Approach D**: This design represents a true out-of-the-box design approach; the product is abstract. It takes a few seconds to digest the form and realize this arrangement of cylinders could actually serve as a reclining armchair.

Another class of Experience Design extends to various types of technology devices and gadgets. *"A technical product is only perfect when it's aesthetically perfect too."* This is the design philosophy of Ettore Bugatti, the founder, designer, and manufacturer of the venerable Bugatti brand.

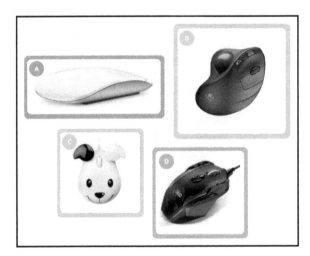

Today, most products are technical products, and approaches to experience aesthetics vary greatly, as illustrated in the design of an input device affectionately known as the "mouse."

The mouse had an important role in the personal computer revolution of the 1980s. It enabled the user to perform direct manipulation of objects on the screen, an interaction pattern known as "point-and-click." It represented a major departure from the command-line interface of prior generations of personal computers.

- **Approach A**: This represents Apple's philosophy of simplicity and elegance. When this model, the *Apple Magic Mouse,* was released in 2009, its visual and tactile experience made it stand out--no buttons. The quality of the materials and the underlying technology allows it to function as a regular mouse despite having only a single button, and its entire top surface hints at the sophisticated technology underneath that supports it. The simplicity of user experience often means that the heavy lifting has to be performed by the system.

- **Approach B**: This represents the ergonomic Experience Design approach to technology. The guiding principle of this approach is that the healthiest and therefore the best user experience comes from designs based on deep understanding of human anatomy and physiology. In this approach, the device's shape and operation match the body's structure, functions and constraints. Repetitive Strain Syndrome has become a serious problem for people and employers. The problem was been attributed in part to product designs that were ignorant or dismissive of the human body. This generated the demand for ergonomic design.

- **Approach C**: This is a "cutesy" fun design approach that transforms the device from a purely functional object to one that is designed to evoke warm emotional feelings; shaped as a cute pet toy, its non-technical appearance stands in contrast to the seriousness of computers.

- **Approach D**: The design of this souped-up, feature-rich device communicates its technical abilities with an angular, streamlined shape and evokes the futuristic, science-fiction imagery of a space craft or weapon. The use of the glowing blue light when the mouse turned on, serves both functional and design functions.

Design has an important role in preserving a culture through the careful design evolution of its artifacts and products. The following image shows two instances of the same product, a newspaper--in this example, the New York Times; image **A** is the printed edition of the paper, and image **B** is the digital edition, as viewed on the monitor of a desktop computer:

The visual design of both instances is very similar, and it is easy to see that the objective of the digital experience has been to maintain continuity with the look of the printed paper, as manifested in the use of a multi-columns grid, and the sparse use of color, which is primarily reserved for ads and photographs.

Why might this design approach be important? For a publication such as the Times, which has had been continuously published since September 18, 1851, the look of the paper goes beyond tradition. The message that the experience delivers to its readers, and to the public in general, is a promise to preserve the same journalistic standards and values that had made this particular newspaper one of the most influential news publications in the world.

The following image compares the design of the New York Times (**A**) to that of another the well-regarded newspaper--*The Guardian* (**B**). The Guardian has been published in the United Kingdom since 1821, although until 1959 it was called the *Manchester Guardian*. The digital edition of the paper looks very different from that of the Times. Its layout and use of color--very much in-line with general approach to web aesthetics--signals continuity through adaptation to changing times.

The same set of design principles drive these two very different outcomes to what is essentially are very similar products-- Under the "skin" of a traditional or contemporary look is a relentless drive to apply the most advanced tools, methodologies, and technologies to develop and deliver a design system that best fits the product, target audience, and individual users.

We can find an interesting equivalent to approaching tradition and contemporary in the design of two familiar websites. The following shows the landing pages of Amazon (**A**) and Craigslist (**B**). As of March 2017, Amazon was ranked fourth in the United States, with close to 75 million daily users, whereas Craigslist ranked seventh, with nearly 22 million daily visitors. These are staggering numbers, and with so many repeat visitors, something about the experience of both sites must be right, despite a very different experience at each destination. As the saying goes: you can't argue with success.

The Amazon experience for desktop computer customers has evolved gradually--some would argue, very gradually, since 1995. Obviously, with hundreds of millions of annual visitors, any dramatic changes to the experience risk causing significant financial damage, if users are disoriented by, or are not happy with, the change.

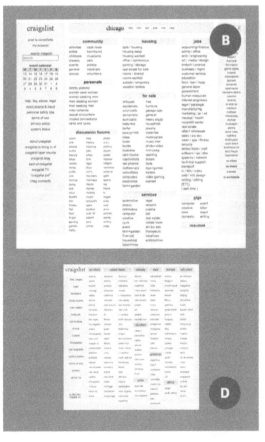

Amazon has advanced its website design, constantly tweaking the visual and interaction sophistication of the website's header, navigation systems, and page layout to accommodate an ever growing number of departments and products. Craigslist's website, which started in 1996 at about the time Amazon did, stuck with its original text-based, hyperlink-heavy design.

Although this experience may appear very outdated in today's hyper visual age, given that the site still maintains such a large number of visitors, there is no doubt that this experience works.

Like Amazon, Craigslist is an example of a company that understands its target audiences, and its website design is meant to provide visitors with an optimal experience. The text interface has several benefits--it is straightforward and easy to understand, text lends itself to fast and efficient visual scanning--important for a classified ad business--page downloads are fast and do not consume much bandwidth, it works on any device with Web-browsing, and finally, the development and maintenance costs of a text-based interface are relatively low.

The preceding image illustrates competing design approaches to transform traditional products through technology. Each of the approaches represents a step in the evolution, revolution, and paradoxically, the eventual extinction of experience.

In contrast to earlier generations of designers, contemporary designers have a wider range of design directions to follow or invent because of the endless opportunities afforded by technology. However, to what extent should technological advances drive the nature of experience?

Can the design of established product categories depart from experience conventions that have been established over decades and sometimes centuries of use? The three watches shown in the preceding image reflect design philosophies and approach to this question.

- **Approach A**: The Apple watch is at once an attempt to revolutionize the category of wrist watches, while attempting to maintain continuity with a design system for the company's existing product line. The product can be configured to look very much like a traditional timepiece, but the face can be customized to any number of unique and very untraditional looks. However, beyond just showing the time, the watch experiences through many other functionalities in apps. This is similar to Apple's approach to the mobile phone, but while the look and feel of the iPhone were revolutionary at the time it was introduced, the watch--coming nearly a decade later--is only an evolutionary step.

- **Approach B**: Withings' approach to smartwatches is very different from Apple's in that the watch' time-keeping hardware makes the product look very much like a traditional timepiece, but its underlying technology provides the user with advanced capabilities. Most significantly, and in contrast to traditional watches, one sets the time of a Withings watch through an app on the user's phone, and not by a mechanical apparatus inside the case. The experience is a blend of modern and traditional.

- **Approach C**: The EmoPulse design might look quite futuristic to contemporary customers due to its wide but thin rounded sheet of molded plastic and glass, which brings to mind an ornamental bracelet that might be seen in a Star Trek episode. It does not look at all like a typical wrist watch. The Apple watch seem bulkier and heavier in comparison, the EmoPulse design promises an experience that attracts attention.

Design questions that come to mind when thinking about these watches are as follows:

- To what extent should designers be carried away by design possibilities that are afforded by new technology? In other words, just because we can, does it mean we should?

- To what degree should designers support a reactionary desire to preserve the product's experience and history, regardless of technological possibilities that make some of the past irrelevant--for example, designing the most amazing experience for a horse-drawn carriage just when Ford began manufacturing the less sumptuous, but revolutionary Model T.

First impressions

While designers are constrained by the desires of those who pay for the design, their influence can be significant because of the design philosophy and the power of the user experience to transform a product.

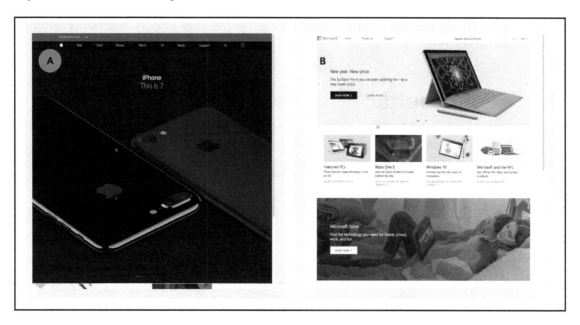

The designer is responsible for conceiving an approach that is technology-driven and yet can be either a departure from the past or a compelling enhancement or continuation of the it.

The last example, illustrated in the preceding image, deals with the question--how important is the impact of the first impression to the overall experience?

- **Approach A**: As exemplified by Apple's home page, this favors a minimalist visual appeal, that is purely aesthetic. Apple sells many products, but the experience choice is to impress the visitor with a welcoming introduction that communicates the company's overall design philosophy of sophisticated yet simple and clean design. Regardless of the varying needs of visitors to the site, there is an assumption of sharing the same design philosophy that binds company and its customers.

- **Approach B**: This represents Microsoft's home page. For a couple of decades, these two companies were on the opposite side of the experience spectrum, and evidence of this contrast can still be traced today. While the site's design is certainly contemporary, it attempts to communicate multiple facets of the company and addresses very different types of audience. The design does not attempt to unify the experience, but rather to apply a generically clean experience to the home page and make it easy for each segment to find its destination under the brand.

The "cookie cutter"

Why reinvent the wheel? Why spend time and money on new experience when it is possible to reuse proven existing ones? Is the experience so important that it must be unique to the product, or, will customers be satisfied with an experience that is good, familiar, and functional, but not very original?

These are very valid questions, and in fact, most product Experience Design follows in the footsteps of some previous approaches. Relatively few companies can afford or are even interested in revolutionizing their product experience because the effort is expensive and time-consuming.

We are all familiar with the cookie cutter, of course. Cookies are associated with pleasure--a fun snack or dessert, and when shaped as animals or geometric forms, they are more pleasing to look at than irregular mound of baked dough. For cookies, having a shape is more satisfying than not having one, and the fact that the cookies are uniform does not minimize the warm and appetizing experience they generate.

The preceding image illustrates examples from architecture and software design that provides another angle to consider the benefits and potential limitations of the cookie-cutter Experience Design--the suburban development (**A**) and user interfaces based on popular design ecosystems, such as Google's Material design or Microsoft's Metro design (**B**):

- **Pros**: This has significantly reduced costs of construction and ongoing maintenance to those who use existing patterns that deliver proven and tested experience. Faster development and builds and some degree of flexibility in the configuration of various patterns allows for sufficient customization and personalization within the design framework. This works well for customers who value the familiarity, reliability and predictability of such patterns.
- **Cons**: It spreads a homogeneous look and feel that make it difficult for the individual person or company to stand out in the crowd. there is less flexibility in the ability to create new design systems that address specific needs that are not provided by the framework.

Accessible design

From concept to finished product, designers face important moral and practical civil-rights questions of equal access to all users:

- Can experience designers place design considerations ahead of the needs of people with disabilities? Is a bold design statement that will do wonders to the product but render the product unusable to a user justifiable?
- Are experience designers responsible for pressing the issue of accessibility on corporations, and advocating accessible design, despite the potential added costs associated with the production of accessible products?

The sad reality is that society, architects and designers included, has ignored the issue of accessibility for the most part of human history. It has been through long civil rights struggles that the needs of people with disabilities have finally been codified. The **Americans with Disabilities Rights** (**ADA**), for example, was signed into law only in 1990. In a nutshell, the law states that:

> *The Americans with Disabilities Act of 1990 (ADA) prohibits discrimination and ensures equal opportunity for persons with disabilities in employment, State and local government services, public accommodations, commercial facilities, and transportation.*

Similar laws exist in many countries around the world. After years of ineffective attempts to encourage organizations to invest in making their products and services accessible, fear of expensive legal action is leading to an increase in the number of accessible physical and digital products.

One of the fundamental priorities when thinking about accessible design is eliminating the social stigma around mental and physical disabilities by ensuring the full inclusion of all people in the same experience by accommodating special needs. In other words, don't segregate users with disabilities-- for example, the common practice at the turn of the century, of creating text-only version of websites, sometimes with less content, for visually impaired users. These site were meant to be processed by screen readers and other assistive-technology devices, and while better than having no access at all, still were a crude solution.

Today on the digital front, leading vendors of operating systems such as Apple, Google, and Microsoft fully integrated a wide array of accessibility features into their operating systems, making it easy for software developers to make their own products natively accessible.

In the United States, as in other countries, ADA has brought a welcome improvement to the physical world, as laws and the enforcement of codes governing accessibility eliminated barriers that rendered many types of public property--including government and commercial buildings, businesses, sidewalks, and public transportation--inaccessible to people with disabilities. The improvements ended up benefiting everyone, not just the disabled--parents with baby strollers, people with shopping carts, and delivery people benefit from mandated sidewalk slopes, for example.

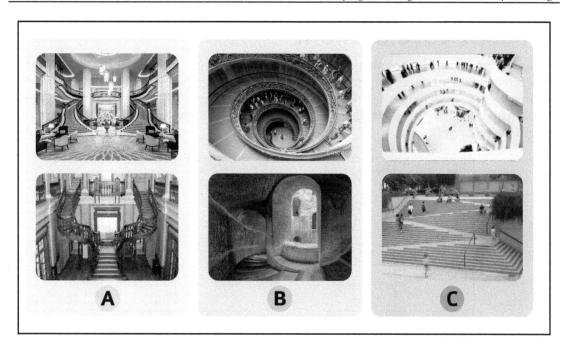

Staircases provide highly visible evidence of the extent of taking into account accessibility considerations in design thinking. The preceding image has a number of examples that illustrate fundamental issues of experience accessibility as reflected in the design of staircases.

Concept development

Concept development is a formal part of the Experience Design process. The purpose of this phase is to help the designer synthesize all the information gathered in previous phases of the project--through activities that are mostly formal and analytical--and define the design approach and solution that address the product objectives and needs in unique and engaging ways.

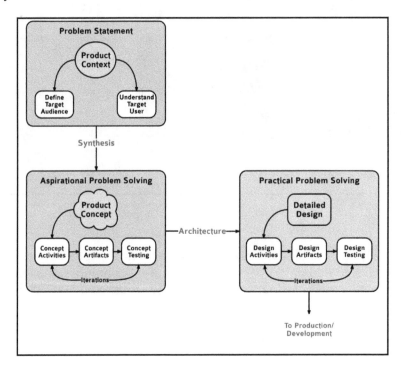

One way to think about concept development is as an advanced form of problem solving, as illustrated in the preceding figure:

- **Define a problem statement**: The early phases of the product design process are focused on discovery and research activities--Company X wants to create a unique experience for its product Y, which will focus on target audience Z, and others. What should this experience be like?

- **Aspirational problem solving**: To answer this question, the designer needs to switch to a different mode of thinking--from research and analysis to synthesis guided by design-thinking and experimentation. Concepts are, by nature, more concerned with capturing the essence of the experience at a high level, or "wide strokes", by defining a set of matching guiding principles that are used throughout the development process.
- **Practical problem solving**: Once a concept has been refined, tested, and approved, the project can shift its gear to the next phase of defining the design's nuts and bolts, that is, transforming a high-level concept into detailed design specifications, that will guide the actual engineering and build of the product. Throughout this phase, the designer extends and, often, diverges from the original concepts to address specific known and new business requirements, technical constraints, and production deadlines.

The word aspirational in the design context can be interpreted to mean a solution that is not burdened by budget, schedule, technical, or any other constraints--a "pie in the sky" exploration of the problem statement. For a limited window of time, the design team is given the freedom to aim at the best possible experience solution for the design problem statement.

The concept development process includes a defined set of activities that are meant to generate concrete design artifacts that can be tested for rejection or continued iteration. The opportunity to think "out-of-the-box" can pay off, if it leads to an approach that sheds current inefficiencies and complexities and improves the overall experience.

There are no set formulas, processes, or methods that are uniformly used for concept development across all product categories or by all design practitioners. That is just fine, because the context of people and problems is variable--some people may have formal training in design and familiarity with the tools, techniques, and methodologies, and yet not be able to come up with a creative solution to design problems. Others, with little knowledge of formal design, may come up with very creative solutions to the very same problems.

Moreover, teams of designers using identical processes and methods might come up with different solutions to the same problem, and in different contexts, the same designer might come up with completely distinct approaches to the same design challenge.

Finally, there are well-established concept development techniques, that have proven to be effective and productive under some circumstances. These include, but are certainly not limited to, the Double Diamond design approach and variations on design thinking methodologies by IDEO, Stanford University, IBM, and Google. Some work well for individuals and others are meant to be used in group settings. Their purpose is to introduce consistency and process to support effective idea generation, which will increase the quality and number of ideas that may be relevant to the project.

It is important to remember, however, that design thinking is an innate human trait, and people have been "design thinking" quite wonderfully throughout the evolution of our species.

Activities

Design is one of the occupations that is unapologetic about its dependency on the good services of a mysterious Muse--the Greek goddess of Greek in charge of inspiration--shown in the following image.

In Greek, the word *mousa* means "art" or "poetry" and according to ancient Greek mythology, the muses were the daughters of Zeus, the "head" god of Olympus, and Mnemosyne, the goddess of memory. Throughout the ages, the muses, who in antiquity encompassed nearly all aspects of learning and creation became, in our times, explicitly associated with creativity.

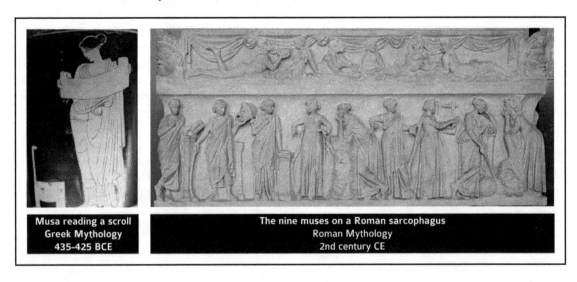

Musa reading a scroll
Greek Mythology
435-425 BCE

The nine muses on a Roman sarcophagus
Roman Mythology
2nd century CE

The business reality means that the need for the inspiration, or rather, the need for exploration of design ideas, is real. Most designers are methodical in their exploration process, using various techniques to iterate and refine through various experimentations.

In design, there are multiple viable approaches to the same problem, but the mix of circumstances that leads to the creation of these options is part art and part science. The blending of art and science is fuzzy and, excitingly, unpredictable--which is one reason design and designers--justifiably or not--enjoy special privileges. They know how to materialize the full experience potential in a product that might otherwise be dull and uninspiring.

The following section is meant to provide a small sample of techniques that are used--with some variation--for the generation and evaluation of design ideas. The methods combine speed, spontaneity, evaluation, and the scoring of multiple concepts and to narrow down to a successful design candidate.

Sketching

Sketching is probably one of the oldest forms of visual brainstorming. The power of sketching stems from several advantages:

- It is possible to generate many ideas in a short amount of time.
- Sketching has minimal requirements--a writing instrument and a surface to sketch on. The proverbial napkin is a famous example. The range of possibilities, from a pencil and paper to mobile apps, is very wide.
- It can be done almost anytime, anywhere.
- No need to be a celebrated illustrator--rough and basic sketches can do the job. It is easy to add notes to clarify.
- It is easy to show, share, and come up with new variations.
- Sketching is cheap.

The following image includes sample sketches dating from the 15th century. It may seem that these examples are very much in contrast to the list above, since today these sketches are considered to be works of art in their own right. Yet, while scribbled by extremely gifted people, they were not created as artwork, but rather, as quick sketches meant to help idea development.

- Leonardo Da Vinci's exploration of a device for lifting weights (**A**)

- Michelangelo's sketch of the Dome of the St. Peter Cathedral, for which he was, at some point, the chief architect (**B**)

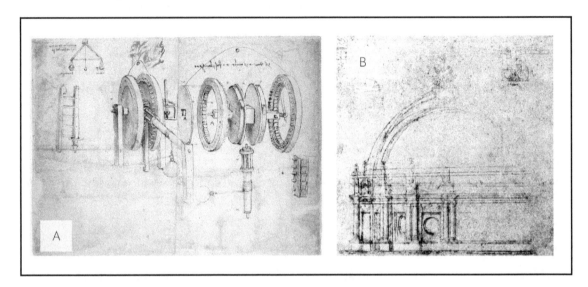

Sketching works well to explore forms, proportions, configurations, and transformations. The following image includes a number of sketching artifacts--samples of usage in architecture (**A**), automotive design (**B**), package design (**C**), and web design (**D**).

The use of these artifacts is typically limited to the designer and is not an expected deliverable. It is an exercise that allows the designer to flesh out some of the core visual properties that the product will express through its physical shape as a three-dimensional object or as a page--digital or printed. As a communication tool, sketching helps discuss the structure and organization of layouts and content, user journeys, and task flows, almost anything, really.

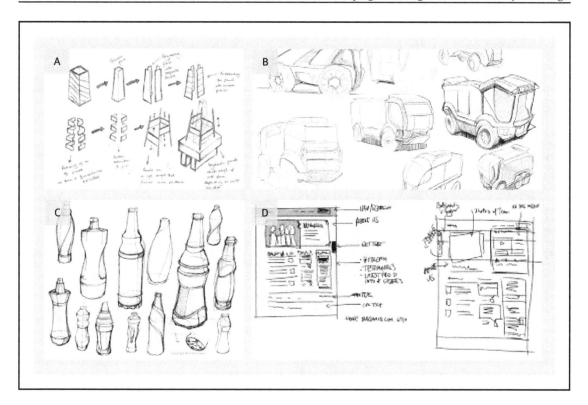

Mind mapping

The early phases of product design typically generate massive amounts of data, the result of discovery activities that included stakeholder interviews, various forms of audience, user and competitive research, and other activities. As was explored in the previous chapters, this information helps define the product, including the desired experience strategy.

The information can also be used for concept development by helping the designer "see the wood from the trees" and the technique to accomplish that is called mind mapping.

In the context of forests and trees, it is interesting to note that, similar to sketching, visualizing knowledge with diagrams has been used for centuries, dating back at least to the 3rd century CA, and is attributed to the Roman philosopher, Porphyry.

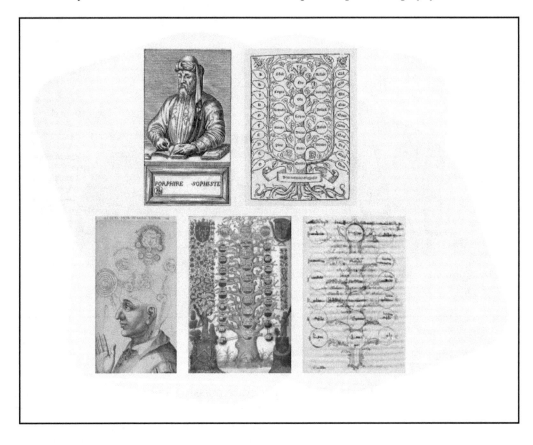

Porphyry, whose portrait you can see in the preceding image, was supposedly the first to organize information--in his case, Aristotle's Categories--in a diagram known as a Porphyry tree, examples of which are also provided in the same image. Today, there are many open source and commercial software tools for authoring and sharing mind maps, such as FreeMind, MindManager, and iMindMap.

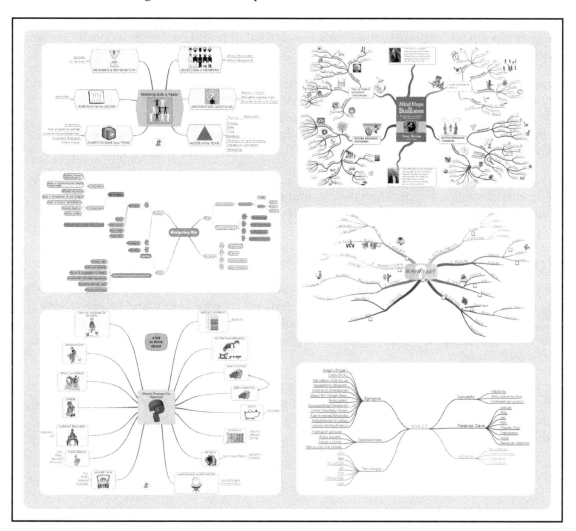

Mind-mapping software products help organize and visualize data in compelling graphic ways, as illustrated in the preceding image. The free-form interaction makes it easy and fast to manually organize a large number of unstructured ideas, thoughts, and other bits of information and turn them into a coherent structure.

Clusters and the items nested in them can be easily named, expanded, and collapsed--items can be moved between groups, groups can be nested in other groups, and so on. The designer can quickly explore various arrangements of data and evolve the concept to a final version.

Mind-maps are significantly more effective than spreadsheets in communicating complex relationships because large amounts of data are presented to business and other stakeholders visually--initially at a high level, as a few clusters of data; the discussion progresses to details, the designer can gradually drill into each of the clusters, and discuss its composition and relationship to the rest of the structure.

Mind mapping is a domain-agnostic data-visualization technique that has endless uses. In the context of software application design, and example developing the information architecture of the application can be considered as an example.

Storyboards

The Bayeux tapestry is an embroidered storyboard of sorts, 230 feet long and 20 inches tall (**A**) . It depicts the events that lead to the invasion and capture of England by the armies of William, the Conqueror. This artifact was created about nine centuries ago, in early medieval Europe, and it depicts several key events throughout England, where important battles took place.

The idea of sequencing events in a pictorial way in order to capture, document, and communicate an event or idea has been used throughout the World for centuries, from Europe, with its tapestries, tiles, and triptych imagery (**B**) to China and the use of scenic scrolls that depicted road journeys (**C**).

In more recent times, we are familiar with the use of storyboards in the movie-making and video industry, and especially in animation. The use of storyboards for concept development in the context of Experience Design has been evolving, as time-based interaction patterns and experiences are being introduced to more products.

Storyboards are a very effective means of communicating a narrative; each tile depicts a key event in the experience process. It is possible to follow the user experience arc as a narrative that flows from initial exposure to the product, to various scenarios of its use. Storyboards are now being merged with journey maps to provide a complementary visual reference to various touchpoints throughout the experience.

Visualizing the experience through storyboards helps designers and stakeholders share a unified understanding of the experience narrative, identify gaps, and simplify processes; it is easy to understand the contribution of each storyboard card to the overall narrative. For example, if a card can be eliminated from the storyboard without disrupting the overall sequence flow, it may mean that the card, and hence the process step it represents, is extraneous.

Designer versus collaborative design

On the spectrum of design conception and development, we find the following two scenarios:

- The designer is at the center of the design conception process, solely responsible for conceiving and controlling the entire design approach. This individualistic approach is common in fashion design and architecture, where the brand of the individual designer is a major selling point of the resulting experience.
  The designer researches the product and user context and then forms a design vision, that is heavily influenced by the designer's biases, preferences, style, and methods of work. In a way, the client is seeking in the designer a transcendental quality that differentiates that designer's work from that of numerous others operating in the same industry. In this scenario, the individual designer is a celebrity, and in a way, so also is the experience--people desire designer products, after all.

- Collaborative design is on the other end of that spectrum; the designer's individuality is less dominant, and the design is not an extension of the designer's ego. Instead, the designer partners with relevant project stakeholders and potential users of the product--all typically nondesigners--to work jointly on the design.
  The designer still owns the process and is responsible for facilitating collaborative design sessions, curating ideas and feedback from the team and iterating the evolving design in prototypes and other forms.

In practice, variations on both scenarios take place but, regardless, the contribution and influence of nondesigners can be significant, and several questions typically follow:

- Why bother with a designer on the team, if the end result is based on so much influence from non-designers? In other words, can business people who collaborate only with engineers be successful?
- How can a designer be successful if non-designers continuously muddle with the design?

- Is there a risk that the inclusion of non-designers will limit innovative experience concepts due to their lack of design experience?

Generally, however, practice shows that collaborative design can be extremely successful if managed correctly; to begin with, collaboration rules, their purpose to establish a clear understanding of who is responsible for what, and expectations as to the degree to which the designer needs to actually implement the feedback from participants in the design should be set.

Collaborative design is potentially more time-consuming; the designer needs to develop and coordinate workshops--not an easy task when busy stakeholders are involved. Activities need to be guided and facilitated in order to be productive and avoid wasting the teams' valuable time.

Another argument in support of collaborative design is that the final experience approach benefits from real-time inputs from people who are closely familiar with the product, and provide the designer with critiques and advice regarding constraints and opportunities that the designer is not aware of.

There are risks to both design scenarios. In the "celebrity designer" model, influential designers often conceive stunning revolutionary design approaches, and yet there is a risk that the design will lead to the failure of the final product, because the designs masks critical business or technical issues.

The following image includes several examples of striking designs by top architects. For a variety of reasons, these designs, despite the success of the experience they generated, were very problematic for the clients who paid for the design. Of course, many of the works by these designers did turn out to be a success.

The risks in collaborative design are often related to the unpredictability of working with non-designers, on tasks that depend on some familiarity with design iteration. For example, designers are trained and experienced in extrapolating the final look and feel and interaction patterns of raw drafts. They work from an almost abstract high level as they introduce more details. Many non-designers need the small details in order to get the intent and full potential of the object. As a result, the designer might be forced to get into detailed design work well before the basic concept has matured enough.

Refining concepts

Although designers are as likely to conceive of concepts in the shower in the office, it is rare that initial concepts are full and detailed at a level that addresses the entire set of a product's objectives.

In some cases, concepts that show initial promise end up being dropped after additional thought is given to how the experience might unfold, technical difficulties, and other limitations. In other cases, the first concept conceived is also the one that leads to the desirable approach.

Then, there are cases where the designer or the design team end up going through multiple approaches, zig-zagging until the right concept is found; occasionally, a good concept is never found, and a compromise is implemented instead. In all cases, it is impossible to predict the path to a successful concept. Often, it is a matter of sheer luck.

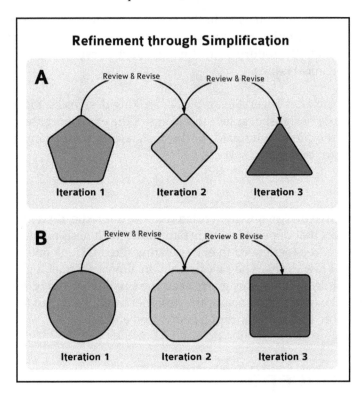

Either way, a promising design concept typically must go through a process of refinement. The preceding figure illustrates two common scenarios of refinement through simplification:

- In case **A**, the initial concept, iteration 1 is represented by a shape with five lines. After a review and feedback, the designer realizes that the objectives can be met by eliminating one of the lines, and thus achieving some efficiencies. After another review and additional feedback, and in the third iteration, the final concept that the designer proposes has only three lines.
  In this example, the refinement process enables the designer to simplify the approach by 40%--a reduction that might have a considerable positive impact on costs and the final experience.

- In case **B**, the designer's initial concept is shaped as a circle. After review and feedback, the designer determines that a different shape is needed to support the experience, and the second iteration morphs into an octagon, a shape that resembles the initial circle shape, but is also decidedly very different.
  After another review and feedback, the designer's third and wining proposal is a square--a simplification of the second concept, but an entirely different experience from both earlier concepts; the third concept has been simplified but also very different from the starting point.

Each iteration of the concept is a step that gets the team closer to the final product. Still, the experience foundations established in the initial concept should be clearly recognizable in the final version.

Prototyping

The word prototype is derived from the Greek word "prōtotupos", which meant "a first or primitive form." In Medieval Latin, the word evolved to mean "original, primitive", and today, it is referred to mostly as a key artifact in the design process of any product, be it physical or digital.

The fifteenth-century Italian architect, Leon Battista Alberti describes in his book *On the Art of Building in Ten Books*, an event from the first-century BC in which Julius Caesar,

> *"completely demolished a house on his estate in Nemi, because it did not totally meet with his approval." Alberti then recommends that practitioners keep "the time-honored custom, practiced by the best builders, of preparing not only drawings and sketches but also models of wood or any other material..."*

Julius Cesar, the ruler of the Roman Empire, was probably not acting in the capricious, short-tempered manner of an autocrat. Rather, we can think of him as a typical client, reacting negatively to a design that did has not been reviewed with him prior to building, and the end result did not meet his expectations.

Prototype help solve a serious communication challenge--How can the designer share ideas about the look and feel of the product with clients and other stakeholders so that the latter can evaluate the fit of the approach to the product's needs, afford feasibility assessments, and approve or modify prior to moving ahead to the detailed design.

Alberti expresses this through this quote:

> *"Having constructed those models, it will be possible to examine clearly and consider thoroughly the relationship between the site and the surrounding district, the shape of the area, the number and order of parts of a building. It will also allow one to increase or decrease the size of those elements freely, to exchange them, and make new proposals and alterations until everything fits together well and meets with approval. Furthermore, it will provide a surer indication of the likely costs, which is not unimportant, by allowing one to calculate costs."*

Despite the reference to buildings, this text sounds very contemporary and relevant to experience prototyping in general. Alberti outlines the benefits of prototyping, such as the ability to articulate the layout, the hierarchy of entities, the organization of elements, the order of entities, and also the ability to use the prototype for the estimation of complexity and cost.

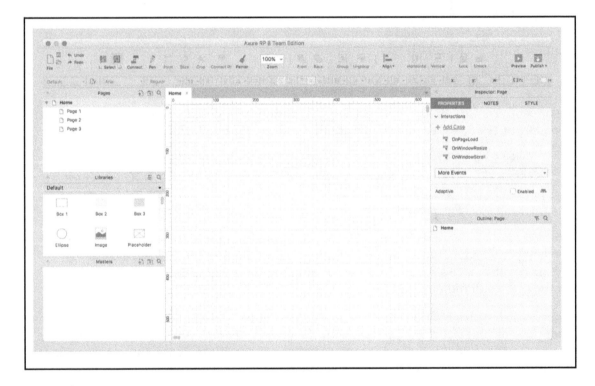

The preceding screenshot is of **Axure RP**, a popular prototyping tool used by UX designers who create user experiences for software, be it for web or mobile applications. The software enables designers at all skill levels to create prototypes with various degrees of fidelity-- from simple click-troughs, which are similar to a PowerPoint slide show, to highly detailed interactive simulations of the intended software.

Prototyping software, in general, should support team collaboration for multi-designer projects, simulate desktop and mobile experiences, and support Macintosh, Windows, and all common browsers.

Some key experiences that designers can communicate with prototyping software products are as follows:

- **Action and response**: The prototype needs to simulate key scenarios that a user would perform, and the product's appropriate responses to actions the user is taking. Scenarios could involve multiple steps and include branching subscenarios based on contextual conditions. The prototype should demonstrate these interaction and the user's ability to complete them in a satisfactory way.

- **Context awareness**: This is a personalized experience based on login; the prototype needs to simulate how the system will render for different users, based on the user role and entitlements. Common examples are e-commerce and banking applications. For non-registered users, such sites provide a "public" face and an experience that is somewhat generic. They may display special offers to entice users to register. A registered user may get information based on previous purchases, preferences they have set in an earlier session, and so on. A paying subscriber will have access to additional content, and recommendations based on their past activity.

- **Scalability and future scope**: Applications are developed and deployed in phases, allowing the company to prioritize its investment in the product, based on strategic goals, practical budgetary constraints, and technical constraints. The prototype is often conceived to demonstrate how future capabilities and functionality will be incorporated in the framework.

- **Localization support**: To reach a global audience, many applications must support the language and sometimes the cultural preferences of the locale of its users are from. The prototype can demonstrate how various elements, such as navigation or buttons, handle languages that are written from left to right and right to left, and accommodate languages that have longer words than English, such as German or Spanish.

- **Error handling**: How does the system communicate to the user various types of user or system errors, and where and how do errors and alerts appear on the screen?

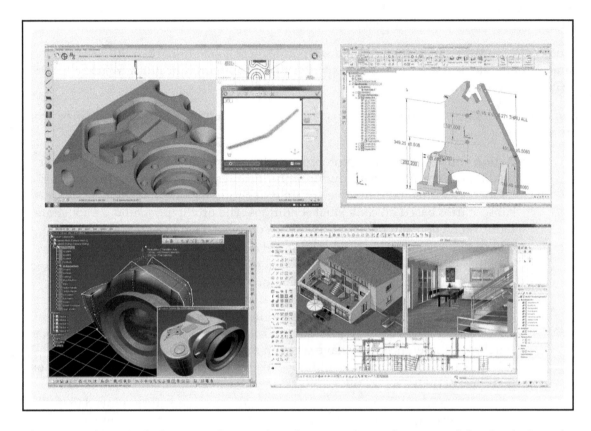

The image above includes several examples of prototyping software used for the design of physical products.

This type of software--CAD (computer aided design), has been around for several decades; originally it was just used by aircraft designers and architects, but is now a common design instrument.

The preceding image shows a three-dimensional method of prototyping in which clay is used to reproduce the product's external features. This technique is common in the automobile industry. Working with clay is similar to sculpture, except that the material is a lot more forgiving than marble.

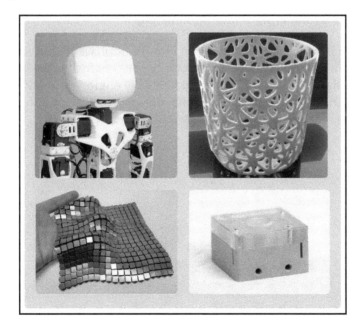

Finally, a few examples of the most recent entry to the prototyping tools, such as 3D printing, are shown in the preceding image. As the price of this technology decreases and with the level of sophistication, detail, and complexity the devices can produce increases, designers are able to experiment with much more risk-taking than before.

Summary

In this chapter we reached another milestone in the experience design journey. Starting with research, designers collect raw materials from many sources, and continue with analysis and synthesis to build a deep understanding of the business, product, and customer space. Then, we switched to a creative phase in which abstract constructs are iterated on until they take concrete forms. Throughout this process, designers are often guided by a design philosophy that informs their approach.

As a concept is tested, revised, and transformed into detailed prototypes and design specifications, the experience itself--the essence of the entire effort--emerges as well. When you think about it, the experience that drives the products we are enticed to purchase and love using, is in a fairly raw state throughout the concept development phase. Yet, that is when major decisions are often made regarding the final experience. The emerging experience has been validated with a relatively small number of people, and now it is expected to generate similar emotional responses and experiences from a substantially larger number of people, sometimes millions of people.

However, before production begins, there is an important phase that involves testing the design by placing it in front of real people that represent the final target user base. Additionally, the design has to be documented to enable engineers to build it, and provide a blueprint that will guide future iterations of the design, so it can be extended consistent and predictable ways. These topics are discussed in the next chapter.

10
Design Testing

"Testing leads to failure, and failure leads to understanding."

- Burt Rutan

This chapter addresses the following questions:

- Given all the work invested in research, experience modeling, and design, what is the purpose of testing?
- How and when to test?
- What to test and who should perform the testing?
- What to do with the findings?

Launching a new product or a product redesign, is a significant investment for most companies. Because design plays a pivotal role in the success of many products, testing its effectiveness is considered an important activity before, during, and after the product is launched. And that is why most companies invest in testing.

Testing focuses on two primary dimensions of the design:

- **Strategic (macro) testing**: This type of testing validates the entire design approach at a high level to ensure that it matches agreed design principles, high-level business requirements, and target audience expectations. This is a macro-level approach that is mostly concerned with marketing aspects, such as competitive edge and market domination.

- **Tactical (micro) testing**: This type of testing is concerned with the details of interaction patterns. It includes a structured examination and micro-level validation of usability, efficiency, and the effectiveness of and satisfaction with the user experience under various conditions of use. In some industries, such as aerospace, automotive, or healthcare, design testing is literally a matter of life and death.

However, the effectiveness of macro testing as a predictor of end-product success is often challenged. Sometimes the experience approach fails the testing, and yet, both designer and company share a strong belief in the appropriateness of their approach. The choice is between taking the safe path and modifying the experience, or following instincts and taking a risky bet.

As was discussed in previous chapters, design is a mix of subjective qualities derived from the arts, and objective qualities derived from engineering and science. The objective-subjective balance makes design challenging to test. People respond to experiences in unpredictable and sometimes irrational ways. Consequently, while testing is unquestionably effective when it comes to improving design engineering and usability, the overall power of testing to predict the contribution of the design to the success or failure of a product is disputable.

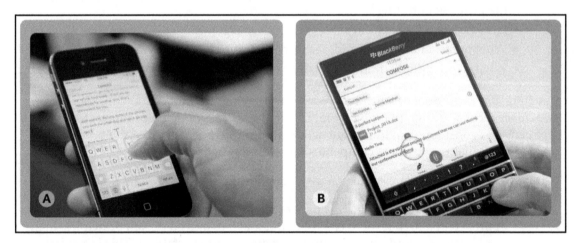

The introduction of the iPhone in 2007 launched a usability controversy. Typing on glass--how usable is that?

To judge by the enormous proliferation of mobile devices equipped with glass screens and by the fact that few have a physical keyboard, one might easily conclude that typing on glass is not only possible, but even superior to typing on a physical keyboard, the experience previously championed by Blackberry.

Getting rid of the physical keyboard, which has been an integral element of cell phone design since the inception of the iPhone, certainly has had advantages. Steve Jobs outlined these in the 2007 iPhone-launch keynote speech:

> "...Here's four smart phones... Motorola Q, the Blackberry, Palm Treo, Nokia E62--the usual suspects. And, what's wrong with their user interfaces? ...They all have these keyboards that are there whether you need them or not to be there.
>
> And they all have these control buttons that are fixed in plastic and are the same for every application. Well, every application wants a slightly different user interface, a slightly optimized set of buttons, just for it.
> And what happens if you think of a great idea six months from now? You can't run around and add a button to these things. They're already shipped.
> So what do you do?
>
> What we're gonna do is get rid of all these buttons and just make a giant screen.
> ...Now, how are we gonna communicate this?... We're gonna use the best pointing device in the world. We're gonna use a pointing device that we're all born with--we're born with ten of them. We're gonna use our fingers.
> We're gonna touch this with our fingers. And we have invented a new technology called multi-touch, which is phenomenal.
>
> It works like magic."

Despite these words, typing on glass can be an unpleasant tactile sensation, and slow compared to physical keyboards. Blackberry devices have been especially popular with business people due to the ease and convenience of typing long emails. Typing long documents on a glass screen has been described by some as "torturous." And yet, here we are: Not going back to keyboards, but witnessing the rise of conversational interfaces as a direct response to the typing-on-glass problem and in an effort to bypass typing all together.

What this story highlights is an inherent tension between experience design and usability testing, between strategic and tactical testing. Sometimes, when tactical testing shows that a design is wrong, strategic design testing forcefully claims the opposite, or vice-versa. Of course, both types of testing may also align in their assessment of the design.

The iPhone experience, for example, had to be considered holistically. From a wider perspective, typing is only one of limitless entertainment and productivity activities a mobile user can perform by engaging directly with beautifully designed apps. Direct and instantaneous interaction between the device and one's fingers further enhances perceptions of having fun and freedom. Compared to this, the input from the keyboard is associated with activities that are more formal, businesslike, and work-related.

In a company different from Apple, if a designer came up with an idea for a device like the iPhone, it is quite possible that after rigorous usability testing, the entire concept would have been scrapped. Indeed, our world today might have been very different.

The example of the type-on-glass screen may raise a concern that experience testing is potentially an innovation-busting activity. For the most part, however, testing is a foundational pillar of the user-centered-design methodology. When integrated into the design process, testing provides a practical and reliable means of improving the design, and the experience it delivers.

Why test?

All modern products are technology products. Design and experience are fused with the science and engineering of products, and it is often impossible to separate the boundaries of design from technology:

- Rapid changes in technology create opportunities to introduce new experience patterns for many existing products. How will customers respond to departure from experiences they like and used to? How does the new design-technology experience compare to the existing one? Are changes needed? Which elements should be changed? What are the priorities in making the changes before launch?
- New products need to be validated to ensure that the experience is safe and satisfactory. Just because a product is new and the experience is new and unique, does not automatically mean that its quality, efficiency, and user satisfaction are good. How do design assumptions correlate to a user's actual impression and experience?

Key justifications for testing help validate these questions:

- Is the product working as intended?
- How easy is the product to use?
- How satisfied are users with the experience?

Encapsulated in these three questions are numerous variations that help designers ensure that the experience delivered is satisfactory throughout the product's life and well beyond first impressions.

As an example, let's consider you, the reader. You have an extensive experience as a usability assessor and judge, right in your own home. The typical home kitchen has several large and small appliances--refrigerator, stove, dish washer, microwave, food processor, coffee maker, toaster, juicer, and so on.

The aggregate number of all potential functions these products help perform is mind boggling--given the enormous range of age, education level, and other demographics of the users who experience the equipment on a daily basis--with no prior training.

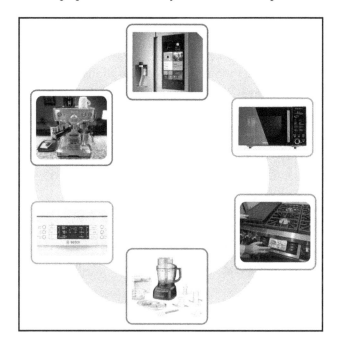

As appliances are getting more advanced, connected, and "intelligent", the combined number of user interface controls that an average person has to master rivals the interface of a small aircraft.

R.T.G.D.M?

R.T.G.D.M is an acronym that stands for--"Read The God-Damned Manual", a complaint attributed to frustrated designers and engineers of perplexing products, who are puzzled by users' helplessness.

The difference between an aircraft and a home kitchen, besides the fact that training is needed to operate the first, is that from a pure experience perspective, the kitchen is associated in many cultures with a positive and comforting atmosphere that people cherish. This is why terms such as "Mom's Cooking", "Homemade", "Home Cooked Meals", are used for advertising restaurant chains, food products, and even kitchen appliances that are mass-manufactured. The promise is to reproduce a cherished homey experience.

Given that the kitchen is also the most dangerous room in the home, usability testing of kitchen appliances helps reduce the risk of accidents due to user-error caused by poorly conceived interactions.

Consider the microwave oven. You probably have one in your kitchen. There is a high probability that you are perplexed by how to get the appliance to perform some of its functions, such as reheat or defrost. In some models, it can be challenging even to figure out how to get it to work.

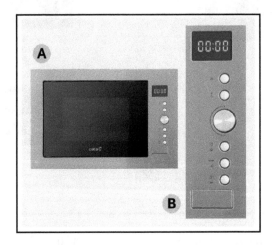

The microwave oven shown in the image above is an example. The overall design can be described as minimalistic, elegant, and "clean". At first glance, the column of round buttons is compelling, and the icons next to each button look familiar, like those used in mobile apps. This appliance offers multiple desirable functions in addition to microwave cooking: convection cooking, broiling, and a combination of these methods.

For the shopper in a store, either online or in a "brick and mortar" location, this appliance seems to offer a great user experience. It looks great, is multi-functional, and the user interface looks simple and easy. The coming years of day-to-day experience often depend on a purchase decision that takes only a few minutes and is based only on a superficial evaluation of the product's visual design and functionality.

Here is an example for a simple usability in which you can participate right now.

Looking at the image above, can you figure out how to use the defrosting function and defrost a frozen cheese cake? My personal answer is,"No! I have no idea which of the buttons to press". A closer evaluation of the product with common scenarios of use, exposes the non-intuitive nature of the interface. The future suggests ongoing frustration and frequent search for the user manual. In reality, most people do not keep the manuals of their kitchen appliances handy. More importantly, these are daily use appliances that should be intuitively usable, without having to read any manuals.

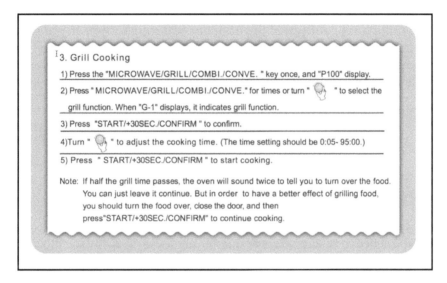

When we need to read the user manual before we can unlock the functionality of routine devices, the user experience is not good, even if the instructions in the manual are easy to follow. Often, however, they are not. The image above shows an excerpt from the user guide of the microwave featured in this section.

To access grill cooking functionality, the user has to follow a sequence of five ordered steps. These steps requires the user to remember a total of eight sub-steps, use three different buttons, and remember two obscure codes:

1. **Step 1** (two things to remember):
    - Press a button (we'll call it X) ONCE
    - Remember the relevant code, "P100" in this case.
2. **Step 2** (three things to remember):
    - Press button X "for times"--here we must assume a typo in the text and the idea is to press that button four times

- Turn another button (we'll call it Y) to the grill function
- Remember that the code "G-1" means the grill function

3. **Step 3** (one thing to remember):
    - Press a third button (we'll call it Z) to confirm

4. **Step 4** (one thing to remember):
    - Turn button Y to adjust the cooking time

5. **Step 5** (one thing to remember):
    - Press button Z to start the cooking

It can be argued quite successfully, that the usability of the microwave in our example is very poor, and that a usability test with actual users might have uncovered the issues, leading to a change in the interface. A good experience design cannot be dependent on manuals, online help, and customer support.

In fact, a key argument for usability testing is that by uncovering perplexing interactions in an otherwise great experience, the company can avoid significant costs from an increase in calls to its customer service centers.

Testing prototypes

Prototypes are design artifacts that resemble the final product, and often can communicate aspects of the experience to stakeholders and potential users. In software and web design it is common to create clickable prototypes, which let a participant in a usability test navigate the application and perform key tasks.

However, should there be testing while the product is being designed, and the experience is just a work-in-progress? And if so, how complete should the prototype be, and what should be tested?

An argument against early prototype testing is that testers can only respond to what is placed in front of them. If what is tested is a prototype of the experience, the response is only valid for the prototype, but may not necessarily apply to the final product. Therefore, there is a risk that changes to the final experience would be made based on inaccurate feedback to the prototype, resulting in a final product that is not as good as it could have been.

The practice of usability has emerged with the web, and became its own specialized practice, with methodologies and techniques. The practice has shown that testing design in progress with prototypes is valuable to the overall design process.

Hi-fidelity and low-fidelity prototypes

Low-fidelity prototypes are early sketches of the initial design idea. In web and software design, these are often static wireframes that range from ideas sketched by hand on paper, basic slides created in software such as PowerPoint, or wireframes created in prototyping software such as *Axure*.

The rudimentary nature of these artifacts is reflect by the term, "low-fidelity". The key value of such artifacts is that they are inexpensive--it is possible to create many variations and explorations of the products relatively quickly, and the means of creation are inexpensive as well.

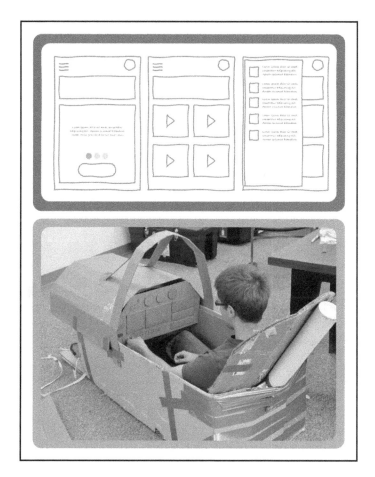

The preceding picture shows examples of low-fidelity prototypes that were created to explore and test the design of physical and digital products. The thinking is that raw design ideas should go through iterations in a raw state, before moving to a more detailed, refined prototype.

It is possible to put these prototypes in front of potential users and engage in research that involves aspects of macro usability, such as the prioritization of desirable features and functionality, layout, position of buttons, and other high-level design aspects, that are not directly dependent on the experience itself. The focus is on what users need or want to do with the products.

Many designers believe strongly in sharing low-fidelity designs that are executed only in grayscale or black and white colors. The theory behind this approach is that adding actual color to such prototypes confuses stakeholders and testers, who would conflate the prototype with the final design and shift their responses to immaterial topics, such as the nuances of the colors used in the prototype.

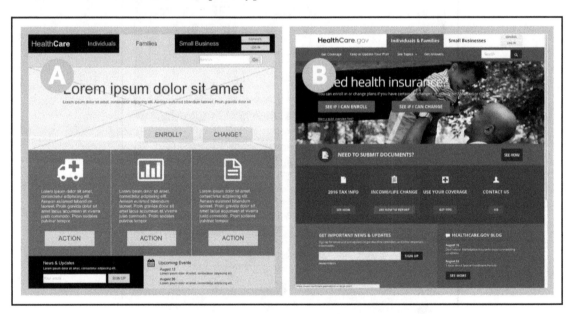

Grayscale prototypes make it easier to concentrate on essential aspects of the experience, such as navigation and information architecture. Only after the designer has validated that an approach is successful, it makes sense to transition to much more detailed high-fidelity prototyping. The preceding picture shows the prototype of the same page as low-fidelity grayscale wireframe (**A**), and a highly detailed version (**B**).

The following picture shows various examples of high-fidelity prototypes. The term points to the prototype's level of detail and general resemblance to the final product. In web and software design, participants in usability testing experience a look and feel that closely approximates the actual experience--elements on the screen are clickable while content and data elements are simulated to respond to tester actions. The results are always reliable and accurate, and the effectiveness of such prototyping is so compelling that some designers argue for starting with high-fidelity prototypes from the get-go, and forego the use of low-fidelity prototypes altogether.

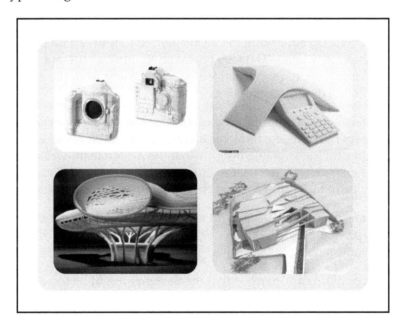

The benefits are clear, as mentioned previously, but so are the risks that the time and effort invested in a complex, detailed prototype too early in the process, would tie the designer to a sub-optimal concept. Cheap, simple prototypes are easy to scrap, while expensive ones, not so much. The agility and flexibility of prototyping as a means of iteratively and frequently testing and adjusting the design must be preserved.

The timing of testing is critical, and the main concern about testing high-fidelity prototypes is that by the time such prototypes are tested and results compiled, it is often too late for the engineering team to make any significant changes to the product without negatively impacting costs and the target release date.

Who should facilitate?

An interesting question is, who should perform the testing and report on the results?

The designer is most familiar with the design--the research that leads to the concepts and ideas being tested. The designer is also most familiar with the product's target audience and user personas. The design being tested is the result of thinking that has emerged from that material. Who then, is better qualified to plan, facilitate, and analyze the results of usability testing?

Usability tests are often scripted, asking the participant to follow certain paths of interaction that map out to high-priority tasks. The tester is asked to think aloud and share with the facilitator their thinking, responses, and rationale for departing from the expected response, or for interacting with the design as expected.

When the designer facilitates such tests, the designer is attuned to opportunities to depart from the script, in response to user comments and behavior that was not expected or that is interesting and might provide valuable insights that the design team was unaware of or overlooked. The designer can ask the user about motivations, expectations, and other aspects that may not be in the script, and use this new information to enhance the design.

The other option is to separate the design and testing responsibilities--designers create the concept and prototypes to be tested, but an objective third-party tester will facilitate the actual usability test, and report on the results.

The argument in favor of this approach is that the designer might be too close to the design, too invested, and thus, biased in favor of their design and oblivious to feedback from test participants. An impartial usability-testing expert is objective, and would ensure that the testing follows the script, and the testing provides consistent and comparable data for analysis.

Some companies have their own design and research departments, where each is responsible for their segment of the process. In other companies, designers plan, conduct, and analyze the research.

Either way, it is important to use methods that are reliable and are known to provide consistent results. Macro testing generally maps to concept testing, and micro testing, to detailed design testing. Process wise, concepts are tested before work on detailed design commences. Because the testing of each of these aspects requires different approaches, some companies end up with a hybrid approach to testing, where designers conduct the concept testing, and the more time-consuming phase of formal usability testing is performed by professional testing and research experts.

Planning usability tests

It is important to clarify to test participants that in usability tests, the design is being tested--not the participant. Because the feedback on the quality of the experience is provided by multiple people, making sure that all testing sessions conform to a consistent protocol, can be important. That being said, it is OK to have some flexibility in each session, to explore directions of research that was not initially planned for, if the opportunity arises.

There are several reasons testing sessions should be planned:

- Planning ensures that all the important experience questions are covered. If it turns out that there are just too many elements to test, this fact will emerge during planning, and alternatives can be developed--for example, having two or more scripts, each focused on a major experience theme. This revelation might require recruiting more participants, and setting more time for testing.
- Once design questions are identified, appropriate testing scenarios can be developed. The scenarios guide the facilitator and the participant in going through the experience in a simulated way that makes the testing meaningful. It can be very difficult for testers to provide good feedback if they are asked to perform tasks that make no sense to them.
- Planning helps ensure that the prototype and other artifacts necessary to conduct the testing are ready and can support all the functionality that needs to be tested. If there is an issue, planning helps develop an alternative strategy.
- Planning is necessary in order to determine how many participants are needed, how many sessions, their timing, the time needed for analysis, presentation of results, and implementation of changes, if usability issues are discovered. Additionally, the need for special testing equipment, facilities, or resources.
- Finally, it is often the case that sessions are conducted in parallel, or in multiple geographical locations, by different members of the design team. The plan ensures that the need for such a structure is in place, and that all facilitators work with the same scripts.

The test

The following is a fictional test of the actual Amazon.com website. This is a very abbreviated sample of potential testing, and one in which you can pretend to be the participant. The idea is to let you experience what website testing might be like. This test has no association to Amazon, the company, and was created specifically for this book, as an example. By the time you read this, the site has most probably changed, but that is immaterial to the general principals illustrated in the example.

This example also points to the fact that testing is not reserved only to new products in development, but is also used to evaluate refinements and updates to existing products.

Test objectives

Detailed test objectives are typically not shared with the participant. Rather, it is an internal statement that sets a baseline for subsequent tests. Objectives that are not met in the first round of testing, need to be re-tested until satisfactory results are achieved. The objectives set are developed in collaboration with business and development stakeholders, to ensure alignment with and, agreement on the scope and focus of the testing.

In this example, let's pretend that Amazon is planning to refine a product filtering functionality on the website. A testing server will be used to present test participants with a functional website, so that the experience will be familiar to the participants. The objective is to test the effectiveness and impact of the new refinement option on the user experience. Success will eventually be measured as an increase in customer engagement with the feature, and potentially--increase in sales. In the test, the designers will check the following:

- Did participants notice the refinement options?
- Which of the filters did they use?
- Do they use multiple filters?
- Which filters might they use regularly and why?
- Which filters might they ignore regularly and why?
- Is the filter list too long, such that users miss some of the filtering options?
- Are users happy with the feature and with the filtering results?

The testing scenario

You are in the market for a new tablet device. This will be a replacement of an old iPad 2 that has become too slow and frustrating to use. The device is shared by the entire family and is stationed in the kitchen, where family members use it for news, recipes, and general browsing. Since your budget is limited to $250, a new iPad is out of your price range, and you hope to find a device at a much lower price. Your task is to find a product that will fit your budget as well as your family needs for the device.

You may have noticed that the scenario does not mention the refinement functionality, or provide any other interaction guidance. Rather, the scenario provides context to the purpose of visiting the site, the goal of the interaction, and goals for task completion.

Before starting the test, participants are asked to "think aloud" and share their thoughts, emotions, and decision-making process with the tester. This verbal feed is as close as testers can get to the participant's inner mental processes.

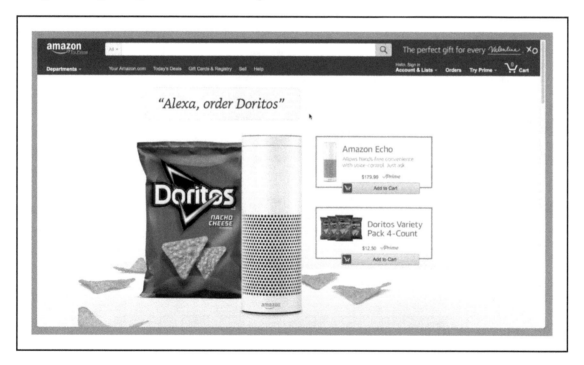

Screen 1

1. The participant is shown the Amazon home page as seen in the preceding screenshot and asked to start interacting.
2. The user starts typing the word **tablet** into the search field and the "type-ahead" functionality presents a menu of options as shown in the following screenshot .
3. The user is asked to ignore the list and type the full word tablet and hit the *Enter* key.

Screen 2

1. The user is presented with the search results screen as seen in the following screenshot:

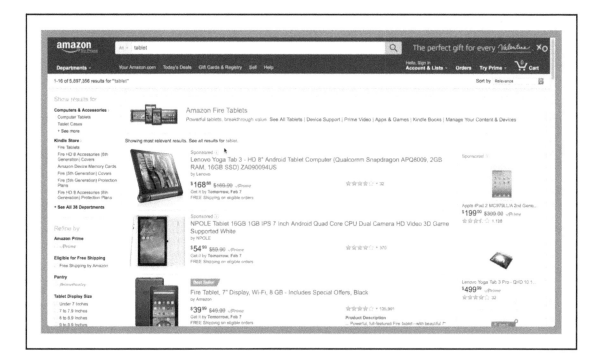

At this point, the facilitator is most interested to know if the participant noticed the refinement options presented on the left pane of the "search results" screen.

If the user starts interacting with various items in the search results and ignores the list, the facilitator notes that. At this point, the facilitator has several options:

1. Let the user continue. It is possible that the user will find the tablet without ever looking at the refinement option. End the test without mentioning to the participant the existence of the filters.
2. Similar to option 1--let the user continue, with the possibility that the user will find the tablet without ever looking at the refinement option. However, at that point, direct the participant's attention to the refinement pane, and ask if the user noticed it, and if the user did, their reason for not taking advantage of the feature.

3. If the user appears to be ignoring the refinement options, stop the test and direct the person's attention to it, have a conversation about it, and discuss the refinement options as shown in the following screenshot:

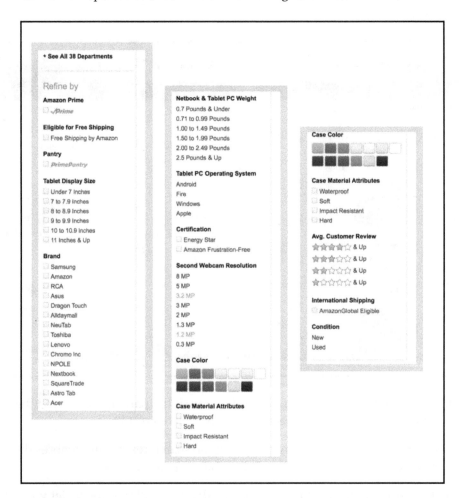

At this point, observe the participant's use of filters. Typically, the user is asked to think aloud, and so, it is possible to capture their thoughts about the various filters.

Documenting test responses

A typical testing session typically lasts an hour to 90 minutes. The longer the session, the higher the risk that both tester and facilitator will get fatigued, resulting in diminished feedback to important topics at the end of the session.

During the session, the participant is asked to perform certain tasks, and the facilitator observes. As mentioned before, the participant continuously shares their thoughts as they go through the scenario--what they see, what they think they should do, why they are choosing a particular path, and so on. Many tasks are typically a compound of multiple sub-tasks that need to be performed in a certain order, such as in a checkout in an online shopping experience.

With each of the tasks and sub-tasks, the participant might have one of several possible experiences, and their success in completing the task, as well as their experience, are recorded. The common results for task completion are:

- **Complete success:** The user was able to complete the task without any guidance. The task was competed quickly, the user was able to identify exactly what it is they need to do, how to do it, and in which sequence. And the user expressed satisfaction with the way the experience facilitates the task.
- **Success:** The user was able to complete the task without any assistance. The user hesitated once or more about which path or action to take, but was able to figure things out independently, and with a reasonable amount of time. The user expressed satisfaction or was neutral regarding the experience.
- **Success with assists:** The user was able to complete the task with minor guidance from the facilitator. The assists were not material to the flow of the task, and the user expressed satisfaction or was neutral regarding the experience.
- **Failure:** The user was unable to complete the task and required explicit assistance from the facilitator. Even if the participant feels in retrospect that the experience, as shown, is good, the failure is marked as such.
- **Error rate:** This is a percentage breakdown by task, of users' success rate--in the aggregate, how many users were able to complete the task with complete success, success, failure, and so on. This measurement helps to flag tasks with problematic experience, as well as those that provide a very good experience, at least in the testing.
- **Time on task:** In testing sessions that capture the length of time the participant spent on each task, it is possible to identify the tasks that are most time consuming, or conversely, isolate cases where the issue can be attributed to a particular participant, but is not a common problem.

During the session, the facilitator captures other reactions the participant has to the experience. These range from suggestions, comparisons to other products, ideas, complaints, and so on.

Recruiting participants

A key component of testing, sometimes overlooked, is the testers--the actual people who agree to participate in the testing effort. In the end, experience testing is all about real people--this is the theory, at least.

In practice, testing with real people is expensive and time consuming. Recruiting can be challenging when design schedules are tight, when relevant audiences are overseas or in remote places, and when the design team is small and limited in budget and time. As a result, many companies end up testing with a smaller set of actual people than initially envisioned.

The screener

Many products, such as smartphones, e-commerce websites, and cars are meant for a wide and general audience. Potentially, almost any person is thus a candidate to be recruited to participate in usability testing. However, a random call for volunteers might yield an enormous list of interested candidates, but no effective means to ascertain if they really qualify.

Some degree of qualification is necessary and practical. For example, testers for an e-commerce website: should have a checking account, credit card, or something like a PayPal account. If they don't, their effectiveness in evaluating the checkout and payment process might be compromised, because most common online shopping websites require the use of a credit card.

Other products target a specific audience, and for these, a random call for participants is also ineffective. The tool to recruit quality participants is called a **screener**, and its name is self-explanatory. The screener is a questionnaire that interested participants are asked to fill out. Based on the budget, location, and timing for the testing, participants are selected among those who met the criteria.

The following is a sample screener based on a form published by the United States Department of Health & Human Services. The form is meant to screen participants for the testing of websites on a desktop computer. It is one of many similar templates companies and governments use, and is used here as an example. The screener can be delivered by phone, by a recruiter, or via a web form. The following version has been adjusted for web delivery.

Introduction

The purpose of the introduction is to set the stage and context for the rest of the form. The screener identifies briefly what the person is being contacted for. Specifically, the introduction makes it clear upfront:

- What is the requested activity (usability test)?
- Which site will be tested?
- The length of the session
- When will the testing take place?
- The compensation awarded to participants

Answers:

- We have been asked to recruit participants for an upcoming Usability test on a [WEBSITE].
- The participants will be asked to use the website and provide comments and feedback about the site and how it functions.
- These 1-hour usability test sessions are being scheduled [DATE RANGE].
- Each session will last approximately one hour and will take place on [DAY].
- As a thank you for your time, you will receive a [$ AMOUNT check eGift cert or Gift Card] at the end of the session.

Validation and vetting

At this point, the person is asked if they are interested in the offer. A simple "Yes" or "No" question respects the person's time by letting them leave the screen now, or continue. For those who continue, the screen lists a number of common activities the person participated in over the past 30 days, such as:

- Travel booking
- Email

- Trade stocks
- Job hunt
- Visit a cooking website for recipes
- Research health or medical information
- Hobby websites
- Current news
- Electronic banking
- Classified ads or auction websites
- Online shopping
- Visit a municipal or other government websites
- Internet searches
- Playing computer games
- None of the above

Responses to the list of activities help associate the person with a particular profile. For example, a user that indicates that the only online activity they engaged with is playing computer games suggests a very different type of tester, from a person whose response includes a varied mix of activities such as online banking, shopping, and so on. Based on the response, it is possible to eliminate the person from the candidate list. For example, a user that responded "None of the Above", might not be suitable to the particular testing.

The next set of questions help segment the person by gender, ethnicity, and age group. The age segmentation helps flag minors--which, even if they are candidates for testing, require additional clearing such as parental consent. The responses to these questions further help segment the pool of candidates, for example, ensuring an equal number of males and females, or a proper representation of ethnicities.

Additional information and confirmation

Next, the designers ask questions that may be relevant to the specific website they are testing. It is best if such questions are in a multiple choice format, which can save a tremendous amount of processing time when reviewing submissions. These questions can ensure that the person responding to the screen, matches the target audience.

At this point, and based on all the gathered information, it is possible to determine if the respondent is eligible to participate in the test. Candidates who qualify are asked to provide their contact information, such as phone and email address. Summary information about the test, its purpose, location, time, and compensation is provided, and a thank you note-- addressed to all those who completed the screener, concludes the session.

Follow up emails and phone calls help ensure that those who indicated their interest in participating will attend. It is very common to lose a significant amount of testers who initially indicated their willingness to participate, but end up bailing out at the last moment, for a variety of reasons.

Testing considerations

Do you know an elderly person who owns a smartphone? If you do, you know how frustrating these and many other technology-driven devices can be to the elderly. Most of the well-known tech companies are proud of their large investments in user research and usability testing facilities. And yet, the difficulty the elderly have with operating devices raises a concern about the true ease of use of their products.

This ties to the topic of this segment--test participants map to user personas. As was described earlier in the book, personas are used early on in the design process, as models of key user-segments. Obviously, with products such as smartphones which have hundreds of millions of users of all ages worldwide, personas can be very limited.

So, if an elderly persona has not been created, it is quite likely that little or no testing will be performed with this segment of the user market. Given the difficulties elderly people have with technology, the industry's claim for ease of use is questionable. The argument that the devices are targeted at younger audiences is discriminatory.

Testing people raises important ethical problems. In many academic and industry settings, approval of testing requires strict adherence to strict protocol, such as the **Institutional Review Board** (**IRB**), also known as an "Independent Ethics Committee", which approves and monitors biomedical and behavioral research. While the history of such tight control is beyond the scope of this book, the purpose of these controls is to protect the human participants from physical and mental damage.

For the most part, experience design testing has been "off the hock" with regards to formal regulatory protocols and controls over conduct of tests. One might argue that experience testing has evolved in an organic way--an honest, harmless effort of designers to improve the usability and satisfaction of users by improving bad design. Whether this is still a totally valid argument, time will tell.

There are, however, important questions around the topic of testing that designers continue to wrestle with, and as usual, there are no conclusive answers. The following are some of the major topics.

Fee versus free

Should participants be compensated for the time and effort they invest in the testing? This is not a trivial question. When the organization that conducts the test is a commercial, for-profit organization, the test participant is providing a service to that company. Other service providers in a commercial context get paid, so shouldn't testing participants be paid too?

The counter argument is a concern that a key expectation from the tester is to be impartial. Getting paid for testing might place the tester in an ethical bind--the tester might feel compelled to "satisfy" the organization by avoiding critical comments and providing only good feedback that the participant thinks the company wants to get.

Cultural conventions or personal circumstances may indeed impact the results of testing if individuals got a fee for their participation. Conversely, if no fee is offered, impartial participants might be willing to donate only a limited amount of their time, and get annoyed with the testing if it gets too long or demanding.

In practice, there are cases where a fee is just expected, as when testing a product intended for professional use, for which ideal participants are professionals who are too busy to volunteer their time, and only a sizable monetary reward might compel them to participate.

Another common approach to compensate participants for their time and effort involves paying for their travel expenses, offering meals and snacks on site, and providing gift cards with a relatively low nominal value.

Insiders versus impartial

Most companies have a readily available pool of people that can be used for testing any time--for free. These are company employees, and sometimes--their extended circle of family members and friends. To save time and money, it is not uncommon to recruit testers within the organization. The thinking is that these employees may not be familiar with the product being tested, and thus, their responses to the experience will be as useful as the responses of outsiders.

This approach can sometimes work, although there is always a risk that employees feel compelled to provide favorable feedback to support their colleagues. Providing negative responses might risk friendships, or, in case of hierarchical company structure, fear of retaliation.

Clearly, testing with target users who are impartial to the company is preferable, but if the choice is between no testing or testing with internal resources, the latter should be seriously considered.

Products have their critics--people who are annoyed by a product's poor usability, or it does not perform the way they expect. For example, people who are forced to use a product they don't like, but the product is mandated by their company.

The same exact product also has fans and champions, who love the product and find it useful and usable. These users are satisfied, and when recruiting for usability tests, it can be very tempting to approach supporters, and not critics.

Casual versus power users

The casual and power users are another example of user types. The product experience sometimes leans in favor of one type over the other--design of a product that targets professionals might focus more on the experience that supports a lot of functionality, while the design of a product that targets casual users might lean towards the 80:20 rule that states that because 80 percent of users typically use only 20 percent of features, the design effort should be focused on making those 20 percent as easy to use as possible.

Testing both types of users makes it possible to validate that the 20 percent of functionality that the casual users needs the most is as close as possible to the most frequent functionality power user need. The smaller the gap, the wider set of users can be satisfied.

There are several challenges for testing with power users, or with users who are very familiar with the product in general. For example, when testing financial websites of apps, it is extremely important to make sure that the screens show accurate data--that figures which need to add up--add up correctly, that decimal points are placed correctly, and that the data overall makes sense--people who work with financial data are easily distracted by inaccuracies in prototypes, and as a result, their feedback may be overly negative.

Low-fidelity prototypes are less effective when tested with experts and power users. Such participants will easily grasp the overall direction of the design and understand the concepts behind it, but a lack of specific details makes the prototype too ambiguous for them to provide constructive, meaningful feedback about the design's nuts and bolts.

Such users can also be resistant to change, when presented with a concept that departs from what they are familiar with. It is often the case that real improvement to a product is dependent on replacing or eliminating existing procedures and workflows--either because new technology renders them obsolete, or because the way the business works is changing as well. Some of this information may not be known to the users who participate in the testing, and if they are having a hard time mapping the new flows to what they are comfortable with, they might resist, and risk implementation of the changes in the final product.

Test settings

Product categories often require unique settings for testing. For example, the riding experience in cars or airplanes can be tested in simulators that submit participants to conditions that parallel real conditions. Driving ranges for car testing are roads that simulate various driving conditions--from smooth paved highways, to bumpy, water flooded dirt roads. Flight simulators range from inexpensive, software-based products that are sold to gamers and hobbyists, to very expensive civilian and military aviation devices that replicate the physical condition of any flight condition. Such devices are very effective in training pilots.

The preceding picture shows a few examples of car and airplane cabin simulators that help car designers study the riding experience in a moving vehicle, at a high-fidelity of precision and predictability. Other physical products are ideally tested in conditions that simulate a relevant use case. In addition to simulations, there are other parameters that impact testing conditions.

Moderated versus unmoderated

Moderated tests involve a test setup in which a participant and facilitator meet--either in a physical location or remotely. The facilitator guides the participant through a series of scenarios that approximate key tasks one would perform with the product. In most cases, the participant is not free to use the product spontaneously, although this is possible.

Typically the sessions are being recorded; the facilitator take notes and engages the participant as needed. When the participant needs help because they are stuck, the facilitator suggests ways to try to resolve the issue. Typically, the facilitator does not provide the answer right away, but rather, provides hints that might point to a desirable way out. Only when the user completely gives up on completing the task, will the facilitator provide the path.

In unmoderated tests, the participant explores a prototype of the product on their own--as the name of the test suggests. The session might be recorded, but often, the participant is asked to log their experience as they go. There might be a script, or the person might just perform the tasks that are relevant to them. The benefit of such an approach is that the participant does not feel stressed about being observed. Moreover, many participants worry- despite being explicitly assured to the contrary--that their performance is being tested and that failing to perform tasks correctly might impact their job. Unmoderated testing alleviates such potential pressure, and in addition, the experience is more closely tied to the natural use pattern the user prefers, as opposed to a scripted sequence that the participant might not be as familiar with.

Lab versus field testing

Depending on the product and testing objectives, designers have options ranging from lab testing, where real-life scenarios are simulated such that all participants can engage and assess the same interactions, to field testing, where user-product interaction is evaluated in real-life settings, but changing conditions make it harder to ensure situational consistency across all testers.

For those who need to approach usability testing with the rigor of scientific research, or because real-life testing is unsafe, such as early testing of new commercial or military airplanes--usability test labs provide an environment for testing under optimal controlled conditions--while the testing participant is performing simulated scenarios in an isolated environment, the session can be observed by designers and stakeholders through double sided glass or streaming, and recordings are used later for detailed analysis.

For example, the Center for Medical Simulation in Boston is a company that specializes in the use of "high-realism medical simulation" to:

> *"...teach surgeons, anesthesiologists, and other healthcare providers.. how to reduce medical errors and provide safer patient care... and help companies evaluate their medical technologies and train clinicians in their use."*

> *"...designing clinical environments and simulation scenarios that replicate situations more likely to reveal use errors. While no one can identify all of the ways that mistakes can be made, high realism simulation is a way to do it better while learning more about a product's usability faster. The end result is lower risk to patients."*

Eye tracking usability testing, mentioned earlier, is a method of recording and analyzing the tester's eye movement, gaze, and focus throughout an interaction. Analysis of such testing helps design aircraft cockpits, and other types of high intensity interfaces. In such environments, the operator is required to make critical, sometimes life and death decisions, while their attention is divided across multiple instrumental data sources as well as external conditions. The test provides evidence to the efficiency with which the operator shifts their focus across needed instruments, and which elements are most looked at. The latter should be placed in more prominent positions if they are found to be in a less optimal place.

Performing eye tracking tests outside of a lab-based simulator and in the real world, involves wearing special glasses that record the objects the user looked at, the amount of time the eyes were focused on certain areas, the path the eyes followed, and so on.

The preceding picture shows a tester equipped with Tobii pro glasses (**A**). With these, it is possible to conduct the tests in a real environment, such as a store, in a car, and so on. The output of the date stream (**B**) makes it possible to generate heat-maps of the products the tester focused on and spent most time looking at.

Software and web-based applications lend themselves to remote testing using screen sharing and video conferencing technology. This technology has become pervasive, inexpensive, and reliable--just when travel, and especially cross-state or international-travel has become expensive and difficult.

Although the design can be modified after the release, as is often the case, there are some design problems which, if not fixed prior to the product's release, risk generating significant negative responses. This is one of the major risks companies worry about and yet, it is often the case that the budget and time allocated for testing is inadequate. As with other aspects of the design process, competitive pressure is on the business to release the product as soon as possible. Companies and designers are faced with choosing one of the following approaches to testing:

- **Incremental testing**: Frequent tests with real users throughout the design and development process, which provide continuous streams of validation data to the team. Some argue that this is the most effective approach, in terms of overall costs and impact on the final results.

- **Milestone testing**: At specific points in the design process, the work is taken for testing--often when it is already too late to make any significant changes before the start of production without missing target release dates.
- **No testing**: In this approach, the team is satisfied that internal quality control testing is sufficient, but the actual design itself is not tested with potential users. This approach is the riskiest, but probably also the most common.

Summary

This chapter concludes the (simplified) product design journey which began with a definition of needs, and ends in testing the resulting product. Subjecting the design to continuous validation and testing is one of the key tenants of experience design. At the core of the approach is the belief that good design is the result of quick iterative evolution of a concept to full design through frequent engagement and participation of its actual end users.

In the final chapter, an exploration of key topics related to the future of Experience Design, and the ways in which our own lives might be impacted by emerging new experiences.

11
The Design Continuum

"There is nothing permanent except change."

- Heraclitus

"Change is an illusion."

- Parmenides

This chapter addresses the following questions:

- What happens to the design once the product has been released?
- In a world of constant and rapid change, how do companies and designers balance the significant investment in the just-released design, with continuous market pressure for new experiences?
- If the new design is very good and effective, what is the point of changing it?

The answers, in a nutshell, are primarily within the domain of design management and design governance. However, first, let's consider the paradox of tradition and trend, and the contrasting properties inherent in the continuous evolution of experience design. Once design X becomes trendy because it is fresh and new, it has often also reached the peak of its social impact, and its decline is imminent because the next fashionable experience-- delivered by competing design Y--begins its journey along the same path.

Design Y may enjoy a brief moment of glowing fame and high demand, and then disappear without a trace, giving in to design Z, and the cycle repeats. However, sometimes, thanks to its experience quality, design X holds on to its success and enjoys persistent demand and deep loyalty even when it is no longer all the rage. Loyalty and longevity is the aim of great design--to emerge from the trendy phase and persist as a proven solution to new problems.

Before a particular design matures into a tradition, it needs to break the rules set by established design traditions, and take over as a new trend. That is the paradox of design evolution.

In the past, the rate of change was relatively slow, and design traditions were highly regarded. In a variety of areas, be it the construction of temples and palaces or the manufacturing of household furniture, utensils, and personal artifacts, patrons asked the designers they hired to apply traditional design patterns to new projects. Traditional patterns pronounced respectability. They legitimized the owners' status through association with sacred things or with the lives of the noble classes, who for centuries had the financial means to commission designs.

Design evolved gradually, over thousands of years, expanding from the institutional to the personal, from the ceremonial to the ordinary, and from the exclusive to the common. With expanding demand came the need to train more designers. At the same time, growing demand also created pressures to bring the cost of products down. These interrelated development required adjustments to the designs of products and the experience they deliver.

Elaborate, time-consuming, hand-made ornamentation gave way to simpler, templated patterns. The extensive use of marble, silk, gold, silver, precious stones, and other high-quality ingredients, the staples of design systems associated with aristocracy and sacred objects, gave way to economical, commonplace substitutes, such as wood, iron, bricks, and plastics.

Several developments had a significant impact on experience design. Widening markets, new artisans, new materials, new technologies, fresh ideas, competition, and international commerce have led to the following:

- The establishment of large design studios led by the prominent artists of their time, design trade groups (guilds), design schools, and eventually formalization of various design specializations as academic disciplines.
- Popularization and expansion of the vocabulary of experience design and its reach into the daily lives of ordinary people. With it faster rate of changes to traditional design patters has become acceptable and, eventually, expected.

Most people need simultaneously to feel unique and have a sense of belonging to a social group. The boundaries between individualized existence and social association are sometimes expressed through the separation of the ordinary from the ceremonial, as it is expressed in the traditions of social or religious groups. For some, the need for individuation is more pronounced than the need for social belonging, for others it is the other way around.

Nonetheless, the tension between unique expression and tradition has been the driving force that maintained a healthy demand for experience design throughout the ages. Uniqueness and individuality drive new experience patterns, whereas the need for belonging and tradition maintains continuous refinement of the existing design patterns.

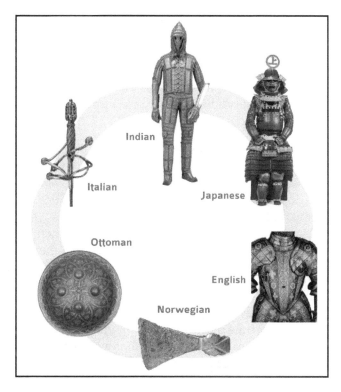

The image above shows examples of military artifacts used centuries ago by warriors and knights, a professional social class in many cultures since antiquity, who found it important to own highly ornamented armor, swords, shields, and other battle-field accessories.

These highly prized items were used as battle gear and also served for ceremonial purposes. Consequently, the highest level of masterful craftsmanship was required. Design and engineering fused to deliver products that could serve as effective weapons but also communicate personal bravery and the social status that separated knights from common thugs.

The elevation of weaponry into a highly symbolic, desirable artifacts worthy of high-end manufacturing and design, is an early example for the transformation of a product from a plain, utilitarian object into a unique meaningful experience. This process has helped designers occupy a special place in society.

The acknowledgment of the unique role of the designer is evident in ancient Greek mythology. One of the Olympian Gods, Hephaestus, served as the God of fire, forges, and blacksmiths and also as the God of metalworking, stone masonry, and the art of sculpture. Indeed Hephaestus was the ultimate designer, the embodiment of the fusion of engineering, craftsmanship, and art.

Until recently, all artifacts were, of course, handmade. Over the millennia, generations of craftsmen evolved the technology and esthetics of the artifacts used by their societies. A specialized class of artisanship has emerged wherever there was a demand for armor and weapons, which was almost everywhere. With this demand also came fame and recognition for these artisans-designers, whose products gained the appreciation and admiration of their powerful and influential patrons.

Similar trends emerged in all aspect of daily life. Highly decorative, beautiful, fully functional and usable items evolved in response to the needs and desires of the elites--the nobility and religious classes. These patrons--as important clients were called in pre industrial times--could afford to order and pay for such luxuries. For the most part, they paid for the expensive materials, from which their desired artifacts were produced--refined gold, silver, and precious stones. These were rare and expensive then, as they are now. The cost of labor and craftsmanship, on the other hand, was marginal then, as it is often today.

While luxury artifacts were unattainable for the majority of people, their existence and high-visibility had a significant social impact. These luxury designs underscored the contrast between the common and the amazing and generated massive aspirational drive. Ambition, desire, envy, and emulation are some of the emotional byproducts that still underline many design approaches and marketing campaigns. The inherent desire to stand out from the crowd through an association with exclusive social groups or organizations, can be expressed by owning a product that communicates that unique experience.

Design continuity

Most traditional design domains emerged as masterful hand-crafting of a singular product experience for one patron. They transitioned to pattern-based mass production during the industrial age. Today we are witnessing a return to singularly produced fully customizable experiences. However, these are not hand-made, but rather driven by manufacturing technologies, such as 3D printing, which make it possible to design, produce, and deliver an experience-of-one to millions of people.

Experience design is rooted deeply in personal biases and social norms. In some cultures, tradition and uniformity are valued, and in others, individualism and change are valued. In all cultures, design is influenced by cross-cultural pollination. The influences may spread quickly or take effect slowly, yin any case, it is safe to say that new design ideas do not eliminate traditional design. Instead, designers fold the new into the wider vocabulary of patterns and techniques from which they draw inspiration when conceiving new projects.

Design is expensive. This book follows the journey that companies undertake toward fusing their products with compelling and engaging experiences. Once their investment in design has been made, companies seek to benefit from it for as long as possible before reinvestment is necessary. This means that, while changes to the product are certain and frequent, the design needs to scale, adjust, and adapt to these changes while preserving all the properties that made it a success. This is a major design challenge.

The following are some of the questions experience designers are confronted with:

- Which elements of design are constant, and which must keep evolving?
- How to preserve the DNA of a successful design?
- How to document design?
- How to govern design in order to preserve its consistency and principles, and yet evolve the design in response to change?

Like the seasons, design trends appear to be replaced and then reappear. In the process, designers contribute evolutionary refinement and optimization to known experiences, or they revolutionize the space with a completely new approach.

However, how can companies do this and still be profitable, given that there is often strong competition in each product segment? How can design scale in a way that targets tens of millions of people, and yet meets the unique desires and preferences of a single individual?

Experience platforms

A platform is a system of systems--an integrated, modular, and specialized technology foundation, which makes it possible to extend a published set of predefined components in a variety of ways, in order to create quickly and at lower costs new product experiences. Experience platforms also include, in addition to various technology foundations, a design system that blends seamlessly with the technology.

Familiar examples of computing platforms are those produced by Microsoft, Apple, and Google. A generic ecosystem of platforms is visualized in the following diagram:

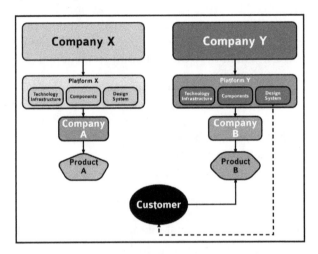

A platform's ecosystem represents a chain of dependencies that bind the platform-maker to other companies and customers. The other companies sometimes tie their success and the success of their products to the platform's success by creating modules and components that enrich and support the platform, but depend on it for their operation.

Let's look at mobile apps, for example, in relation to the three dominant computing platforms--Microsoft, Apple, and Google. App makers must decide on the operating system for their product. If they want their app to be available on iPhones, they need to design according to the iOS specifications and the esthetics associated with the platform. Making the app available on all platforms, although a technically viable option, can be significantly more expensive to create and maintain, especially if the objective is to preserve the distinct user experience of each platform.

Once a platform decision is made, the app maker's focus is naturally on improving and evolving the app by adding new capabilities and enriching the user experience. However, this important effort is diluted because the app developer must also follow closely the ongoing changes in the underlying platform. Each update might cause unexpected problems with the app, and each new version of the operating system carries with it the risk that significant revisions to design and code would be required to maintain compatibility across new and previous versions of the underlying software and hardware platform.

As more companies adopt the platform, competition grows and prices go down. Customers evaluate the landscape of products supported by the platform and are influenced by price and design. The following is a generic chain of events:

- Companies *X* and *Y* each develop their technology platform. Let's consider Microsoft and Apple, for example. Each platform has its own set of technology infrastructure, components, and a distinct design system.
- Each of these platforms is also highly influenced by a distinct philosophy of experience design, which influences the approach to its architecture and use; for example, Apple's closed system versus Google's open system.
- Company *A* chooses to develop a productivity application using platform *X*, and company *B* decides to build a similar application but is committed to platform *Y*.
- The customer in the market for such a productivity application has the benefit of choice between two competing products. Often, the decision in choosing the product--*A* or *B*--relies solely on the experience that the underlying platforms--*X* or *Y*--support.

This is the reason why today, technology-platform vendors are investing so much in their experience design. They recognize that their competitive edge rests on providing a better user experience.

Although their platforms provide consumers with very similar types of experiences, each of these platforms offers its own branded design system for expressing products and deliver experience in hardware and software. Most importantly, though, the goal is to develop loyal fans.

Loyalty is key in experience platforms, because usually platforms are not compatible with each other, and consequently, the customer must choose one and stick with it. Sometimes customers are not even fully aware that they are making a long-term commitment to a specific platform. This is the case with Apple, Microsoft, or Google experiences. Once the choice is made, the consumer is often tied to the platform's ecosystem because many related products, such as peripherals and accessories, must be compatible with the chosen platform.

The underlying framework of each design system is governed by tightly controlled specifications published by the platform's owner.

The preceding screenshot from Apple's website points experience designers to the company's hardware-specific **Design Guides**. Currently, Apple creates four distinct types of hardware platforms, and each has its own experience design system that is fused into the operating system so that the experience is optimized for the capabilities of that hardware. The following are interaction methods supported by Apples' hardware platforms:

- Desktop and laptop computers run **macOS**. The interaction experience is based on use of input devices such as:
    - Keyboard and mouse
    - Touch and gestures via the Touch Bar (on some new Macbook Pro models) and Touch Pad.
    - Voice commands
    - Attached tablets and styluses
    - Assistive technology devices, such as screen readers

- iPhone and iPads run **iOS**:
    - Touch and gestures via the device screen
    - External keyboard
    - Voice commands
- Apple Watch runs **WatchOS**. The interaction experience is based on the use of input devices such as:
    - Touch and gestures via the device screen
    - Voice commands
- Apple TV runs **tvOS**. The interaction experience is based on the use of input devices such as:
    - Apple TV Remote Control
    - Apple Remote App (via iPhone or iPad)

The user experience of products within each of Apple's hardware categories is tightly coupled with, and influenced by, the hardware. However, Apple, Microsoft, and other companies in similar situations work continuously toward delivering a consistent, unified experience across the entire spectrum of their hardware offering. These companies can do that because they control the platform.

The historic progression of platform design and its evolution shifts from generally available and free platforms, to platforms that are a part of the public domain, to platforms that are exclusive property of a corporation and require licensing and purchase.

These shift contributed in recent decades to the gradual raise in prominence of the open source movement, a movement which evolved as an alternative to commercial, proprietary platforms. Companies and consumers now can choose between commercial platforms and open source solutions, which are often significantly cheaper or even free.

The beauty of open source is that at least according to the movement's vision, its platform is open to the design community at large. Practically anyone who cares to work on it, can do so free of charge. The platform, loosely guarded and guided by active volunteers, evolves organically, with numerous contributions.

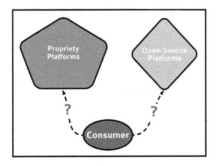

For some companies, choosing an open source platform is a simple business decision because they can avoid being financially or legally tied to a proprietary platform and its maker. Also, the opportunity to further extend the platform is compelling. Other companies are concerned that open source components might lack the internal coherence that is inherent to a commercially designed platform. Without design integrity, the end product might be infused with experience inconsistencies, resulting in frustrated customers.

Either way, platforms offer customers and users several important benefits, which are illustrated by the next example--the Kitchen Aid Stand mixer, shown in the preceding image. Since its introduction in 1919, the Kitchen Aid Stand mixer has become an iconic kitchen appliance. Over the years, the company added a plethora of attachments, which transform the mixer into an entirely different appliance, such as a juicer, meat grinder, pasta maker, cheese shredder, sausage stuffer, grain mill, and an ice maker.

Compared to other mixers in the market, the Kitchen Aid is expensive. Yet, the customers enjoy unique long-term benefits because they can endlessly expand their culinary range by purchasing attachments instead of purchasing multiple single-purpose appliances. Customers can save money and valuable countertop and cupboard space. The design element that makes this possible is not the mixer's unique esthetics, solid cast iron stand, or its powerful motor. Rather, it is an attachment hub, which extends horizontally forward from the tilt-head and passes powers from the motor to the attachment. This is no longer a mixer, but a food preparation platform, which extends its core component.

Experience platforms tend to be industry-specific, such as computing, automobiles, large appliances, and so on. In the automobile industry, car makers base the underpinnings of distinctive car models on a global platform. Each of these models offers a unique experience--the car type, dimensions, the exterior style and interior layout, materials used, and their grade of finish might all be different. The country, target audience, and price might be vastly different and yet, a closer look reveals the shared frame, engines, and other parts that are identical.

The preceding image shows Subaru cars--the Impreza, Crosstrek, and WRX--that share the same platform and many of the parts, but target very different types of customers. The following is a quote from a recent Subaru announcement about its latest global platform. The language used is very technical, but even without understanding the technical terms, you will be able to appreciate the significance of the platform for this company:

> *"The new Subaru Global Platform, together with the Boxer engine, Symmetrical All-Wheel Drive (AWD) and EyeSight® that represent Subaru's core technologies, constitutes the basic foundation of the next generation of Subaru vehicles... (the) new platform incorporates new frameworks with optimized cross sections and highly stiffened joints ... to significantly enhance straight-line stability, agility and ride comfort while suppressing noise, vibration and harshness ... Specifically, the new platform increases rigidity of the unitized body structure by over 70 percent.*
>
> *A lower center of gravity and revised suspension systems contribute to the biggest-ever leap in Subaru's performance evolution... Greater hazard-avoidance capability is another benefit of the Subaru Global Platform's inherent handling agility.. the resolute straight-line... is also an important constituent of the autonomous driving capability this platform can support in future Subaru vehicles."*

The vehicles in the previous image share a substantial number of components. These are manufactured by numerous vendors who design and manufacture thousands of components for the platform--from engine parts, to airbags, breaks, sound system, and so on.

In a global economy where manufacturing and designing are spread around the globe and partnerships among competitors are common, shared experience platforms make a lot of sense because development of an entirely new platform is extremely expensive. The companies save significantly on the "nuts and bolts", but compete on the experience manifested in the finished product's look and feel. The customer benefits too from products that are offered in a range of prices, but overall cheaper, and a wider variety of experience options.

The company that controls the platform is responsible for evolving it. If there is a defect in the design, there is a risk that the damage would cascade and impact the experience of everyone who is using a product based on the platform.

Historically, in the computing world, when companies wanted to create computing products, either hardware or software, they had to make a very deliberate choice among these options:

- Committing to a single platform--coming to the market with a software or hardware product that can only run on an Apple- or a Microsoft-driven platform, for example.
- Trying to offer cross-platform products that work with leading platforms--that meant the expense of having design and development teams that are familiar and the risk of developing what would be the same product.
- Taking the open source approach.
- Coming up with an entirely new platform of their own.

All things being equal--access to raw technology such as programming languages or computers, engineering skill, and business drive--the one major differentiator that influences the direction companies take these days is experience design; specifically, the fusion of modular experience design systems with their underlying platform, and the power of modularity to scale and support the evolution of new experience patterns.

Design systems

Design systems are everywhere. Some emerge to address the production needs of platforms and products, but most sprout organically. In fact, you have created several design systems yourself. Your wardrobe is an example. If you are wearing men's clothes, you may have an assortment of items in categories such as coats, jackets, sweaters, sweatshirts, t-shirts, shirts, pants, underwear, socks, sleepwear, and active wear. In each category, you have items in subcategories, such as light and heavy jackets, long-sleeve shirts, short-sleeve shirts, and so on. When you shop for new clothes, the choices you make are based on:

- Needs--such as weather conditions--work, or leisure
- Constraints, such as budget and availability
- Preferences, such as colors, fabrics, and brands
- Consideration of the cloths that you already have

Excluding gifts from others, the collection you have curated is a personalized design system. Every day, you mix your finite set of options into various combinations that you feel are appropriate for the circumstances. Each of the various combinations projects a public image of yourself. An emerging trend indicates that individuals are beginning to see themselves as brands. In this context, individuals are products, which a design system of clothes helps communicate.

In this section, we will explore four types of design systems--the first type was described just now. It evolves organically. Most people--conscientiously or not--are constantly creating their design systems in their wardrobes, the pantries where they keep preferred cooking ingredients, and in many other daily settings. The next type of design system is depicted in the following image (the Lego bricks). This is a form of atomic design, meaning that the system is made of a small set of core elements, which users can combine in infinite ways.

Consider the Lego bricks, the original ones--this ingenious toy was introduced in the late 1950s and has since won the title "Toy of the Century" twice. Lego pieces interlock with any other Lego pieces. Originally there were only a few basic sizes and colors. Nonetheless, even then, the combinations were limited only by the player's creativity and imagination.

The preceding image shows a shapeless assortment of Lego bricks and examples of what one can build out of them. Infinite construction possibilities make Lego a popular imaginative play for all ages, at all levels of interest and sophistication.

The bricks themselves are generic plastic pieces. When they are disassembled, it is a meaningless pile of plastic. It is the infinite combinatorial possibilities, one brick at a time, which create amazing experiences in two ways. The first occurs during play. It is the assembly and construction of bricks into forms. The second is the end result.

Viewed more broadly, design systems are a bit like palindromes--words that can be read backward and forward, such as rotor, civic, pop, and eye. How so? Design systems have to be created with one or more products in mind in order to be useful for the design of other products. The design of these future products will in turn evolve the original design system.

The third type of design systems is produced by platform makers, as described earlier, and by companies that want to consolidate an assortment of design patterns spread among multiple products, into a unified, consistent, and cost-saving library of approved patterns. Either way, a design system specifies the following:

- The product's look and feel, regardless of its operating system
- Aspects of the experience that are tightly coupled with those underlying product technologies that dictate interactions such as touch, voice, and so on

Apple, Tesla, Nest, and many other companies that make the delivery of experience an explicit feature of their brand and products. They have recognized the importance of, and the need for, documenting the architecture and hierarchy that governs their design:

- A systemic approach to design makes it possible to insure an internal consistency that is independent from the whims of individual designers.
- It is easy to spread the system, because any designer who likes it can easily adopt its guidelines.

When designers and developers follow these guidelines, updates and new capabilities of the system cascade down to the elements that were used by the designer.

The preceding screenshot is from Apple's **macOS Human Interface Guidelines** and Google's competing design system, known as Material Design. These documents define each company's experience design philosophy as well as the implementation of this philosophy in their hardware and software platform. These are a valuable resource for any practicing designer or design student, even if they don't design in any of the platforms.

The guidelines cover every aspect of the user interface, from basics to advanced topics, from color-palette guidelines to animation and other types of interactivity. Designers who work on products that are based on the platform are advised to comply closely with experience principles and standards, which were set by the platform's designers. The thinking is that, after all, the platform is the foundation for the experience, and consequently, its native design system is most organically suited for:

- **Companies**: Provided with the fastest ways to deliver new products with the guaranteed experiences, which are natively supported by the platform
- **Users**: Provided with recognizable interaction and design patterns, which leverage knowledge they gained through experience with other products built with the platform; new applications are, thus, easy to learn and to use

The promise and benefits of design guidelines are as follows:

- Reduced risk to the company developing the product.
- Faster design and development process, which can be approached like Lego construction--the design building-blocks are preset and standard, but the resulting new design can be unique and compelling in its own right.
- Proven experience framework--no need to "reinvent the wheel' for each product. This translates to significant reduction in development costs.

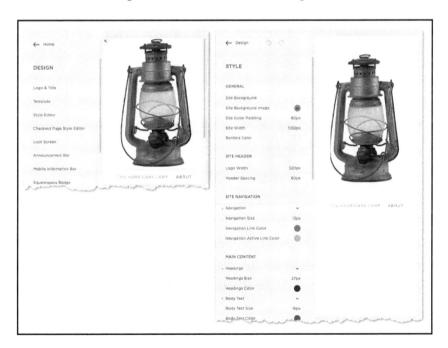

The fourth type of design systems are practical combinatorial products. Compared to the abstract atomic units in the Lego design system, or to clothing items in an organic system in which each component is fully independent and functional on their own, these systems are made of atomic elements that have an assigned functionality, so they are not abstract, but they are only usable as part of the assembled design.

For example, the IKEA's PAX wardrobe system, a sample of which is shown in the following image, offers frames, hinged doors, sliding doors, handles, knobs, interior organizers, and lightning components. Each is available in an assortment of color, size, and styles, as shown in the following image.

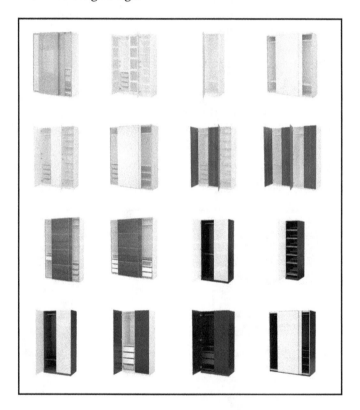

Both company and customer benefit from this type of design system approach to product experience. Production, shipping, and storage of components are cheaper because each individual element is simple, there is no assembly, and the inventory takes significantly less space. The costs of updating and evolving the system are lower, because new materials, colors, elements, and functionalities are added progressively and replace components that don't sell well or go out of fashion.

Such systems are incredibly flexible in addressing needs, constraints, and preferences of a wide customer base. First, a system like PAX can scale to fit any room size and desired width and height. The choices of color and style are limited, but the number of resulting combinations is not. Customers can purchase only as much as they need or can afford, extend their item as their needs and budgets grow, and replace a component if it breaks or to refresh the design. Because the products require self-assembly, they are cheaper.

In a global economy, products are often conceived and designed in one location and manufactured in another location, often overseas. To support world-wide distribution, multiple variations on the basic theme are created, reflecting the necessary adaptations to appeal to various local markets. Brands want to protect the product's core design signature while accommodating localization needs.

Brand style guides emerged first as a simple and practical way to document, communicate, and control the consistency of the brand's representation across all internal and external instances where the brand's identity was used--advertisements, publications, packaging, and the product itself. Experience designers who work on any of these are guided by directives that include the company's logo, tagline, approved colors, and so on, as well as exact placement and variations based on background colors.

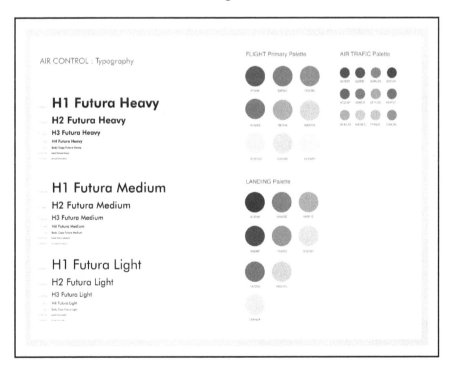

The web and mobile apps have rapidly expanded the use of marketing style guides to software applications. In addition to maintaining brand identity, the use of style guides expanded to specifying the look and feel of shared components, such as web pages, headers, footers, navigation elements, menus, and so on. The screenshot above, is an example of a style guide.

As new members join the design and development team and extend the functionality of a website or application, they follow the style guide. As new components are added, there is often a need to expand the style guide in support of the new capabilities. New patterns are added after considering the existing ones and the best ways to maintain continuity.

The design guide should be perceived as a "living" document that has to be adjusted over time to reflect changes in the application. If a guide becomes a "bible," it does not support the emergence and spread of new styles and designers may feel constrained and restricted from trying out new engaging experiences because those are not in the guide.

Wrapping up

The nature of experience is still a mystery despite being both universally shared and a highly personal feature of human makeup. Dedicated academic research into the science of emotions only began about three decades ago, and theories about the relationships between perception, emotions, and thoughts continue to evolve, shedding new and often surprising light on human motivations and behaviors.

What is known for certain is that we have an innate desire to expand and repeat positive experiences and an innate urge to shorten and shun negative ones. These behavioral preferences have real consequences for companies, and provide the guiding rails for experience design. Organizations are increasingly motivated to invest in design, design is becoming an integral part of product development, designers own a central responsibility for product success, and people are more aware of the role of design in their lives, and they demand better experiences.

For some practitioners, experience design is just a job, something to do in exchange for a paycheck. Others enjoy problem-solving through design, or want to express their passion for imagining the most innovative, user-friendly experience as a means to help people interact with products. For some, experience design is a way to influence, and for others, it is the mysterious fusion of art, science, and technology. Finally, many people who are not design practitioners have little awareness of the degree to which experience design shapes a great deal of their daily life.

Experience design is not an object, such as a car, house, or refrigerator, that can be clearly defined. It is the practice that helps make these items desirable and usable for those who use them. It is a set of evolving practices and methodologies fused tightly into the psychology and physiology of individuals and societies.

Many new products today are portrayed as 'innovative', 'disruptive' or 'revolutionary'. But, as the quote attributed to Igor Stravinsky goes "*a complete revolution... you'll come exactly to the same point*" - the origins of experience design can be found in antiquity, and from there, we can trace the continuity, references, and renewal of early ideas in modern life.

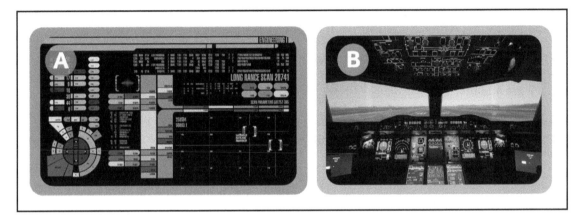

The image above shows the command center of the USS Enterprise from the TV series Star Trek (**A**), and the cockpit of the Super Jumbo Jet Airbus 380 (**B**). The command controls of the Enterprise flight deck were imagined in a Hollywood studio at about the same time that the Airbus 380 was conceived, nearly 30 years before computing power existed to support the modern jet's sophisticated controls. In computing time, 30 years are like eternity, and yet there are a lot of common experience elements that the two airborne vehicles share, such as data visualization on digital displays and interactions via voice commands and touch screens.

The relationships between people and the intelligent machines they build, has occupied the imagination of science fiction writers for generations, and now it is supported by actual science and commercial reality. Products that are endowed with powerful chips, fast algorithms, and the label "artificial intelligence" mark a shift from an interaction experience model in which the user guides the product, to interactions in which the product can predict our needs and fulfill them before we know them.

The following is a quote from a recent e-mail I received from a company regarding one of its predictive analytics offerings:

> *"What if you could understand what people want before they knew themselves? You may be closer than you think--you've already collected a wealth of enterprise data on customer buying patterns and preferences. Predictive analytics can help you use those insights to turn prospects into profitable customers."*

The idea that a corporation, organization or government can "understand" what people want before they know it, is disturbing when we think about the abuse of technology, and compelling when we think about putting it to good use. Herein lie the darker aspects of experience design, which are clustered in its powers of influence.

Currently, the bleak possibilities are restricted to dystopian fiction and action movies, but it is not too difficult to imagine "Big Brother" dystopias becoming a reality. Some would argue that we are already there.

Manipulating people's emotional states of mind by anticipating their needs, pales in comparison to the possibilities DNA manipulation, which can produce specially formulated babies or organs.

Experience design can hardly be more personal or more impactful than the design of one's physical appearance. The roots of cosmetic plastic surgery can be traced to ancient Egypt about 5,000 years ago. The "father of plastic surgery", the Indian physician Sushruta made important contributions to the field about 2,800 years ago. Until recently, surgery was about modifying existing limbs and the use of prosthetics has been limited to people who have lost their own. However, it is possible that in the future, people would replace their natural eyes by *iEyes* from Apple or acquire bionic ears powered by Amazon's Alexa. After all, these products will surely promise and deliver a much superior experience than our natural organs, and they will be tailored to the unique specifications of the individual customer.

It is very entertaining to think about the commercial potential. With the *iEyes* bionic eye, you could change your eye colors to fit your attire, your mood, the furniture in the room, and so on. You will have great eyesight with zoom and macro capabilities, and the ability to stream movies. Better yet, with the *iEyes* you could replace the boring reality your natural eyes see, with a perfect, beautiful landscape, filter out stuff you don't want to see, and so on. The *iEye* will be easy, fast, and painless to install and upgrade every year or two for a better model. Admit it--who would not want the *iEye* 8?

Index

W

9 781787 122444